Job Interviews

FOR

DUMMIES®

3RD EDITION

by Joyce Lain Kennedy

BICENTENNIAL

1807

WILEY

2007

BICENTENNIAL

Wiley Publishing, Inc.

Job Interviews For Dummies®, 3rd Edition

Published by
Wiley Publishing, Inc.
111 River St.
Hoboken, NJ 07030-5774
www.wiley.com

Copyright © 2008 by Wiley Publishing, Inc., Indianapolis, Indiana

Published by Wiley Publishing, Inc., Indianapolis, Indiana

Published simultaneously in Canada

For general information on our other products and services, please contact our Customer Care Department within the U.S. at 800-762-2974, outside the U.S. at 317-572-3993, or fax 317-572-4002.

For technical support, please visit www.wiley.com/techsupport.

Wiley also publishes its books in a variety of electronic formats. Some content that appears in print may not be available in electronic books.

Library of Congress Control Number: 2007941166

ISBN: 978-0-470-17748-8

Manufactured in the United States of America

10 9 8 7 6 5 4 3 2 1

WILEY

About the Author

Joyce Lain Kennedy is America's first nationally syndicated careers columnist. Her two-times-weekly column, CAREERS NOW, appears in newspapers and on Web sites across the land. In her four decades of advising readers — newbies, prime-timers, and those in-between — Joyce has received millions of letters inquiring about career moves and job search and has answered countless numbers of them in print.

Joyce is the author of seven career books, including *Joyce Lain Kennedy's Career Book* (McGraw-Hill), *Electronic Job Search Revolution*, *Electronic Resume Revolution*, and *Hook Up, Get Hired! The Internet Job Search Revolution* (the last three published by Wiley). *Job Interviews For Dummies* is one of a trio of job market books published under Wiley's wildly popular *For Dummies* branded imprint. The others are *Resumes For Dummies* and *Cover Letters For Dummies*.

Writing from Carlsbad, California, a San Diego suburb, the country's best-known careers columnist is a graduate of Washington University in St. Louis. Contact Joyce at jlk@sunfeatures.com.

About the Technical Reviewer

James M. Lemke has earned a reputation as a leader in talent strategies and processes. He is director of organizational development for Opportunity International. Previously, Jim spent 15 years as a human resources consultant. His client list included: Real Networks, Southern California Metropolitan Water District, Northrop Grumman, Southwest Airlines, Jet Propulsion Laboratory, United Arab Emirates University, and the White House. Jim has held executive positions with Wachovia Bank, TRW, UCLA, Walt Disney Imagineering, and Raytheon. He resides in Mesa, Arizona. Contact Jim at jlemke@opportunity.net.

Author's Acknowledgments

"We're better together" is a philosophy proven yet again in this richly informed book. The largess of helpful information you find within these pages is to a large degree due to my luck in sourcing many respected minds in the employment space. Contributors to whom I am especially indebted are individually credited in chapter pages. Applause to one and all.

Additionally, thanks a billion to the following individuals who worked long and hard to make this book happen:

Traci Cumbay, intrepid editor and clear-eyed train engineer who kept this ambitious work running on track; she's earned her rave reviews, chapter by chapter.

James M. Lemke, above-the-title technical reviewing star whose brainwork is indispensable to every book I write.

John S. Gill, college student, computer genie, and editorial whiz kid who I predict has a big future ahead of him; after he graduates, he'll have to fight off recruiters.

Muriel Turner, Alberto Mendez, and **Kelly James,** each of whom kept my landfill . . . er, I mean *office* . . . from crashing and burning; I appreciate you.

Gail Ross, literary agent–attorney and friend who continues to help me make the right moves in the world of publishing.

Publisher's Acknowledgments

We're proud of this book; please send us your comments through our Dummies online registration form located at www.dummies.com/register/.

Some of the people who helped bring this book to market include the following:

Acquisitions, Editorial, and Media Development

Project Editor: Traci Cumbay

(Previous Edition: Kelly Ewing)

Acquisitions Editor: Lindsay Lefevere

Copy Editor: Traci Cumbay

Editorial Program Coordinator: Erin Calligan Mooney

Technical Editor: James M. Lemke

Editorial Managers: Michelle Hacker, Carmen Krikorian

Editorial Assistants: Joe Niesen, Leeann Harney

Cover Photos: © Michael Prince/Corbis

Cartoons: Rich Tennant (www.the5thwave.com)

Composition Services

Project Coordinator: Patrick Redmond

Layout and Graphics: Reuben W. Davis, Alissa D. Ellet, Joyce Haughey, Melissa K. Jester

Anniversary Logo Design: Richard Pacifico

Proofreaders: Laura Albert, Tom Arany, John Greenough

Indexer: Estalita Slivoskey

Special Help: Carmen Krikorian

Publishing and Editorial for Consumer Dummies

Diane Graves Steele, Vice President and Publisher, Consumer Dummies

Joyce Pepple, Acquisitions Director, Consumer Dummies

Kristin A. Cocks, Product Development Director, Consumer Dummies

Michael Spring, Vice President and Publisher, Travel

Kelly Regan, Editorial Director, Travel

Publishing for Technology Dummies

Andy Cummings, Vice President and Publisher, Dummies Technology/General User

Composition Services

Gerry Fahey, Vice President of Production Services

Debbie Stailey, Director of Composition Services

Contents at a Glance

Table of Contents

Introduction

*H*uman nature hasn't changed over the past eight years since the previous edition of *Job Interviews For Dummies* appeared in 2000. We humans still like to do business with people we like, and we still like people who are like us. But almost everything else about the interviewing process is transitioning in ways you need to know about to be a top contender for the jobs you want.

Changes in job interviews — those crucial meetings that seal the deal on who gets hired — range from the interviewing medium itself (online video interviewing) to who's asking the questions and judging your answers (young and younger). Even classic techniques used in salary negotiation that once worked with predictable outcomes (more money) now need tweaking.

Job interviews continue to be a slice of performance art. They're staged theatrical sketches rather than X-rays of life histories. (Read more about that in Chapter 1.) That's why theater and drama are once again the theme of this book, and I hope you have some fun with it.

Why, you ask, should you expect a little fun and humor when finding out what it takes to sail out of an interview with prospects of a five-star job offer? Isn't interviewing for a chunk of your future serious stuff? Sure it is, but in decades of quizzing leading authorities on interviewing secrets, I've never found anyone who says that discovering how to score at the job Oscars can't be fun business as well as serious business.

A lighthearted approach may even help you. In my opinion, Julie Andrews had the right idea in the hit 1964 movie *Mary Poppins* when she sang: "A spoonful of sugar helps the medicine go down."

I hope you have some fun in this edition as you get ready to be a ShowStopper.

What Is a ShowStopper in Job Interviewing?

In the drama of job interviewing, a ShowStopper performance is one that wins so much enthusiastic, prolonged applause that the show is temporarily interrupted until the audience quiets down.

A ShowStopper meeting causes the employer interviewer to mentally shout "Bravo! More!" Your stunning impact quickly translates to a preliminary decision in your favor. If follow-up interviews, testing, and reference-checking support that reaction, a job offer is on its way to you. The employer may continue to see other candidates to round out the interview process, but in reality no one else stands a chance of landing the job after you figuratively stop the show.

Job Interviews For Dummies, 3rd Edition, is packed with the essentials of performing ShowStopper interviews. These include

 ✔ Strategies and techniques.

 ✔ Sample dialogue and research tips.

 ✔ The best answers for make-or-break questions and reporting of news of current events in the interview world.

When you want metaphorical standing ovations with clapping and shouting for more, follow the guidelines presented in these pages.

About This Book

A handbook of contemporary interview arts, *Job Interviews For Dummies*, 3rd Edition, contains the wisdom of hundreds of leading interview experts whose brains I've been privileged to pick for many years. (Okay, if you must know — 40 years of hearing from the best and the brightest.)

By absorbing the lowdown I pass on in this guide, you can interview your way into a job by outpreparing and outperforming the other candidates.

Conventions Used in This Book

To assist your navigation of this book, I've established the following conventions:

 ✔ I use *italic* for emphasis and to highlight new words or terms that I define.

 ✔ I use `monofont` for Web addresses.

 ✔ Sidebars, which are shaded boxes of text, consist of information that's interesting but not necessarily critical to your understanding of the topic.

Terms Used in This Book

Is there another word for synonym? Would a fly without wings be called a walk? How is it possible to have a civil war? These one-liners from comedian George Carlin (www.georgecarlin.com) hint at the importance of words.

I use the following terminology in this guide to label specific roles and organizations:

- ✔ A *candidate* or *job seeker* is a person applying for a job. (Another once-common label, *applicant,* has fallen into disuse because of a federal regulation that defines an applicant as one to be counted in discrimination monitoring. But applicant means the same thing.)

- ✔ An *interviewer* is someone interviewing a candidate for a job. An *interviewee* is a candidate being interviewed for a job.

- ✔ A *human resources* (or *HR*) *specialist, HR manager,* or *screener* is an employer sentry who is conducting a screening interview. A *hiring manager, decision-maker, decision-making manager,* or *department manager* is a management representative who is conducting a selection interview. (Read about the differences in screening and selection interviews in Chapter 5.)

- ✔ A *company, employer,* or *organization* is the entity you hope to work for, whether private and profitmaking or private and non-profitmaking. *Agency* implies employment in the government (public) sector.

- ✔ A *recruiter* (also called a *headhunter*) is an intermediary between the employer and you. *Internal recruiters* work inside the company, either as regular employees of the human resources department, or as contract employees. *Third-party recruiters* or *independent recruiters* are external recruiters, some of whom are employed as retained recruiters on an ongoing basis, while most are employed on a transaction basis as contingency recruiters and are paid only when a candidate they submit is hired.

- ✔ A *career coach* (also called a *career consultant*) helps job seekers gain workplace opportunities. (A career counselor and a career coach represent two different professions, although their work sometimes overlaps.)

Foolish Assumptions

I assume you picked up this book for one of the following reasons:

- ✔ You've never been through a competitive interview and you're freaking out. You could use a couple thousand friendly pointers from someone who's interviewed many of the marquee minds in the job interview business and lived to write about it.

- You've been through a competitive interview and assume the company sank like Atlantis because you never heard a peep from those folks again. Or maybe you could have done better and heard back if you had known more about what you were doing in this interview thing.

- The most important interview of your career is coming up. You realize now is the hour to dramatically improve your interviewing success. You need help, and you're willing to work for it.

- You've been through a slew of job interviews over the course of your career and have a hunch that some important things have changed (you just don't know what exactly) and you want to catch up with the help of a trusted resource.

- You want to be in the interviewing know and are sure that authors of *For Dummies* books give you the goods. You rely on *For Dummies* books to get the facts you need to succeed without jumping through verbal hoops until your eyes pop out of your head.

I further assume that you're someone who likes reliable, comprehensive information that gets to the point without rocking you to sleep. And I assume even further that you like your expertise with a smile now and then.

How This Book Is Organized

Before he was famous, superstar George Clooney auditioned for a television stereo commercial with a six-pack of beer tucked under his arm; he had researched the type of actor the advertiser wanted for the role, one whose attitude revealed the casual poise of a couch potato. He got the gig.

Later Clooney explained the contribution of performance in both theatrical auditioning and job interviewing. He noted that the actor who lands the job isn't always the most talented but the one who makes the best impression: "You get the job when you walk in the door. Because in a weird way, we're not selling acting. What we're selling is confidence."

Appearance. Performance skills. Confidence. All are winning — and learnable — traits in job interviews as well as theatrical auditions. This book shows you these traits and much, much more in the following five useful categories.

Part 1: And the Interview Winner Is . . . You!

Of special interest to time-challenged readers, this part opens with an overview of what's happening right now in job interviewing circles, beginning with the theme of this handbook: *interviews are theater*. A spotlight on new topics is next, including the beginning of interactive video interviewing from home with Webcam hookups, followed by a report on the growing recognition of interview variations in a global marketplace. The conclusion is a wealth of interview formats that you may encounter.

Part II: Backstage Researching and Rehearsing

In this part, I show you how to explore the backstage preparation that drives interview success. You learn how to research employers, understand job tests, negotiate salary, overcome stage fright, look smart with questions you ask, say the right things before you leave an interview, and evaluate a job offer.

Part III: Actors' Studio: Casting Your Character

Are you a new graduate getting ready for your debut career interview and concerned about coming across as a clueless beginner? An experienced person who feels miscast and wants desperately to change careers? A job-search veteran whose presentation persona may need a touch of recasting? I show you how to tailor your interviews for job offers, whether you're a rookie, career refugee, or prime-timer.

Part IV: Lights, Camera, Talk! Answering Questions

How should you deal with the heart and soul of the interview: the questions? Turn to this part to find out. Here you get an advanced-level education in a ShowStopper's response to each major question employers are almost certain to ask. The answers are presented in a long-story-short style that puts you out in front of a competitive chorus.

Part V: The Part of Tens

In these short chapters, I present quick surefire tips on how to get invited to the post-interview VIP employment party, as well as an irreverent group of statements that superstars of history might have made on a job interview, if they'd had one. I also run down some of the personality types who might be on the other side of the interview desk.

Icons Used in This Book

For Dummies signature icons are the little round pictures you see in the margins of the book. I use them to focus a searchlight on key bits of information. Here's a list of the icons you find in this book:

This icon reminds you that prior preparation prevents poor performance on stage.

You see this icon beside moves or lines that leave 'em clapping. It translates to critical acclaim for what you do or say.

This icon flags news you can use that you won't want to forget.

Bravo! This icon heralds star-quality lines and moves that prompt job offers.

A bad review for a poor performance, this icon signals situations in which you may find trouble if you don't make a good decision.

Advice and information that can put you on award-winning pathways in your interview follows this icon. It tips you to interviewing best practices.

Where to Go from Here

On the stress scale of life, job interviewing ranks with making a speech before 500 people when you can't remember your name or why you're standing in a spotlight at a podium. The spot where you start in this book depends upon your present needs:

- ✔ If you have a job interview tomorrow, quickly read Chapter 1 for an overview. And do jiffy research by going to the employer's Web site and getting as much basic information as you can. Don't forget to read the press releases.

- ✔ If you have a few days before you're on deck for an interview, read Chapter 1, and then flip through the Table of Contents to the chapters dealing with your most pressing concerns.

✔ If you have plenty of time, read the book from cover to cover. Practice recommended strategies and techniques. After you master the information in these pages, you have a special kind of insurance policy that pays off for as long as you want to work.

Part I

And the Interview Winner Is . . . You!

"The magazine didn't hire me, but they are paying me $50 to print my resume on their joke page."

In this part . . .

Interviews are theater, and in this part, I start off by showing you how that's true and what it means for your role in an interview — giving you the rundown on interviews from rehearsal to curtain call.

This part also gives you the details about where interviewing stands now — the scenarios you might encounter (video interviewing, opportunities abroad) and the styles of interviews that stand between you and your new job.

Chapter 1

Job Interviews Are Reality Shows. Really!

Are you on edge about that big job interview in your future? Try putting unnamed fears to rest by anticipating the worst thing that can happen to you. Among unappealing scenes are these possibilities:

A. Blowing the interview and feeling like a total loser for days after stumbling and mumbling your way through the ordeal.

B. Feeling glued to a hot seat as they beat the answers out of you and realizing that you're going to be sick if you don't leave immediately.

C. Slip-sliding as you come through the door, physically falling on your good intentions (hey, this is a PG–rated guidebook), and losing all hope of leaving behind a professional impression.

Situations A and B are common. Even C isn't unheard of. Perhaps you saw the video of Miss USA taking a tumble and bottoming-out as she made her grand entrance in a recent Miss Universe competition. It happens to the loveliest of us.

Still worried? Exhale. You've come to the right book. Take the suggestions to heart that I offer within these pages and horror situations A and B won't happen to you. As for your odds on situation C, that's between you and your inner-ear balance.

This work is dedicated to making sure that nothing you can control goes wrong. I offer proven tips on how to take the duck tape off your mouth, dry off your sweaty palms, and step out into interview spotlights with a quality of confidence you never thought could be yours. Dim the lights and raise the curtain on your quest for a new gig.

Interviewing Is Theater

Job interviewing is major furniture in the employment drama. Because it's the do-or-die step in the difficult process of getting hired, leading career coaches spend the majority of client-coaching time on interviewing drills.

Once you're inside an office and engaged in an interview, your entire future may rest on how successful you are in presenting yourself to a stranger across a desk in 15, 30, or 60 minutes.

These self-presentations have been described as everything from school final exams to mating rituals, but here's the real secret:

Job interviews are show biz. Like reality shows on TV, interviews are based on reality but in fact are staged. And, as in reality shows, only one survivor beats out the competition to win the prize.

The most successful interviews require solid preparation to learn your lines. At each meeting, your goal is to deliver a flawless performance that rolls off your tongue and gets the employer applauding — and remembering — you.

And because interviewing is show biz, you're allowed to have some fun learning your stagecraft.

Actors teach law students how to act

Actors and acting coaches are showing up in law school classrooms to coach students at law schools across the nation on story-telling, posture, tongue-twisters, and how to establish rapport with clients, according to one of them, the University of Dayton in Dayton, Ohio.

The theatrical simulation programs not only teach students how to sharpen verbal interviewing skills but give them insight into how their mannerisms, listening skills and even posture may affect the people they are trying to work with and influence.

At the end of the semester, the future legal eagles receive a DVD for job interviews that shows them in action.

Why "Be Yourself" Can Be Poor Advice

A scene in the movie *Children of a Lesser God* reveals a speech teacher (William Hurt) and a deaf janitor (Marlee Matlin) duking it out in a jolting battle of wits.

In a climactic verbal battle, the janitor signs to the speech teacher, "Let me be me," to which the speech teacher replies, "Well, who the hell are you?" There is no answer.

The troubled janitor isn't the only one who has trouble with that question. The bromide — "Be yourself" — is very difficult to articulate with consistency. Be yourself? Which self? Who is the real you? Our roles change at various times.

Your role: Job seeker

Jerry is a father, an engineer, a marathon runner, a public speaker, a law student at night, and a writer of professional papers. Will the real Jerry please stand up?

Jennifer is a loving daughter, the best salesperson in her company, a pilot, a tennis player, and a football fan. Will the real Jennifer please stand up?

Jerry or Jennifer could duck the which-self question by asserting unchangeable inborn traits: *I am the same as my feelings. If I suppress or alter my urges I am being untrue to myself. I am not being authentic.*

Wrong! Shuck the superficial thinking. If you enjoy improving yourself, isn't that a form of "being yourself"? Remember too that each of us has all kinds of urges, some of which are lofty and admirable while others are base and unattractive.

Don't make the mistake of pretending you're stuck with one identity — that's not who you are.

Who you are at this particular time is a person playing the role of job seeker. The stranger across an interviewing desk is playing the role of interviewer.

Playing the role most appropriate to you at a given time, and playing it effectively enough to get you the job you deserve, isn't dishonest. To do less courts unemployment — or underemployment.

 When you give a ShowStopping interview performance, you aren't being phony. You're simply standing back from the situation and looking at it with dispassionate eyes, seeing which type of information and behavior is likely to result in a job offer and which is likely to leave you out in the cold. You can't do so if you are too busy staying true to your most easily assumed self-identity.

Outtake: Forget about being "natural"

What about being *natural?* Isn't natural better than artificial? Not always. Is combed hair natural? Shaved legs? Trimmed beard? Polished shoes? How about covering a cough in public? Or not scratching where you itch?

Being natural in a job interview is fine as long as you don't use your desire to be natural as an excuse to display or blurt out negative characteristics.

Never treat a job interview as a confessional in which you're charged with disclosing imperfections and indiscretions that don't relate to your future job performance.

Nor should you treat a job interview as social dialogue in which you share cultural, sociological, political, sexual, or other viewpoints. Don't download your personal beliefs on interviewers in the name of "being yourself" or "being natural" — or, for that matter, "being honest."

Society cannot survive totally natural behavior. Neither can your unrefined behavior survive at job interviews. To really know someone in a brief encounter of 15, 30, or 60 minutes is simply impossible — even when you repeat that encounter multiple times. How can you compress a lifetime into 15 to 60 minutes? You can't, unless you present your biography with the same 30-seconds-per-story speed that television news uses to cover the state of the world.

Instead of real life, each participant in an interview sees what the other participant(s) wants seen. If you doubt that, think back: How long did you need to really get to know your roommate, spouse, or significant other?

If you insist on being natural, an employer may pass you over because of your unkempt beard, unshined shoes, or because you don't feel like smiling that day.

The price for ignoring self-improvement is too high. All the things you've done to date — your identification of your competencies and skills, your job-lead management, your resume, your cover letter — are pointless if you fail to deliver a job interview that delivers a job offer.

New Faces, New Factors in Interviewing

Are you having trouble staking out your future because you can't close the sale during job interviews? This mangled proverb states the right idea:

If at first you don't succeed . . . get new batteries.

Recharge yourself with knowledge of the new trends and changing developments that impact your job interviews. For the one-minute reader, here are highlights of contemporary happenings.

Expect new kinds of interviewers

If the last time you trod the boards of job interviewing you went one to one with a single interviewer, usually a white man or woman, get ready for a different set of questioners, like these

- ✔ A veteran team of six managers — individually or collectively
- ✔ A hiring manager (especially in technical and retail fields) who is two decades younger than you
- ✔ Someone of another color or heritage

Turn to Chapter 5 for a broader picture of group interviews, and to Chapter 17 for a good tip on interviews with younger bosses.

Watch for new calls for a fast start

Because you can't count on being on the job more than a few years — or, in contract assignments, a few months — the hiring spotlight lasers in on competencies and skills you can use from Day One. The question is: *What can you do for our company immediately?*

You can come across as ready to blast off if you do enough research on the company's goals (increase revenues, reduce costs, acquire new market share, land larger accounts, create a technical breakthrough), think about how you can help the company reach those goals, and are ready to speak the insider jargon of the industry.

If the job you're applying for isn't at the professional or managerial level, research the nature of the company's business, assume that it wants to make or save money, and stock up on a few good words used in the industry.

Scope out more ways to show your launch speed in Chapter 2.

Find out about the new way to meet

Although the video interview has been tried since the 1970s without becoming a mainstream hiring technique, it may work this time around because the tools to do it are better than ever. Webcams attached to computers make it easy and cheap for an employer and job seeker to see and talk to each other no matter where each is hanging out — around a block or around a globe.

A surge of video interviews is expected to supplant the familiar phone *screening* interviews (discussed later in this chapter and also in Chapter 5). Other "vids" will be used as substitutes for traditional fly-in meetings to avoid the expense of physical travel.

Get your technology lift in Chapter 3.

Focus on fitting in

Disappointed job seekers who ask employers why they didn't get hired are often told they aren't the best "fit" for the job. *Fit?* What exactly does "fit" mean in employment? That question seems to be on more lips than ever as some seemingly well-qualified people don't receive job offers while others who are less qualified are welcomed aboard.

In the workplace, "fit" essentially refers to how an individual fits into a company's culture. Company culture is expressed in the values and behaviors of the group, which forms a kind of "tribe" or, to use an analogy from high school, an "in crowd."

The culture typically flows from company or department chieftains: If the boss wears long sleeves, you wear long sleeves; if the boss shows a sense of humor, you show a sense of humor; if the boss works until 6 o'clock, you work until 6 o'clock.

An expert consultant on the inner workings of workplace fit, Mark A. Williams, further explains the concept:

"Fit is the elusive match between your profile and that specific combination of unspoken and informal social, behavioral, and cultural criteria unique to every organization. By answering questions such as *who do I feel comfortable with?* and *who seems most natural in the role?* or *who's most likely to blend into our culture?* your next employer will determine who gets the job."

When you're given the not-the-best-fit-for-the-job rejection, the reason is

- A convenient short and legally safe answer
- A cover story, or
- The hiring decision makers perceive that you won't fit in well with the "tribe."

When the reason really is the fit issue, decision makers may think you can do the job but that you won't do it the way they want and, furthermore, they just don't feel at ease with you.

Rather than lose sleep over a fit-based turn-down, move on. Do better pre-interview research. At least you won't waste time on companies well-known for being a fortress of round holes when you're a square peg.

Bone up on fit and corporate culture in Chapter 6, and in Mark A. Williams' book, *Fit In! The Unofficial Guide to Corporate Culture* (Capital Books, 2007).

Cut out the loyalty oath

Answers to certain questions are pretty much the same year after year, but watch out for one humdinger requiring a new response: Why do you want to work here? The old "I'm looking for a home and I'll be loyal to you forever" statements don't play as well as they once did.

Companies typically no longer expect that you will stay with them forever — nor do they want you to. They may not even want to see your face a year from now. Doing the math, managements don't want to have to deal with high health insurance and pension costs. Many employers now solicit contract employees — no muss, no fuss in getting them out the door when a project's finished, or when a decision is made to outsource the work.

Rather than pledge eternal fidelity, talk about your desire to do the work. Talk about how you are driven to funnel substantial amounts of productivity into the job quickly. Talk about wanting to use your superior technology skills. Talk about your interest in work that excites you, work that matters. Talk about work that — with its combination of work-life balance and stimulating tasks — is too tempting to pass by.

But fidelity? Pass on that as a theme song; it won't make the charts.

Stock up on what you *should* say instead of talking about loyalty in Chapters 18, 19, 20, and 21.

Revisit the dramatic pause

In face-to-face live interviews, allowing a few moments of silence to pass, pausing to look at the ceiling or glance out an open window — taking time to think — can make you look wise and measured in your response. Pauses can raise the ante by reflecting disappointment in a salary offer. Pauses can suggest that you're reluctant to travel 50 percent of the time but you're a team player and will consider the requirement.

A pause is effective body language and works great in live face-to-face interviews. But today's interviewer may call on a telephone or use online video interviewing where dead air time can make you appear dull-witted rather than contemplative.

Moral: Exercise judgment in using the reflective pause as a communications tool. (When you just don't know the answer immediately, that's another story; stall by asking for clarification.)

Rely on Chapter 3 for details on video body language and Chapter 8 for salary negotiation.

Polish your storytelling skills

Behavior-based interviewing is said to predict future performance based on past performance in similar situations. The behavioral interviewing style is not new but it seems to be more popular than ever.

Advocates of the behavioral style claim that it is 55 percent predictive of future on-job behavior, compared to traditional interviewing at only 10 percent predictive. The reasoning is "If you acted a certain way once, you'll act that way again." Hard proof of this claim is hard to come by. But, for you as a job seeker, it doesn't matter the least bit whether the claim is true or false. The behavioral style is such a big deal with employers today that you need to know how to use the style to your advantage.

It works like this: Interviewers ask candidates to tell them a story of a time when they reacted to such and such a situation. *How did you handle an angry customer? Can you describe an example of a significant achievement in your last job?* The more success stories you can drag in from your past, the more likely those interviewers using this approach will highly rate your chances of achieving equivalent success in the future.

Read more about behavior-based interviewing in Chapter 5.

Learn new lines for small-business jobs

Have you grown up professionally in a large-company environment? If so, carefully consider the answers you give when applying to small companies. That could happen sooner than you think if you're forced into an involuntary change of employment. Prime-timers in countless droves are discovering that the small company sector is where the action is for them.

Emphasize different aspects of your work personality than those you emphasize when interviewing for a big company. Interviewers at big companies and small companies have different agendas.

Among the reasons that owners of small ventures reject former big-company people are these stereotypical perceptions: People who come out of Big Corporate America often are though to be

- ✔ Unaware of the needs of small business
- ✔ Too extravagant in their expectations of resources and compensation
- ✔ Too spoiled to produce double the work product their former jobs required
- ✔ Unwilling to wear more than one job hat at a time
- ✔ Deadwood, or they wouldn't have been cut loose from the big company

Chapters 17, 19, and 21 can help you with this issue.

Get ready for the global job interview

For professional jobs, the basic format of interviews globally is Western-style accomplishment-oriented, but cultural interviewing differences among nations still matter. Newcomers to the United States may be surprised to learn, for example, that they aren't expected to dress up in pinstriped suits to interview for a technology job, nor are they encouraged to speak extensively of family and other personal issues.

Americans who hope to work overseas for the first time may be surprised at such local customs as those of China, where interviewees are expected to nod, showing that they're listening and understanding the Chinese speaker who is communicating in English, or of certain European countries where a female candidate might be asked directly, "Are you pregnant?"

Chapter 4 tackles the emerging body of buzz about international interviewing.

Ten Concepts to Make You a Star

To get hired, press to impress! Read these ten super tips to make the hiring gods choose you at job interviews.

Amplify your preparation for top billing

Preparation makes all the difference in whether you get the best offers as you face intense scrutiny, probing questions, and employers who are afraid of making hiring mistakes. You must show that you're tuned in to the company's needs, that you have the skills to get up to speed quickly, and that you're a hand-in-glove fit with the company.

Fortunately, never in history has so much information about companies and industries been so easily accessible, both in print and online.

Chapter 6 gives tips on researching your audience.

Distinguish screening from selection interviews

As hiring action is concentrated increasingly in smaller companies, the separation between screening and selection interviews fades, and the same person may do both types. But traditionally, here's how the types, which I cover in Chapter 5, differ.

Screening interviews

In large organizations, interviewing is usually a two-stage process. A human resource specialist screens out all applicants except the best qualified. The screening interview is frequently handled by telephone or online video interviews rather than in-person. Survivors are passed to a manager (or panel of managers) who selects the winning candidate.

Screeners are experienced interviewers who look for reasons to screen you out based on your qualifications. Screeners can reject, but they cannot hire. They won't pass you on to hiring managers if your experience and education aren't within the specifications of the job.

When you're being interviewed by a screener, be pleasant and neutral. Volunteer no strong opinions. Raise no topics, except to reinforce your qualifications. Answer no questions that aren't asked — don't look for trouble.

But do remember smile to a lot. You're in your close-up.

Selection interviews

By the time you're passed on to a hiring manager or panel who makes the selection, you're assumed to be qualified or you wouldn't have made it that far along the channels of employment. You're in a pool of "approved" candidates chosen for the selection interview.

At a selection interview, move from neutral into high gear if the person doing the interview will be your boss or colleague. No more bland behavior — turn up the wattage on your personality power. This is the best time to find out whether you'll hit it off with the boss or colleagues or fit into the company culture.

Verify early what they want and show how you deliver

Almost as soon as you're seated, ask the interviewer to describe the scope of the position and the qualifications of the ideal person for that position.

You've already done this research when you're going for ShowStopper status. Use this question to confirm your research. If you're wrong, you must know immediately that you need to shift direction.

If you're dealing with multiple interviewers, direct your question to the senior panel member and wait for an answer. Then gaze around the group and ask, "Does anyone have something to add to the description?"

Confirming your research or gaining this information on the spot is the key to the entire interview. This technique permits you to focus on the factors upon which the hiring decision is made, without taking verbal detours that don't advance your candidacy.

Take the steps described in Chapters 2 and 5 to hit marks that show you're it! You're the one.

Connect all of your qualifications with a job's requirements

If a quick glance at your notes reminds you that the interviewer missed a requirement or two listed in the job posting when describing the position's scope and the ideal person for it, help the interviewer out by tactfully bringing up the missing criteria yourself. Keep it simple:

> *I see from my notes that your posting asked for three years of experience. I have that and two years more, each with a record of solid performance in —*

Your purpose in doing this is to demonstrate that you take this job possibility seriously, an attitude that the employer will applaud. Winning job offers by targeting your interview performance to a company's requirements is a logical follow-up to the resume targeting strategy that I explain in my book *Resumes For Dummies,* 5th Edition (Wiley, 2007).

Check out additional information about presenting yourself as the logical hire in Chapters 2 and 18–22; additionally, depending on your status, get must-read advice in Chapters 15, 16, or 17.

Master a one-to-two-minute commercial about yourself

Almost certainly you will be asked to respond to some version of the "Tell me about yourself" question. You're not helping yourself if you respond with the kind of question a 13-year-old might ask: "What do you want to know?" That approach makes you sound unprepared and naïve.

Instead, memorize a short description of your background (education, experience, and skills) that matches your strengths to the job.

After briefly relating the facts of your background, add a sentence or two about your curiosity, commitment, and drive to build mountains atop your already good skills base. A few well-chosen words enliven a dry recitation of facts with a splash of your personality.

Simply follow the techniques that I give in Chapter 18.

Seal the deal with a branding brief

Personal branding is becoming known for something — Jon Stewart for political satire and Tiger Woods for golf, for example. You don't have to be famous, just consistent in your efforts to develop your brand. Your personal brand develops along with the buzz about you — good or bad, your professional reputation, and how you're distinguished by characteristics and achievements — all salable distinctions in the marketplace.

Try to perfect a *branding brief* that tells your "story" — one that rolls off your tongue — in about 20 to 30 seconds, or in 100 words or less:

> *After I graduated from San Diego State University, I worked in the insurance industry until I took a break to start a family. That accomplished, I went back for refresher education and now, thoroughly updated, I'm looking for a new connection in either the insurance or financial fields.*

A branding brief may also be called an *elevator speech, personal branding message,* or *profile summary.* By any name, you can use this summary with networking contacts to obtain an interview, or you can use it inside an interview (in your closing statement, for instance). Additionally, a branding brief can be included as part of your longer one-to-two-minute commercial that I describe earlier in this section.

Find more ideas on preparing a branding brief in Chapter 18.

The difference between a commercial and a branding brief is length and content. A commercial is longer and more inclusive of details than is a cut-to-the-chase branding brief.

Win two thumbs up from the hiring manager and you're in!

As I discuss earlier in this chapter, given a choice of technically qualified applicants, employers almost always choose the one they like best. Despite the best efforts of supporters of "scientific" interviewing techniques to eliminate hiring by mutual chemistry, the vast majority of experts continue to say that more people lose job offers for personality factors than for lack of capability.

The psychological principles involved in winning friends and influencing interviewers have been around since the pharaohs ran the pyramid projects. For your purposes, remember this one:

> *We like people who are like us.*

How do you encourage the interviewer to think "you and me against the problem" rather than "you against me"?

Beyond pleasantries, mutual interests, connecting with eye contact, and other well-known bonding techniques, watch for special opportunities:

- ✔ Suppose your interviewer looks harried, with ringing telephones and people rushing about interrupting your talk. Flash a sympathetic smile and commiserate: *It looks like you're having one of those days.* The subtext of your comment is *I understand your frustrations. I've been in a similar place. You and I are alike.*

- ✔ Or suppose you're showing a work sample. Ask if you can come around to the interviewer's side of the desk to discuss your sample. You are looking at it "together."

Forget about age, color, gender, or ethnic background. Do whatever you reasonably can to make the hiring manager believe the two of you are cut from similar cloth.

To rewrite the famous 20th century Broadway wit and playwright Damon Runyon:

The part goes not always to those we like, nor the hiring to our twins, but that's the way to bet.

Pick up still more intel about the value of likeability in growing job offers in Chapter 2.

Allow interviewer to direct the improv

Some job search advisers seem to suggest that you take charge of the interview, directing the discussion in your favor. Not such a hot idea. Wrestling the interviewer for control can easily backfire when you appear to be usurping the interviewer's prerogative. As they say in show biz, you're stepping on the director's lines.

But what to do when a big void exists in what you're being asked to relate? The answer is the question. You can ask many variations of the "Would you like to hear about X?" inquiry and get your story told without seeming to take charge.

Chapter 11 reveals how to look good with questions you ask.

Show sensitivity for the hiring manager's dislike of interviewing

From supervisors to top executives, hiring managers tend to see interviews as encroachments on their already impossibly busy schedules. But they know they have to conduct them.

Suggest follow-up interviews be done on weekends or during the evenings to take the pressure off the interviewer's prime business hours.

Verse yourself in ways to make a hiring authority be glad he took time away from other duties to interview you; see Chapter 25.

Try not to talk money until you know they want you

When the salary question comes up at the beginning of an interview, say that money isn't your most important consideration — nor should it be at this point.

Admittedly, stalling salary talk until a better time is much more difficult today than it was a decade ago. But you should be holding out for the market value of the new job, not settling for an inadequate figure of your present or previous employment.

Only when you know the scope of the position and its market value — and that the company wants to hire you — are the stars in alignment to bargain in your best interest.

Read Chapter 8 for in-depth guidance on salary negotiation.

Take Home an Oscar from Any Interview

Rookie? Prime-timer? Clerk? Chief executive officer? No matter. You can do exceptionally well by following certain performance routines that succeed in any interview scene. Some of these suggestions are basic and familiar, but most people who haven't been on the interview tour for awhile can use the reminders.

Sing "I really, really like you!"

A likeable, relaxed, friendly smile carries you a long way on a carpet of good-will: You seem like an agreeable person, and everyone likes to work with agreeable, sunny people. By the time you're invited to meet the decision maker, the employer has probably put you through a screening interview and believes you're qualified to do the job. Now the decision maker's question is: *Do I like being around you?*

When you find that you and an interviewer have something in common — perhaps by noticing sports trophies or pictures in the office — comment on it. You'll seem affable and likable. People rarely hire someone they don't like.

Soak up opening moves that make interviewers see you as an agreeable person in Chapter 12.

Style your body language

Interviewers observe everything about you: not only your dress and inter-view answers, but your body language, facial expressions, posture, carriage, and gestures. If you're a rookie, think dignity. If you're a prime-timer, think energy. In between? Watch political candidates on TV for hints of what looks good and what doesn't.

Confirm that your body language is sending the "hire-me" message with tips in Chapter 10. Chapter 9's up-to-date data on dress and appearance add even more non-verbal firepower to your candidacy.

Be a treat: Act upbeat

Steer clear of negative words (such as *hate, don't ever want, absolutely not,* or *refuse*). And avoid such risky topics as the knock-down, drag-out fights you had with that bonehead you used to work for — never knock the old boss. Your prospective new boss may empathize with your old boss and decide to never be your boss at all.

Chapters 7 and 16 throw more light on avoiding a maze of negativity and looking as though you are a serial complainer who will never be satisfied.

Start your interview off on the right foot

Some advisers say that the first five minutes are the critical period of your job interview; others say that your window of opportunity for acceptance is only during the first 60 seconds. Why take a chance on who's right? Here are four tips to help you make a good impression right off the bat:

- Find out in advance what to wear (see Chapter 9) and where the interview site is located. Make a trial run if necessary.

- Be on time, be nice to the receptionist, read a business magazine while you're waiting, and — surprise, surprise — don't smoke, chew gum, or otherwise look as though you lack couth.

- Develop a couple of icebreaker sound bites, such as comments about a nice office, attractive color scheme, or interesting pictures.

- Don't sit until you're asked or until the interviewer sits. Don't offer to shake hands until the interviewer does.

During the interview, use the interviewer's name (but never use a first name unless you are old friends) frequently. And remember to make a lot of eye contact by looking at the bridge of an interviewer's nose. (Divert your gaze occasionally, or you're perceived as more creepy than honest.)

Track down more suggestions for making yourself a memorable candidate in Chapter 12.

Remember that you have a speaking part

Communication skills are among the most desired qualities employers say they want. Answer questions clearly and completely. Be sure to observe all social skills of conversation — no interrupting, no profanity. Just as you shouldn't limit yourself to one- or two-word answers, neither should you try to cover your nervousness with surround-sound endless talking. Aim for a happy medium.

Take in Chapter 18 for a savvy start on how to talk about yourself.

Agree to take pre-employment tests

No one likes those annoying pre-employment tests. Job seekers keep hoping they'll drop off the face of the earth but they're with us still. When you want the job, you're going to have to suck it up and test when asked. No test, no job.

Race to Chapter 7 for survival clues when you hope to be the last one standing after test time.

Flesh out your story beyond a college degree

Education is a fulcrum for movement throughout your career but relying on it alone to pull you through a competitive job search is a mistake. The mistake grows larger with too many mentions of an illustrious alma mater, assuming that the school's marquee power is a hall pass to move forward.

For example, a couple of mentions of Harvard in an interview are plenty; interviewers get it the first time. They wonder whether the Harvard background is the singular "accomplishment" a candidate offers.

Instead, spell out your accomplishments with true examples — what you learned and what you can do with your degree that benefit the employer.

In marketing a three-dimensional you, think of your education as one dimension; your experience as a second dimension; and your accomplishment record as a third dimension. All are important.

Wait. Back up. If the interviewer is also a Harvard grad, three mentions is perfectly okay. And if three is good, maybe four or five is better.

Chapter 5 is headquarters for storytelling tips; Chapters 18-22 show you how to fill in the blanks for your campus experience and beyond.

Bring a pen and notebook with you

Making a note here and there is advisable, as long as you don't attempt to record a transcript. To illustrate, you need to jot down reminders to get back to the interviewer when you can't answer a question from memory.

Brownie point: Writing down what someone says is flattering to the speaker.

Keep your ears up and your eyes open

Don't just sell, sell, sell. Take time to listen. When you're constantly busy thinking of what you're going to say next, you miss vital points and openings. So work on your listening skills. When you don't understand an interviewer's question, ask for clarification.

Observe the interviewer's moves. Watch for three key signs: high interest (leaning forward), boredom (yawning or glazed look), or a devout wish to end the interview (stacking papers or standing up). After assessing where you stand with the interviewer, take the appropriate action:

- ✔ High interest suggests you're stopping the show and should continue.

- ✔ The remedy for boredom is to stop and ask, *Would you rather hear more about (whatever you've been talking about) or my skills in the ABC area?*

- ✔ When the interviewer is ready to end the meeting, first ask if the interviewer has any reservations about your fit for the job; if so, attempt to erase them.

  And then go into your interview closing mode (Chapter 13). Gain a sense of timing and keep the door open for a follow-up contact by asking three questions: *What is the next step in the hiring process? When do you expect to make a decision? May I feel free to call if I have further questions?*

Fighting back on interview exploitation

You can lose your intellectual property through abuse of the job interview.

In the so-called *performance interview* for professional and managerial jobs, candidates are required to prove themselves with projects that demonstrate on-job skills, problem-solving capabilities, and communications abilities.

The employer asks for a proposal of how you would handle a company project or requests that you design a process the company can use. You're told to be ready to "defend your ideas" at the interview.

Unfortunately, sometimes the free-sample demand is incredibly time-consuming (say 80 hours) and costly ($200 and up in materials and research). You do your best but suppose you don't get the job? In an example of shoddy ethics, your work samples may be given to the victorious candidate who then steals your viable creative ideas. In the following sections, I give you a few examples from stung readers of my newspaper and Web column.

Portfolio scam

When applying to an advertising agency for a copywriting job, the owner asked me to leave my portfolio for review. He kept the portfolio and called on all the clients whose work was shown in the portfolio! Since then, I always respond to requests to leave or send my portfolio with this statement: "I need to be there to clarify the work shown. I will be glad to bring it, and we can discuss my work at your convenience."

State government rip-off

When I applied for a significant and highly symbolic job with my state government, I was informed I had been selected but had to go through the formality of an interview with a key aide to the governor. As requested, I took materials and a plan for approaching the job's goals to the confirmation interview. A long, official silence followed before a form letter arrived stating that a less-qualified professional, to whom I was a mentor, had won the

position. The victor showed me the state's plan of action: mine.

Consulting caper

My husband, an expert in human resources, spent two long days interviewing in a small town with the owner of a family company and his son. He gave them an unbelievable amount of advice and information to help their meager HR program, process management, and integrated product development. All we got out of that was reimbursement for a 200-mile car trip, a bad motel, and meals. That was our first realization of how small businesses in particular get almost-free consulting work.

Training trickery

I was a candidate for a city's new training division chief. I had to spend several hours in the city's computer labs designing programs and leaving them on CDs. I knew that with my education and experience, I had done well.

A long-term firefighter with zero training experience got the job with the city and used my materials for new employees!

Protecting Yourself

How do you avoid abuse without taking yourself out of the running for a job you want when you're not sure about the real interview agenda? Here are two ideas:

✔ You can copyright your plan and place a valid copyright notice ©, along with the publication date and your name, on its cover as an indication of your underlying claim to ownership. For free information, contact the Copyright Office online at www.copyright.gov, or by mail at Registrar of Copyrights, Copyright Office, Library of Congress, 101 Independence Ave. S.E., Washington, D.C. 20559.

For easier reading, see an excellent guide, *The Copyright Handbook: What Every Writer*

(continued)

(continued)

Needs to Know, 9th Edition, by Stephen Fishman (Nolo Press; www.nolo.com).

✔ You can bluff, hoping to create a theft deterrent by slapping a copyright notice and "Confidential — Property of (Your Name)" on your plan's cover.

When you're desperate or really, really, really want the job but don't have the time, inclination, or money to respond in full measure, offer something like this:

I'm glad that you see I have the brains and talent to bring value to your company. I'm happy, too, that you have the confidence in my work to ask me to handle such a potentially important solution to your marketing challenge. With my background, I'm sure I could do an outstanding job on this assignment. But you do realize, I hope, that such an important project would require 80 to 100 hours of intensely focused work. I'd enjoy doing it, but, quite frankly, I have several other job interviews

scheduled that I really can't shift around. Do you think a sample of substantially smaller scope would serve as well for your purposes?

With a statement like this, you

✔ Remind the interviewer that you're a top candidate

✔ Promise superior results

✔ Bring a reality check to a sensitive interviewer about what's being asked of you

✔ Let the interviewer know others are interested in you

✔ Propose to do much less work until a job offer crosses your palm

You can, of course, flatly refuse to part with advance goodies. In a seller's market, you'll probably be considered anyway. But in a buyer's market, the likelihood is that you'll be passed over when you decline to turn in a hefty free sample.

When Interviewers Chase You

When you're hot, you're hot — but even then the essential dynamic of a hiring episode is immutable: The employer has to be sold on you before a job offer will be yours to accept or reject.

Leverage is the ability to decide the outcome in a situation when you control what someone else wants. In job searching, leverage is your ability not just to get a job, but to get a job on your own terms.

Until a job offer materializes, until your deal moment actually clocks in, stay on message in the selling of your qualifications for the position. It's much easier on the ego to reject an offer than to be left standing at the starting gate.

You find the tools to decide whether you should accept or pass on a job offer in Chapter 14.

Surviving a snippy interviewer

Short of taking out a restraining order, what should you do when an interviewer's manner is offensive?

That depends upon who's doing the talking. When the interviewer is the person who would be your boss, be certain that you're not misunderstanding intent. If conversation really is disrespectful, bail out unless you want to spend most of your waking hours dealing with a difficult person. Show class. Just say "Thank you for your time. I don't think this job is a good fit for me." (Payback: It may leave the interviewer regretful that you're the good one who got away.)

But when the interviewer is doing preliminary screening, give the employer the benefit of the doubt by assuming that the interviewer doesn't represent the entire company and will be working five floors below you in a subbasement. Here are a few coping techniques:

- Smile and make a light remark: "Oh, do you think so? That bears watching."

- Respond with a two-second non-answer, and then quickly ask a question: "That's an interesting observation. It reminds me to ask you what role would the person in this position play in the new company product launch."

- Pretend the rude remark is a dropped call that you didn't hear, pause, and talk about your accomplishments or skills.

- When an interviewer keeps interrupting or contradicting you, look puzzled and ask for clarification. "Perhaps I'm not following you correctly. Could you please restate the question or explain what you mean by — ?"

When all else fails, remember the words of English writer Joanne Kathleen Rowling, author of the Harry Potter books: "Yet, sadly, accidental rudeness occurs alarmingly often. Best to say nothing at all, my dear man."

Building Lifetime Confidence

This first chapter serves as an overview for the entire book. The remainder of these pages is wide and deep with the details that can help you gain a lifetime of confidence in your ability to sail through reality-show interviews and receive the best job offers.

Winning candidates are memorable

Comparing *American Idol* winners to job interview candidates, Phoenix career coach Joe Turner (www.jobchangesecrets.com) says it's the total package that counts. "You don't have to be the best singer, just the *most remembered* decent singer. Same for the job interview. You don't always have to be the best candidate with the top skills. You do have to find a way to be the *most remembered* hirable candidate."

Chapter 2

Tailoring Your Qualifications for Targeted Job Interviews

*N*ew television shows used to get an entire season to catch on with viewers before being bounced to TV's boneyard, but these days they're lucky to snare an eight-week schedule to prove their popularity.

Similarly, job tenure, once gold-watch eligible, today is often reduced to project-oriented employment that may end after fewer than three years. That's the word from Paul Hawkinson, legendary editor-in-chief of *The Fordyce Letter*, the third-party recruiting industry's premier newsletter.

Drawing on Hawkinson's deep recruiting industry knowledge in a telephone interview, I asked him: How does shorter job tenure affect interviewing strategy from the job seeker's side of the desk? His answer illuminates the enhanced value of today's targeted job interview. (A *targeted job interview* demonstrates that you have the skill qualifications that the job requires.)

"Employers now want three things: skills, skills, and skills," Hawkinson explains. "They want immediate ramp-up by new hires. They want people who don't need break-in time. They want productivity and performance from Week One."

"In fact," Hawkinson continues, "employers are so focused on connecting the right skill sets to the job for a fast start that I joke about not being surprised if one day new employees are hired by parts numbers and bar codes tattooed on their heads."

Hawkinson's amusing explanation of the intense interest that employers have in effecting a fast start for new hires may explain why neither he nor I hear much these days about a once-popular recruiting philosophy: Hire for attitude and train for skill — the belief that what people know is less important than who they are. A somewhat different and almost opposite philosophy seems to be emerging: Hire for skill and pray for attitude.

Connecting the Dots: Showing You're the Right One

As I explain in my book *Resumes For Dummies,* 5th Edition, sea changes have taken place over the past several years that affect who gets interviewed and why. The outdated all-purpose resume is being replaced by the targeted resume that is tailor-made for a specific employment goal. A targeted resume, by addressing a given opportunity, makes it easy for an employer to see how your qualifications are a close match to a job's wish list and want to meet you in person.

The identical strategy applies to your interview: When you're in a room with an interviewer, try to make it easy for the interviewer to believe that you have all (or nearly all) of the skills and attributes that the interviewer is trying to recruit for the position. Emphasize that you meet the specs — point for point.

Susan Joyce, CEO of Job-Hunt.org, explains the concept of matching point for point this way: "Employers react favorably when you connect the dots showing that you can deliver almost all of the abilities and results that they're asking for."

Good vibes are always welcome

In this chapter I urge you not to assume a decision maker is aware that your qualifications are a strong match for the job's requirements. People forget, they become distracted, or they may not get the message from preliminary interviewers. So you have to tell them again to be sure your message is delivered. But while skills are critical, they aren't all it takes to get hired.

Personal chemistry (motivation, personality, style, energy, attitude, and so forth) and fit in the workplace's culture are important decision factors as well.

Presenting Your Qualifications in a Targeted Interview

While reflecting on how best to illustrate the ins and outs of a targeted job interview, I had a light-bulb moment. Why not step outside familiar career fields — engineering, retailing, financial services, and so forth — to shake things up a bit with a make-believe movie script of an interview in the high-adventure field of deep sea diving in dangerous waters? Although the lyrics will be different in targeted interviews in familiar fields, the music's the same in all career fields.

I began thinking about deep-diving professionals after reading a newspaper story about the work of Scott Cassell of Escondido, Calif, (www.sea-wolves. com). Cassell is arguably the world authority on the Red Demon (Giant Humboldt Squid) that man eats as calamari — that is, unless the calamari eats him first.

Admittedly, the fictional script that follows isn't a white-hot page turner, but I hope you find it an interesting and novel introduction to the targeted interview.

Hunt for Red Demon: The screenplay

FADE IN

Contemporary kitchen of thirty-something couple. Todd Turner, the leading man in this screenplay, is sitting at a table reading his laptop screen. In good physical shape, Todd obviously works out. His attractive wife Susan drinks orange juice. Todd swings his laptop screen toward Susan calling it to her attention.

TODD

Suze, look at this posting.

Susan crosses over to look and we see these words on the screen:

Need ace underwater camera operator to lead shoot of feature film: Hunt for Red Demon. Tells story of death-defying conflict with Giant Humboldt Squid, also known as Red Demon. More dangerous than sharks, these deep-sea predators are man-eaters. Minimum 10 yrs diving experience and camera work. All diving licenses required. Insurable. Contact Ralph Russo at studio production office.

SUSAN

Are you going to apply? You have 14 years of diving experience but you have only 4 years of film camera work. And just last week you explained to me that now it's a big deal to focus on how you offer the qualifications that match a job's requirements. Aren't those things (pointing to the laptop screen) requirements?

TODD

Yeah they are, but you bet I'm going after this one. And although I only have 4 years of film experience, I've got 11 years of videocam experience. They should see that combo as equivalent — heck, more than equivalent! I'm going to call right now to set up an interview.

INT. FILM STUDIO PRODUCTION OFFICE — LOS ANGELES — DAY

Our POV is from the back of interviewer Ralph Russo's head as we see Todd walk through the door with a smile on his face. Todd is wearing a custom-made suit of chain mail and aluminum panels over his wet suit.

RALPH

Please be seated . . . if you can. That's, uh, an unusual suit . . . custom-made for diving, I suppose.

Scott struggles somewhat comically to slide into the chair and finally succeeds. The interviewer and Todd share a chuckle, bonding.

TODD

I hear you're a diver yourself so you'd know that Scott Cassell is the one who first came up with this one-man armory. You're right; this protection is specially made diving gear that's saved my life more than once. After a close call with a hungry Humboldt, I had one custom-made.

RALPH

I'm glad you recognize that those Humboldts are dangerous creatures. Our research team says that they're typically 3 to 7 feet long but can be as long as 14 feet and weigh more than 700 pounds.

TODD

That's what I thought, too, but I saw a video showing a mammoth Red that's estimated to be 54 ft. I wouldn't be looking forward to doing a tango with that fish. I'd rather go down Moby Dick's gullet.

Ralph holds up a half dozen storyboards with Giant Humboldts making a grab for a fisherman's boat oar and points to them.

RALPH

I think audiences will come to see this action and adventure thriller. Those suckers have eight muscular arms and two feeding tentacles — like a sharp parrot's beak — that they use to attack their prey with more than 40,000 needle sharp teeth at once! That's gotta hurt.

Nodding to agree, Todd looks directly into Ralph's face as he continues.

TODD

Absolutely, I take those fish seriously. They don't just nibble when they grab you and pull you way down; they shred you! They're trying to eat you in tiny, delicate pieces! I'm told that fisherman in Mexico would rather fall into the water with a feeding frenzy of sharks than Humboldts. I'm well aware of the danger. I carry my own insurance but you can never have too much coverage in this business. Health-wise, I'm certain that I'm insurable for your film.

RALPH

That's great. As you know, insurance is not optional. If we come to terms, I'll ask you to get a quick physical for the insurance people. Concerning another must-have, I see on your resume that you've had lots of diving experience . . . you want to elaborate on that?

TODD

Sure. I was a rated commercial diver at 18. I've been diving ever since — 14 years. And of course, I'm fully licensed and certified. Never had a problem or accident.

RALPH

What about camera work?

TODD

I've been doing underwater film for four years — but wait (holds up hand like traffic cop) I've also got 11 years of deep water videography. In fact, I've got some samples with me, including a short documentary that plays periodically on TV. Can we take a look at them now? I think you'll agree that I meet every single one of your requirements — diving and camera experience, licensing, insurable, and as you can see from my "uniform" I'm a cautious guy who knows how to stay alive while I'm getting the shot.

RALPH

I can't argue with those facts, Todd. You're right on the money. I assume that you brought along street clothes?

Todd nods "yes."

Then why don't you change and then we'll walk over to Projection and look at your film and videos. Do you work with an agent?

Telling your qualifications tale, again and again

In the preceding section's screenplay, Ralph Russo the interviewer was a screener, checking out Todd's credentials and bona fides before passing Todd on to others, probably the producer and director of *Hunt for Red Demon*.

The passing of Todd up the food chain (sorry, too bad to resist) raises a question: Do you need to tell everyone at a company who interviews you how your qualifications are a close fit with the competencies and skills that the company's trying to bring aboard? Although doing so seems repetitive, don't assume everyone knows that you're a handsome hand in a groovy glove. You may have to repeat yourself several times — if you can do so without sounding like a broken Blu-ray disc.

Interviews for professional and managerial jobs typically stretch over two or more meetings, as I describe in Chapter 5. Your qualifications for an open job generally are vetted in the first, or screening interview, which likely is conducted by an HR representative. This interviewer can screen you out of the candidate pool, or if you're a qualified candidate, pass you up to the next level: the selection interviewer.

The selection interview(s), usually conducted by the manager to whom you would report, may assume you're qualified or you wouldn't have been passed on to a decision maker. The hiring manager tends to be more interested in how you would fit in with the others on the manager's team.

But sometimes, especially with technical candidates, the hiring manager wants to make sure your qualifications are right on target. Perhaps the hiring process stretched out over weeks, even months, and the hiring manager has to an extent, forgotten what you offer, failed to read your file from HR, or just needs reassurance that you can do the job.

Be alert for signs in a selection interview that you need to shore up the hiring manager's appreciation of your matching skills and experience. You can do it with a simple question technique: "I noticed that one of the requirements you're after is experience in construction project management in foreign countries. Would you like to hear about my office park experience in France?"

Making Up for Missing Qualifications

Suppose you anticipate connecting the dots and come up a requirement or two short. What *not* to do is stand there looking as though you came to the wrong address, shake your head, and admit "I don't have experience in the hotel field" and shut up.

When you can't connect every dot, give a *compensatory response.* Compensatory responding means staying on the stage by offering a substitute qualification when you lack a specified qualification in the job description. Compensatory responding doesn't always work, but it works often enough to make the effort.

In the above example of lack of experience in the hotel field, after you say "I haven't worked at a hotel," add a compensatory response: "But I do have experience in the restaurant field, and I know a good deal that is common to both of these related hospitality industries. Both fields need employees who are experienced in providing attentive customer services, careful accounting and financial processes, and quality materials supplies. Do you agree that my experience is relevant to the requirements of this position?"

Another example of a compensatory response is in education. Suppose the job requirement is a specific education credential that you don't happen to have, such as a bachelor's degree in business administration with an emphasis on marketing. Don't automatically raise the issue, but if it comes up, or if you must show that you're a qualified candidate, explain that you have the equivalent qualification by virtue of alternate education, such as a bachelor's degree in psychology, and/or experience, such as campus marketing experience promoting school events.

I discuss a number of other questions and suggested answers to help you size up well in a measure of the job's requirements in Chapters 18–22. Research improves your odds even when you're not a perfect 100 percent match for the job. Why? Because you'll be talking about topics that the employer wants to talk about — job requirements identified as those needed to solve the employer's problems.

Just as no one's perfect, your work and education history won't match up point for point with the requirements set out in every job interview you attend. And there will be times when despite diligent research and planning, you just can't come up with a compensatory response that makes sense. Yet, despite these factors, you have persistent and realistic feeling that you can handle the job. What can you say on the spot to plug the hole in your history?

When you're up against a rigid requirement that you absolutely can't meet and that you're pretty sure is going to mean curtains for you in the interview, try this last-ditch compensatory response:

> *Let's say that you were to make me an offer and I accept, what can I do when I start to further compensate for my lack of [requirement] as I work hard to relieve your immediate workload?*

Essentially, you're playing the likeability card. You're asking the employer to revert to the philosophy of hiring for attitude and training for skill. You're using the likeability qualification to plug your requirement gap.

As Paul Hawkinson observes "Likeability is a factor that can turn the tide in your direction. Although skill level and applicable experience trumps at the beginning of the interview process, I've seen dozens of less-than-qualified people hired because the employer *liked* them better than the perfect candidate with the personality of a doorknob."

When crossover skills miss the connection

Realistically speaking, what are your chances of success in claiming that you're a good match to a job's requirements on the theory that your skills transfer from one industry or company size to another? Sometimes your assertion works like a charm. Sometimes it doesn't. The theory of crossover skills (also called transferable skills) holds promise only when applied truthfully.

The Fordyce Letter editor-in-chief Paul Hawkinson explains: "It's easier to find a job within the industry where your experience lies. The weapons engineer with 20 years of experience will find it difficult to work outside of the defense industry at the same salary. And 20 years of selling cosmetics does not prepare or qualify someone to sell industrial equipment.

"Along similar lines, a highly specialized employee with a very large company just may not find a market for his or her skills in a smaller firm where versatility is admired."

When you're debating whether your skills transfer and you can do the job, channel Jawaharlal Nehru, India's first prime minister: "A theory must be tempered with reality." Don't waste your time trying to peddle smoke and mirrors in moving your skills from one venue to another when it's a lost cause.

Chapter 3

Going Wireless for Your Interview

*A*nd just when you thought that Webcams were chiefly useful for live peep shows or for nanny surveillance in homes with wee tots, you discover that Webcams can be used for job interviews that take place when, for one reason or another, the interviewer and the candidate can't physically be in the same room. More gee-whiz technology is moving warp-speed into the interviewing space.

What a jolt! Now that most people have finally become accustomed in this digital age to e-mail, camera phones, Web sites, instant messaging, job boards, resume databanks, online employee referral systems, Web-based talent communities, job blogs, BlackBerrys, business-oriented social networks, Podcasting, and iPhones, the next big technological wizardry for job seekers is banging on our doors, ready for roll-out.

The forces in the driver's seat of the new wonders are the same ones fueling the online video industry's rocket growth overall: high-speed Web access and cheap technology.

Video screening saves hiring costs

Why are videos being introduced as employment screening filters? Beyond the fact that employers now use video because they can, companies try to curb time and travel expenses in their hiring practices. Suppose, for instance, that a company starts with a pool of 100 resumes. Perhaps a dozen will be moved to the first-cut pile, from which interviewers make a round of phone calls. The phone calls reduce the candidate pool to perhaps six. The surviving half-dozen candidates move to the next step and receive video job interviews. From those video interviewing results, two or three finalists are invited to an in-person meeting, from which the victor will be selected. Add zeros to the numbers in this example and without winnowing controls, recruiting costs soar and company financial executives get cranky.

I won't keep you in suspense: Here's a heads-up on four major trends that are likely to soon affect the way you do interviewing business. How soon? Your guess is as good as mine, but here's the way the wind is blowing:

- ✔ **Extreme wireless:** An explosive boom in new wireless connectivity, the cutting-edge technology — said to be 50 times faster than today's wireless technology — will carpet the United States in 30-mile stretches, essentially creating a nationwide hot spot, as well as firing up comparable broadband access around the globe.

- ✔ **Webcam bonanza:** At the same time that tens of millions of people are getting their keyboards on enormous amounts of super-speed broadband, cheaper Webcams and smart phones are popping up, permitting consumers to savor the full Internet experience. People everywhere already are using free, live, interactive picture-and-voice chats to stay in touch with new and old friends across the country or around the world.

- ✔ **Video vogue:** The trends of abundant high-speed Web access and cheaper technology have cleared the way for a burst of growth in online video interviews that screen candidates for employment. Thus far, most video job interviews are replacements for the familiar phone screening interview.

- ✔ **Global go-go:** People, money, and ideas cross borders more freely than ever, creating an international force sparking interviewing technology. (I cover international dimensions in job interviewing in Chapter 4.)

The following segments flesh out the ways video techniques are applied to job interviewing today and how you can benefit.

Casting calls and screening interviews

"Employers conduct screening interviews to decide whether a prospective employee should be interviewed face to face. The screening interviewer seeks to determine appropriate product background, job experience, competencies, skills, and if a fit might exist between a candidate and the company's corporate culture.

"These factors can be a lot to address in a typical 30-60 minutes screen. Your best strategy to move forward to the next step in the hiring process is preparing for a screen as you would for a traditional one-to-one interview. Because employers screen to filter out candidates who aren't up to the job, that means they are looking for reasons *not* to bring in people for interviewing. Don't be screened out — prepare!"

*Mark S. James, CPC, President and CEO Hire Consulting Services (*www.hire consultant.com*) Career Transition Coaching*

Can You See Me Now?

Online videoconferencing has been around for years but until now has been used chiefly by corporations with deep pockets for collaborative or distance-meeting purposes. That's changing as traditional videoconferencing systems are also being used as a cost-effective and logical way for employers and candidates to meet and greet each other. Locations at which formal videoconferencing systems are found include the following:

- ✔ Corporate offices
- ✔ College career centers
- ✔ Hotels and airport
- ✔ Recruiting and staffing firms
- ✔ Public room vendors and brokers
- ✔ End-to-end commercial conferencing firms

As a job candidate, never pay for the costs of a video job interview. That expense belongs to the employer.

Moving away from traditional videoconferencing facilities, some employers are engaging video interviewing service firms such as HireVue (www.hirevue.com) to handle the employment screening process from A to Z. HireVue records the interview either at a company office or offsite with a Webcam (or sends the Webcam to the candidate) and provides a tutorial on the technical aspects of the video interview. Each candidate for the same position is asked the same questions. Typically a candidate is given 30 seconds to read a question and about two minutes to answer it. Hiring managers compare recordings of the sessions to see how each candidate answers the questions.

In addition to traditional videoconferencing facilities and independent video interviewing service firms, Webcams at home are the breaking news for job interviews. The reason is cost and available technology.

In the 1980s, color cameras required studio lighting and maintenance costing $5,000 to $100,000. Today a basic Webcam runs as little as $25–$30; pretty good models can be had for $60–$75; and advanced models go for $100–$150. Laptops increasingly come with Webcams built in. Although Webcams keep improving and are better than they were, the picture quality isn't as good as film, and there's still a slight audio delay of a second or two, sometimes causing a lip-sync lag.

What is a video interview?

Video interviewing (a form of videoconferencing) is a live, two-way electronic communication that permits two or more people in different geographic locations to engage in face-to-face visual and audio exchange. Miles separate them: sometimes few, sometimes many, and sometimes oceans.

In the new Webcam-dominated world, the caller and the person on the receiving end need only a computer and a monitor, a Webcam, a microphone and Internet access to do a job interview. Or a more ambitious job interview can be conducted on more sophisticated equipment, such as a television camera (rather than a Webcam) and projected on a television screen (rather than on a computer monitor).

Either way, interviewing skills are front and center in a video version.

The gamut of video interviews

Here's how the *who* and *how* of video job interviews shake out:

- **High end** means traditional technology and assistance used in permanent set-ups (like a TV set) in conference centers, corporate offices, and public rental rooms. High production values typically include costly equipment and professional staff to handle all technical concerns.

- **Mid-level** includes intermediate technology outsourced to a specialty video firm by an employer. The middleman contractor may invite job candidates into an office, operate with traditional equipment, or send them a Webcam to use at home for the interview if the candidate does not own a Webcam. Video firm staff provides instructions and tips to job candidates.

✔ **Low end** refers to new Webcam technology used directly between an employer and a candidate who turns a Webcam on himself or herself with no guidance or technical assistance. This is the category where the vast majority of job seekers find themselves: raw beginners at technically setting up or using Webcams. And after mastering the technical aspects, video newbies are inexperienced on the performing requirements.

Consider video interviewing as a new skill set to master. If you can afford it, get video job interview coaching. If not, practice early and practice often, using friends as interviewers. Study TV personalities for presentation behavior. And read and relish the how-to-do-it suggestions in the upcoming section "Rock the Video Interview."

What's video's upside? Downside?

Certain advantages and disadvantages of video interviewing are obvious, but others are sure to turn up as employers and job seekers gain more experience in using the technology. First, a look at the pros:

✔ **Time-saving:** In certain situations, you may get a job faster because of video interviewing. Recruiters and hiring managers can conduct first-round interviews more quickly online using video interviewing than they can scheduling in-person interviews. Video interviewing is a time-saver particularly in instances where you can't easily break away from your present job to travel to an interview or where several groups of company executives must weigh in on your hiring but are in different locales; video interviewing allows several locations to connect at once.

✔ **Convenience:** When you're currently employed, you won't have to miss work to interview if you can respond at your convenience.

✔ **Distance-jumping for short-term employment:** Video interviewing is a boon to prospective interns and contract workers who want jobs far away; a company isn't going to fly you in for a three-month summer internship or contract gig but may hire you on the basis of an online video interview.

✔ **Modernity:** Not many candidates have used video interviewing yet. If you can show that you take technology in stride (especially if you're over 40), you get bonus points. You image as a good fit in forward-looking companies.

But nothing is perfect. Take a look at some of the drawbacks that video interviewing presents:

✔ **Lag time:** A lag time occurs when data is compressed and sent from one location to another. You have to remember to allow for the delay and not step on the interviewer's lines. Additionally, the interviewer may inadvertently cut you off in mid-sentence.

- ✔ **Connectivity:** Sometimes the connection isn't great and you have to strain to hear what people are saying.

- ✔ **Lighting:** If the lighting is off, you may look too green or pale like a corpse.

- ✔ **Performance pressure:** When it's your turn to speak up, you have very little time to look away, down, up, or sideways to process your thoughts. When the "green light" goes on, the pressure on you is somewhat like a contestant at a quiz show: talk or walk.

- ✔ **Learning curve:** Being judged in front of a camera takes some getting used to. Glimpses of awful screen tests of actors who later became famous confirm the point. While camera success may be ducks-to-water for a few people, more typically candidates start out feeling unnatural. Time and practice make them less so.

Making an on-camera impression

The *content* of a video interview is much the same as an in-person interview. But the *execution* differs. Consider these sample reactions:

- ✔ A candidate, a cool 20-something manager who isn't easily thrown off center, told a magazine that his video interview was "kind of nerve-wracking" and a totally different feeling from sitting in front of someone for a live interview.

- ✔ An employer reported on a comments board that a lot of things don't come across the camera and that certain factors are accentuated: "Posture, dress, comfort with uncertainty, facility with technology — all those things get highlighted and bolded during a Web interview."

Online, you can't use handshakes and ingratiating small talk as you enter and leave an interviewer's office to help imprint favorable memories of you. To compensate, include a memorable statement — a sound bite. Somewhere near the end of the interview, an experienced candidate says something like this:

Of the many things I've accomplished in my career, (name a top achievement) stands out as the most significant. Do you see a strong connection between my favorite accomplishment and what it will take to be very successful in this position?

An entry-level candidate can aim to become unforgettable by saying something unexpected like this:

I know that many employers consider my generation to be lacking in writing and critical thinking skills and are not pleased that some of us write company e-mail as if we were texting cell-phone messages with our thumbs. That's not me. I'm good with technology but I'm old fashioned. I spell my words correctly and include all of the letters. And I believe you will be happy to know that I use my head when I write — not just my thumb. When can we get together and speak face-to-face?

Rock the Video Interview

"Companies hiring at all levels, from entry-level to experienced professionals, are becoming more comfortable using technology (as you can see from the growth in Internet recruiting) and video interviewing is becoming the next step in the online recruiting process for many recruiters and employers," says Alison Doyle, the author of *About.com Guide to Job Searching: Tools and Tactics to Help You Get the Job You Want* (Adams Media, 2006).

Doyle is also the guide for About.com: Job Search (`www.jobsearch.about.com`) and a career center manager at Skidmore College in Saratoga Springs, N.Y. The career expert recognizes that video interviewing can be intimidating to job seekers:

> *It's hard enough to interview face-to-face, let alone in front of a camera and microphone. It can seem like a scary proposition, even for those of us who are familiar with technology and use it on a regular basis.*

Not to worry. As French Renaissance writer Michel de Montaigne famously said: "A learned person is not learned in everything but the capable person is capable in everything." This section is dedicated to making sure that capable you are not intimidated when you interview remotely.

Before the interview

As with all interviews, don't walk in cold to professional videoconference facilities. And don't sit down at your desk Webcam unprepared. The following suggestions brief you on what you should know.

Time limits

Find out whether you're on a clock for the interview. If the interview is scheduled for 30 minutes, consider it a rigid cut-off and don't plan on overtime.

Advance work

Send materials for show-and-tell in advance in case the interviewer wants to ask questions about an updated resume or project; you can't slide materials through the screen.

Content review

Review potential questions that you're likely to be asked. (See Chapters 18–25.) Be ready to relate your qualifications to the job's requirements. (See Chapter 2.) Memorize examples of accomplishments that illustrate what you can bring to the company.

Note taking

Making a few notes during an in-person interview is flattering to the interviewer. But the jury's still out about whether you should take a notebook to video interviews and jot down points that will help you respond with clarity. The criticism of note taking is that it is more pronounced and disruptive onscreen than it is face-to-face. Others disagree, saying that glancing at your notes may make you seem more conscientious.

Technical check

When you're not interviewing at home, arrive 15 minutes early at the interview site to deal with any technical issues that may arise. Request an overview of the interviewing event and a refresher on the use of the equipment. Ask the technician how loud you should speak into the mike and how to use the picture-in-picture feature that shows you in action.

When you're using your own video equipment, check your camera angle (set at eye level), speakers (place out of view), and microphone (set high enough that you don't have to keep bending down but not in front of your face).

Appearance

To avoid a contrast issue, you can't go wrong with solid colors that aren't too dark (black) or too light (white, yellow). Although you may see an anything-goes range of colors on High Definition or digital TV, the technology for the average computer monitor isn't yet that advanced.

Additionally, busy patterns distract from your face. So do definitive stripes and plaids. Watch TV newscasters to form your own wardrobe preferences. Otherwise, wear the same clothing you would wear to a same-room interview. (See Chapter 9.)

Background

Plan for an uncluttered look. Eliminate such distractions as too many books, wall hangings, memos taped to the wall, and so forth. Avoid background motion — second hands ticking on a clock or cars passing on the street outside, for instance.

Dress rehearsal

When you're interviewing at home, arrange a test interview with a friend. Can you hear him and can he hear you? Can you see her and can she see you? Is the framing of your screen about right (head to waist) or is the focus on your face so tight that every pore looks like a moon crater? Do you remember to lock up the family cat so it doesn't leap into the picture and to send the kids outside to play so they don't walk behind you?

Record yourself to see how you're coming across on camera. This tip, more than any other, will improve your interviewing performance.

During the interview

You're almost prepared to command the screen. Now review these finer points gleaned from others who have gone before the cameras before you.

Movements and posture

Calmness is classy and shows confidence. No way should you check your personality at the door, but do try to be fairly still. Smooooth. Avoid overly broad gestures — you're not directing traffic. Ration your gestures to underscore important information.

Microphones have an irritating habit of picking up all the noise in the room. Don't shuffle papers or tap a pen. Noises that you may not notice in a same-room interview can become annoying in a video interview.

Occasionally glance at the picture-in-picture feature on the monitor to check your body language and hope you don't catch yourself scratching, twisting your hair, or jangling your keys. Slouching and other bad-posture sagging make you look even worse on those small screens than they do in person.

Facial expressions and speaking

The first thing you say is *Hi, I'm John Gill. Nice to meet you.* (And if you're not John Gill, use your own name.) Speak normally, but not too fast. When nervous, some people don't stop for air, and their best lines are left on the cutting room floor, unheard or not understood.

Be conscious of a sound delay. A couple of seconds will lapse between the interviewer's statement or question and when you hear her or him. At the end of an interviewer's words, pause before you reply.

Look directly at the camera as often as possible when speaking. You can look around occasionally but avoid rolling your eyes all over the room as though you can hardly wait to make your getaway. Some people look down at the desk. Don't, especially if you have a bald, shiny spot on the top of your dome. And don't bend over the microphone. Imagine that the interviewer is sitting across the table from you.

The three most important things to remember in a video interview are (1) smile, (2) smile, and (3) smile. Have you noticed that even when reporting disasters of nationwide proportions, TV anchor people don't always wipe the smile off their faces? Why do you suppose that is? *Smile!*

Virtual handshake

Unless your interview space is on fire, it's not your prerogative to end the interview. Always allow the interviewer to indicate when time's up. In cases where the interview format is controlled by a technician, you're given signals to close it down.

Since you can't shake hands through a monitor, at the end of the interview, deliver a sign-off statement indicating you understand that the interview is over. You can say something as simple as *Thank you for interviewing me. I enjoyed it. Let's talk face to face very soon.*

For other sign-off ideas, review Chapter 13, and check out Chapter 14 to be prepared if lightening strikes and you're offered the job during the video interview.

When you're in a professional setting, push the mute button and leave the room. When you're at home, mute the mike and close the camera.

When You're on the Phone

Mobile phones (a.k.a. cell phones) have exploded into the world's ears in less than a quarter of a century. About 80 percent of the world's population has mobile phone coverage now, a figure projected to jump to 90 percent by 2010.

The mobiles have progressed from rare and expensive status icons used by corporate suits in the early 1980s to today's common and low-cost personal possessions used by everyone. Mobile phones worldwide now number more than 2 billion, outnumbering land-line telephones in many nations. In the United States, some young adult households have cell phones and aren't sure what you're talking about when you mention land-line phones.

Massive numbers and rapid adoption seem to be only the beginning of the secret life of cell phones. Today's smart phones can be used for two-way videoconferencing. Exactly *when* this killer application will be applied to job interviews is unclear. In the meantime, the telephone, wireless or tethered to land lines, continues to be a popular and powerful audio medium for conducting screening interviews.

Hold the phone

Almost everyone knows someone who's been contacted by a recruiter for a screening interview (see Chapter 5). In looking for reasons to rule you out, recruiters home in on your possible lack of qualifications for the position. They ask about your experience, skills, competencies, education, your inconvenient geography, and whether your financial requirement is too low or too high for the job's predetermined compensation range.

Sometimes recruiters purposely try to catch you off guard, hoping surprise strips away the outer layers of your preparation, exposing genuine, unrehearsed thoughts and feelings. Recruiters also see unanticipated calls as useful for measuring your ability to think on your feet.

Because most people don't prepare for screening phone interviews as rigorously as they prepare for face-to-face meetings, the casualty fallout is heavy. When the caller is trying to reduce the list to a few finalists, expect a future hang-up on your candidacy if the screening call doesn't go well.

If you don't like surprises, take the steps I outline in the upcoming sections.

Keep your phone well-stocked

Stash one phone in a quiet room stocked with all your interview essentials. Must-haves include

- Current resume
- A list of professional accomplishments
- Background information on the employer
- Questions about the company and position
- Outlines of brief stories that illustrate your qualifications, competencies, and problem-solving abilities
- A calendar, with all scheduled commitments and open dates
- A notepad, pen, and calculator
- Water and tissues

Phone interviewing when you're at work

If your current employer doesn't know that you're looking for a new job, close the door and speak to the interviewer for only a couple of minutes, asking the caller if you can set up an in-person interview right then — or if you can talk in the evening when you're at home.

Make phone appointments

Whenever possible, don't answer questions on the fly when the call comes in. You won't be prepared and you won't do your best. Schedule an appointment for your phone interview. Say that you're walking out the door to a meeting across town and will call back as quickly as you can:

> *Thank you for calling. I appreciate your attention. I'm very interested in speaking with you about my qualifications. Unfortunately, this is not a good time for me — I'm headed out the door. Can I call you back in an hour?*

If a recruiter insists on calling you back rather than the other way around, do what you would do for any other interview: Be ready early as a reminder to interview as a professional. Change out of your jeans and into the type of dress you'd wear in a business meeting. Most importantly, treat the call as an overture to an in-room meeting.

Project a winning image

When the call comes, heed the following suggestions, most of which come from Mark S. James, a leading executive career coach (www. hireconsultant.com).

- ✔ **If you have a home office, use it.** An office just feels more businesslike. You may find it helpful to face a blank wall to eliminate distractions of gazing out a window or spotting dust on your favorite painting.

- ✔ **Gather essential information.** At the start of the conversation, get the caller's name, title, company, e-mail address, and phone number. Read back the spelling.

- ✔ **Market yourself.** Assume the role of "seller" during the interview. If you sell your skills and abilities effectively, the listener sees value in bringing you in for an interview.

- ✔ **Strike the right tone.** Be enthusiastic but don't dominate the conversation.

✔ **Have an answer ready.** Be prepared to answer the "tell me about your-self" request early on; keep your answer to two minutes.

✔ **Ask smart questions.** Demonstrate industry knowledge by asking "intelli-gence" questions: *The industry seems to be moving toward [emerging technology]. How does your company plan to compete?*

✔ **Don't rush or drone on.** Speak clearly and be aware of your pace — not too fast, not too slow. Don't ramble or over-explain. Keep your answers short and succinct; if the interviewer wants more information, she'll ask for it.

✔ **Use check-back phrases.** After answering a question, you can add such follow-on phrases as *Does that answer your question? Have I sufficiently answered your question about my managerial experience? Is this the kind of information you're seeking?*

✔ **Be a champion listener.** Prove that you're paying attention by feeding back what the interviewer says: *In other words, you feel that — .* Interject short responses intermittently to acknowledge the interviewer's comments: *That's interesting . . . I see . . . Great idea.*

✔ **Get specific.** Describe your ability to benefit the company by using spe-cific dollar amounts and percentages to explain your past accomplish-ments. Let them know *how* you did it.

✔ **Divert important questions.** Tickle interviewers' interest by answering most of their questions. Then, when they ask a particularly important question, give them a reason to see you in person. Tell the interviewer that you can better answer that question in person:

That's an important question — with my skills (experience) in _____, it's one that I feel I can't answer adequately over the phone. Can we set up a meeting so that I can better explain my qualifications? I'm free on Tuesday morning — is that a good time for you?

Decide beforehand which questions can best be put off. You can use this tactic two or three times in the same conversation.

✔ **Punt the salary question.** Phone screeners often ask you to name an expected salary. Play dodge ball on this one. You don't know how much money you want yet because you don't know what the job is worth. You find more techniques to avoid premature salary talk in Chapter 8.

✔ **Push for a meeting.** As the call winds to a close, go for the prize:

As we talk, I'm thinking we can better discuss my qualifications for (position title) in person. I can be at your office Thursday morning. Is 9:30 good, or is there a better time for you?

Another statement:

(Interviewer's name), based on the information you have given me, I am very interested in pursuing this work opportunity and would like to schedule a time for us to meet in person. What looks good for you?

When the interviewer agrees but can't set a specific time, simply suggest when you are available and ask when would be a good time to follow up. Remember, what you want is an in-person meeting. Assume you'll get it and give the interviewer a choice as to the time.

✔ **Say thanks.** Express your appreciation for the time spent with you.

✔ **Write a thank-you letter.** Just because the interview was via phone doesn't negate the wisdom of putting your thanks in an e-mail. Make it a sales letter restating the qualifications you bring to the position.

Which Way to the Future?

Technology and globalization are drastically changing not only how people do their jobs, but how they get them. The following three examples are based on real and existing technology. Do they describe the future of job interviews in the 21st century, or are they merely fun and games?

Have your avatar talk to my avatar

An avatar is an animated graphic character; you see them wandering around on Web sites, such as www.secondlife.com, a computer-based virtual world, which has held an avatar job fair in which real companies interviewed job seekers.

Job seekers designed any kind of avatars they wanted (hair color and clothing) and sent their characters to each company's virtual office, where they shook hands with avatar recruiters. The avatars with winning ways during the interviews were invited to a face-to-face, non-avatar interview. No word on how many candidates are being hired through avatar interviews.

Holy hologram: I see right through you

Remember back to Star Wars when robot R2-D2 projected the hologram of Princess Leia screaming "Help me, Obi-Wan Kenobi; you're my only hope." Holograms are no longer a galaxy far, far away. Researchers at the University of Southern California have developed a 3D holographic display where three-dimensional images can be viewed from 360 degrees. Can you imagine future online interviews where the computer monitor is a hologram? In the future, you may be conducting interviews with a whole new viewing angle. Of course, you can see through holograms like ghosts with today's technology. Today a hollow head, tomorrow a fully fleshed-out body.

Video: Resumes are not the same as interviews

Despite vendor-driven drum-beating for video resumes, the overwhelming majority of professionals in the employment field whom I interviewed cite two major problems that video resumes will have to overcome if they are ever to become widely adopted, as well as a third problem that additional experience and familiarity with the medium may resolve.

The first hang-up is that reviewing video resumes (rather than online or paper resumes) is a time monster. Far too much time is sucked from the schedules of busy recruiters and employers to make watching visually-enhanced job resumes an efficient use of their talents.

The second issue: Companies worry that video resumes will invite lawsuits by candidates who claim bias based on race, gender, or age — which may be unrevealed on digital resumes but revealed on video. "Anything that shows upfront that a job seeker is old, fat, or ugly is a risk," says HR expert Jim Lemke, this book's technical reviewer.

A third disqualifying factor is that most home-produced video resumes are amateurish and don't show off the candidate to best advantage.

The video resumes most likely to succeed, recruiters tend to believe, are those featuring candidates in performing and creative fields.

The paramount difference between video resumes and video interviews is *control*. The job seeker controls the video resume; the employer controls the video interview.

Don't dare lie: Your mind is an open book

I'm not making this up: A team of top neuroscientists in Germany and England say they have discovered technology to look deep inside people's brains and read their intentions before they act. (Browser search online for "The brain scan that can read people's intentions.") So much for trying to keep your thoughts to yourself.

The neuroscientists claim that high-resolution brain scans aided by special computer software can identify patterns of activity that flags lying and violent behavior. Does this mind-reading machine actually work? One test resulted in an impressive 70 percent accuracy rate. The obvious first usage of the modern truth-telling marvel is the interrogation of criminal suspects. If the mind-peeping technology passes what is sure to be a firestorm of ethical concerns, what's next — brain scan plans for job interviews? Imagine this somewhere in tomorrow's employment norms:

> *Please come in and talk with us about our open position. And oh yes, sign this waiver agreeing to stand brain-naked before our interviewer.*

Chapter 4

Interviewing on the World Stage

*U*nited States. Germany. France. United Kingdom. Kenya. United Arab Emirates. South Africa. China. India. Australia. Russia. Mexico. Norway. Spain. Turkey. Japan. Philippines. Brazil. These and many more far-off places may be a workplace destination for someone on the wing — perhaps you.

A flow of workers has always moved among the world's developed nations. But today's employment practices make that international exchange of talent more vigorous, speeded-up by look-me-over technology that includes interviews by e-mail, land-line phones, airline flights, and, coming soon, interactive online video interviews and the ubiquitous wireless phones I describe in Chapter 3.

Changing the Global Interviewing Game

Old-style job interviewing for foreign nationals is getting an update, too. Interviewing styles are no longer as tightly bound to the customs of individual and disparate nations as they were only 15 or 20 years ago. Back then, job interviewing customs between cultures could be strikingly dissimilar — a slight bow upon shaking hands was attractive in German interviews but not in British interviews, as a single example. Times change. Germans no longer automatically bow upon introduction.

What's driving the homogenizing of interview practices across much of the planet? In a word, modernization. Western-style employment practices, sparked especially by American-based multinationals, are narrowing variances in how candidates are interviewed and evaluated in many countries. Studies show that employers everywhere want all job seekers to have technical knowledge in their fields, and they look for cross-cultural adaptability for those who are foreign-born.

Employers in workplaces ranging from the United States to India and the United Arab Emirates to South Africa want you to show them that you can competently do the jobs, and preferably have done the jobs, that they're trying to fill. That's why the interviewing strategies I present throughout this book are widely applicable almost anywhere for mobile professionals in the global workforce. That's the word from Jim Lemke, this book's technical reviewer, who has worldwide travel and work experience.

Lemke's day job is in human resources management for one of the world's largest microfinance organizations. As he hires professionals for the organization's offices in 28 developing countries, Lemke sees the homogenizing interviewing model up close: "Companies such as Nestle, Barclays, Coca Cola, and Cisco are all looking to expand in developing countries and need bright, young professionals with Western training who have the required work qualifications and who know how to present themselves."

Another career expert, Dr. Ron Krannich, who closely monitors the global workforce, agrees that with the exception of small- and medium-sized companies, especially those outside the major cities, today's employee selection interviews are looking more alike than unalike:

"The world's employers increasingly expect to see the 'sales' model that Americans use in job interviewing. I use the term to mean confidently emphasizing positive accomplishments about you rather than making neutral or negative statements. But here's an important caveat: Be careful not to come across as overly aggressive in nations that are traditionally more accustomed to low-key interviewing styles," says Dr. Krannich, who heads Impact Publications (www.impactpublications.com), an international publisher of career and travel books.

Looking at Remaining Cultural Norms

Although poles-apart interviewing styles are in decline, that trend doesn't mean they've disappeared entirely. They haven't. For example, although business wear is the uniform for professional candidates interviewing in India, a few women continue to apply for work wearing a native form of dress, the sari. So going with the flow of cultural expectations in a country other than your own can still be a tense, waiting-to-exhale experience.

Take handshakes, for example. In the United States, a healthy grip as you pump hands is considered a friendly and straightforward gesture for women as well as men. But in Saudi Arabia, unmarried men and women do not touch, a cultural issue that presents a dilemma for a Saudi woman candidate being interviewed by a male in America. Handshaking isn't a big problem for women in Muslim and many other non-Western countries because in those places it's not a basic part of a job interview.

Making eye contact is another point of difference that survives between cultures. When interviewing in the United States, you're expected to make a lot of eye contact showing honesty and sincerity; failure to look your interviewer in the eye can be perceived as a sign that you are evasive or lying. In Latin America, too much eye contact may suggest a lack of respect or a challenge to authority.

If you're a professional worker who hopes to add far-off places to your resume, it's never too early to begin planning your moves. There's plenty to plan. Aside from the myriad considerations stretching from education and experience qualifications to legal documents allowing you to join another nation's workforce, think through what you must do to convince a foreign interviewer that you "get" the host country's culture and that you fit right in.

Interviewing Across Cultures

To jump-start your understanding of cross-cultural interviewing norms, here are generalized observations about conditions you may encounter in far-off interviews. The following verbal snapshots are a starting point for your further research aimed at understanding specific mores in individual nations, regions of the country, and individual companies:

- **Important protocol variations:** Find out in advance how much interviewing formality to generally expect in a particular nation before moving on to pinpoint research about the region and the company. The tone of the interview may be more or less formal than you would expect at home. Joking in an interview is risky in your own country but in another land you may seriously offend if the interviewer interprets your humor as a sign that you won't take the work seriously or that you're a superficial clown.

- **Personal questions and privacy:** In the United States, laws discourage privacy-penetrating questioning that may lead to discrimination (see Chapter 24). However, employers in a number of nations have no qualms or legal restrictions about asking personal questions of candidates. Understand in advance that you may be expected to answer questions about your age, health, or marital status.

- **Critical language skills:** Language fluency is a main component of cross-cultural adaptability for professional employees. Inability to speak the language or understand accents is going to prove an almost insurmountable obstacle to being hired. (Consider taking a menial or unpaid job for a year, as well as taking lessons, to improve you language skills before applying for professional jobs.)

  English is the lingua franca of international commerce and you may be able to stick with it to be hired in some countries, but, in most cases, you'll get greater approval by speaking the local language, bad grammar and mispronounced words notwithstanding.

- ✔ **Self-promotion American style:** Americans are taught to "sell" not tell when interviewing for employment, to emphasize accomplishments and minimize shortcomings. Making the best case for being hired is the self-marketing strategy and tactics I advise throughout this book. But in some cultures, being too assertive in tooting your own horn is perceived as being nervy, brash, and brazen. In those cultures that prefer an understated performance, employers may want you to volunteer only the skeleton facts of your education and work history, such as previous schools, previous employers, years of employment, job titles, and responsibilities.

- ✔ **Appropriate dress and grooming:** Although local conventions in dress and appearance continue to impact how candidates dress for interviews in a number of countries, most professionals now dress in suits or other business wear. The default mode is conservative. Employers in fashion-conscious European nations, such as France, Spain, and Italy, especially appreciate interview attire that shows business savvy and worldliness. (For interview dressing in the United States, Canada and many other Western nations, see Chapter 9.)

Tracking Down Country Research

Develop a job search plan for each country of interest. The plan should include foundation research you need for most interviews (see Chapter 6). Add to that base and customize it with information about cultural subtleties for each target country, region of the country, and potential employer of interest. Because hiring customs in the world's nations are still evolving, seek the latest data by researching online and by networking your way to people in-country.

International Web sites

The following Web sites provide information for your cross-cultural job search:

- ✔ **Going Global** (www.goinglobal.com; note there is only one "g" in the middle of the address): This site offers country-specific, annually updated interviewing advice for 30 countries. Visit the site's home page where you can use the Quick Search feature (upper right hand side of the page) to find information on interviewing in individual countries. A sample content page for each country is free; you can download the country's entire guide of about 85 pages for under $20.

Questions that probe expat expectations

Employers of expats (expatriates) of any nation are likely to ask questions about your ability to adjust and function in a foreign setting. Can you be happy in an unfamiliar place without becoming homesick? What if your spouse and children hate the place and flee back home? If you can't stand the climate, will you pack up and leave within several months? Survival questions to expats may be direct or implied as the following examples show.

Are there any factors that might limit your ability to take on this assignment, such as health or your family situation?

Are you realistic about living overseas and working under different conditions? How about in developing nations where the living isn't as easy and convenient as back home?

How do your spouse and children view this assignment — are they on board?

In addition to for-fee country guides ordered by the general public, you can read the information for free if you have access to any of the some 300 libraries and university career centers around the world that subscribe to the Going Global service. These institutions are listed on the Going Global Web site.

✔ **Job-hunt.org** (www.job-hunt.org/international.shtml): This site contains a list of international job resources that are most useful for job postings, but you can mine the resources for country-specific interviewing intelligence.

✔ **Transitions Abroad** (www.transitionsabroad.com): This site offers magazine articles and books about working, studying, traveling, living and volunteering in countries other than your own. Selected articles are free but others are available only if you subscribe to the magazine. Additionally, the site contains a blog called the Wide World Café.

International social networking

Reaching across national borders and oceans to get country-specific interviewing tips wasn't a practical approach a dozen years ago. Today tapping into personal and professional online networks to discover the rules of the road in foreign interview rooms is easy. A bit time-consuming but easy. Here are a few suggestions about tracking interviewing conventions the digital way. A marketing professional who wants to work in Denmark would take the following steps:

1. **Start with contacts you already have.**

   Your contacts know people you don't know and their contacts know people they don't know, and so on. Send a brief e-mail message to each contact stating your desire to prepare for a job interview in Denmark.

Say that you would appreciate it if the recipient is able to lend any of the following kinds of assistance:

- To help you directly or to forward your message to one of their contacts in your quest for knowledge about the interviewing protocols and customs common in Denmark.

- To help you arrange a more substantial informational interview with a resident of Denmark who, like you, is a professional or business person. In an online informational interview, whether by e-mail or two-way videocam, ask a series of questions you write out before the interview. Remember, you are exploring only typical job interviewing in Denmark at this informational interview — not every aspect of the job or employment there. You can, of course, arrange for a follow-up interview if your Denmark contact is agreeable.

2. **Check out professional member organizations in the field of work you seek, such as the International Association of Marketing Professionals.**

   Post your request for assistance for current information about interviewing protocols in Denmark for your profession on a forum, chat room, or blog. You probably have to be a member of the organization to access the organization's site.

3. **Try popular business-oriented social network tools.**

   Conduct a keyword search on a site such as LinkedIn (www.linkedin.com) or Xing (www.xing.com). Use a term relevant to your objective — say, "Denmark corporate marketing" or "Denmark human resources" or "Denmark manager" — to see whether you can connect with LinkedIn or Xing users who could prove helpful by providing the latest interviewing information.

Preparing for the Global Job Interview

Whether your interview takes place in a glamorous, cosmopolitan city or a little-known town on the slopes of a mountain or in your home bedroom on a cell phone, the secret to your global search success is preparation and practice. In addition to getting the country-specific environment right, you still have to sell yourself as an ideal candidate for the position you seek. Chapter 5 catalogs the types of interviews you may encounter as you move on up in your life.

Chapter 5

A Chorus Line of Interviews by Type

Action/adventure. Comedy. Mystery. Martial arts. Musical. Romance. Suspense. Thriller. You know the old saying: "Variety is the splice of life in filmmaking." (Yes, you can groan now.)

Variety, in today's job market, is similarly abundant in job interviewing dramas. As you move along what you hope will be a red carpet to fortune and fanfare (or at least to a decent job), do become familiar with the various shapes, forms, and fashions of interviews and understand how to do well in each.

This chapter helps you do just that as it spotlights the most common styles of job interviews today. For convenience, I divided them into four clusters describing the

▸ *Objective* for the interview

▸ *Interviewer* number, from one to dozens

▸ *Technique* and interview forms that shape your participation

▸ *Location* where the interview takes place

Mastering Interviews by Objective

Interviewers set up different kinds of meetings for different reasons, as the leading player in the following story illustrates:

A woman with a dog was leaving a movie theater when a reporter stopped her and said, "I'm sorry to bother you but I was amazed that your dog seemed to get into the movie so much. He cried at the right scenes, yawned during the ho-hum spots, and laughed his head off at the funny parts. Don't you find that unusual?"

"Yes," the woman replied. "I find it very unusual, considering that his objective in coming here was to find out whether the movie was as bad as the book!"

I run down interview objectives in the upcoming sections.

Screening interview

Interviewing is a two-stage process in large organizations. The two stages are *screening* and *selection.* Screening precedes selection.

The purpose of screening — or first-cut interviews — is to weed out all applicants except the best qualified. Live (in-person) interviews to screen applicants typically are held at the employer's work site, independent employment services, college career services, and job fairs.

Interviewers increasingly rely on technology — such as telephone and Webcam (video online) interviews — to screen applicants. (Turn to Chapter 3.) They use the technology as cost-cutting moves to help assure that candidates aren't underskilled and overpriced before their companies invest too much time talking with them at length.

The screener, usually an employee of the company inside the human resource department, or an outside, third-party (independent) recruiter, quizzes all comers and passes the survivors to a person who makes the final selection.

The person who makes the selection — that is, the person who has hiring authority — is usually the department manager or the boss to whom the victorious candidate reports.

Questioners who screen typically are more experienced in interviewing processes than the questioners who select — they've studied and practiced interviewing strategies and tactics. The best screeners have made interviewing an art form. Their job is to gather facts and keep out candidates who aren't qualified for the position, or who may be qualified but who have a poor employment history.

When screening takes place at a professional level (rather than leaving the task to an untrained receptionist or office assistant), the screeners are experts at finding out what's wrong with you — exactly why you should be kept out of an employer's workforce.

But screeners determine only whether you have the minimum qualifications for the position. They don't decide whether you're the best candidate. Typical subjects for the screening interview include

- ✔ Questions about your job history
- ✔ Questions about your salary history or requirements
- ✔ Questions about your transferable skills — ability to do the job
- ✔ Inquiries about inconsistencies on your resume (work history gaps)
- ✔ Probes designed to reveal lies in your resume
- ✔ Questions to reveal what kind of person you are — reliable, trustworthy, team-oriented

Screeners usually aren't concerned with evaluating your personality or thought processes. They have one basic responsibility before putting you on the approved list and waving you up to the next interviewing level: to be sure that you qualify. They do so by validating your experience, education, skills, and track record.

Screeners are gatekeepers; they're criticized for allowing unqualified candidates to slip through the gate. They especially don't want to take a hit for passing along a flat-out loser. That's why screeners want the facts, just the facts.

Keep your answers straightforward and save most of your dynamo-drama moves for the selection interview.

When the facts confirm that you're qualified for the position, the opportunity to participate in a selection interview is favorable. As long as you don't volunteer reasons for the screener to send you away, expect to be passed to the decision-maker — who assumes that you're qualified or you wouldn't be showing up in the interview pool of candidates.

What if you and the screener don't seem to be on the same wavelength? Unless you're plying the human resources trade, it doesn't matter — you won't be working together.

Screeners can't hire you, but screeners can send you to the showers.

Selection interview

Suppose that you're hired, but fail to live up to expectations. Is the screener in trouble? No. The selector made the hiring call.

In the selection interview, almost always a live interview, sometimes called the *decision interview,* you meet with a supervisor, department head, or another person who has the authority to hire you. Often this interviewer will be your potential boss, so you too will be making judgments during the interview. (Sometimes the selection decision is made by more than one person, as I tell you in the section "Group interview.")

Selection interviewers are rarely pros at interviewing and often just go with their intuition, hoping the task is over as quickly as possible so that they can get back to their "real" work.

Because the selection interview may take several detours, be ready to ask leading questions to get the interview back on track and to set up an opening to describe your qualifications in light of the position.

Even if the questioner seems like the kind of person you'd share a beer with, don't relax. Your interviewer is trying to decide which candidate is the best investment for the company — because a wrong choice could cost the company thousands of dollars in training time, correcting mistakes, and firing to hire again. Selection interviewers are looking for

- **Strong presentation of personality:** How you blend with other employees, as well as your general likability and motivation to work

- **Specific details of your competencies and skills:** How your qualifications allow you to do the job better than other candidates

- **Specific details of your job experience or education:** How you've not only done — or been trained for — a similar job, but how you'll apply that background to the new job

- **How you handle specific job scenarios:** How you think under variable or stressful conditions and solve challenges

Assuming that the person conducting the meeting will be your boss or a colleague with whom you have to get along, the selection interview is where you move from neutral behavior into high gear. This is where you reveal the best of your personality (you're not holding yourself in, as you were during the screening interview). And this is where you take note of how you and your potential boss blend. If your gut instinct tells you the blend is oil-and-water, think carefully before saying yes to this job offer.

Even when everything else is tempting, your future will go better when you and your future boss are "using the same software."

In a classic Western spoof, *Blazing Saddles,* actor Harvey Korman plays a gang leader recruiting bad guys to ruin a town. Interviewing Cleavon Little, who wants to be his sidekick, Korman initially worries that they're not "using the same software."

Korman asks Little to describe his qualifications as a villain. When Little tells him that his past work was stampeding cattle, Korman is about to blow him off with a comment that stampeding cattle isn't a big thing in gangland. Little smirks knowingly, then says, "Through the Vatican?" Right then, Korman decides that Little and he are two villains of a kind, shouting "kinky!" and hiring him on the spot.

Combination interview

Small firms often combine the screening and selection interviews. The resulting combination tends to be long and grueling, and not only tests your match to the hiring requirements but also measures your stamina and motivation for the job.

From the very first exchange, pull out all the stops in selling your top qualities and displaying a pleasant personality because you won't get a second chance.

Promotion interview

Moving up from the inside as an internal candidate often is easier than gaining access as an outside candidate. But it's not a sure thing.

Approach a promotion interview as though you were heading out to a new company. Research diligently, as I describe in Chapter 6, to be able to talk about industry trends and other big issues.

When you're the only insider wrangling for the job, use your knowledge of the company's policies, plans, and culture to point out that you alone can hit the floor running — which no outsider can actually do. Then identify several current company problems you could deal with immediately.

Should you emphasize your 20 years of loyal service with a show-and-tell of your successes at a time when your company is handing off generational control from boomers to Xers? The right answer, although it may seem counterintuitive to you, is not exactly. You have to do more. The familiar "tried-and-proven" strategy won't have legs during a time when new captains are determined to justify taking the wheel by steering in different directions.

A youth-oriented management doesn't care about the glories of Ancient Rome or Ancient You — what they care about is whether you can do the work ahead — now and tomorrow.

So while you include the accomplishments of the past ten years (no more than that), reframe the discussion to focus on work samples and skills that highlight your ability to do the new job. Give examples of your flexible personality. Identify times when you welcomed new tasks and responsibilities. Help them see you as "the way ahead," not as "a tribute to yesteryear."

Recruiter courtesy interview

A *retained recruiter* gets paid whether or not the recruiter matches a candidate to a position. They typically run the other way to avoid seeing job seekers who come unbidden to their offices. (Time is money.) But you may know someone who is a client or friend of a retained recruiter who can get you through the door with a courtesy interview.

Unless your interviewer is recruiting for a position that's perfect for you (which is very unlikely), focus on providing the recruiter with information that may qualify you for a future search. Some rules to follow:

- ✔ Always give the recruiter a current resume.
- ✔ Get straight to the point; don't take more than 20 minutes of the recruiter's time.
- ✔ Explain your experience, achievements, and skills.
- ✔ Thank the recruiter for time invested in you.

Don't play the role of a coy, amateur job seeker. The retained recruiter is doing you a favor. You wouldn't ask for a courtesy interview if you didn't need a job. Your conciseness and ability to communicate efficiently count. Review your resume and get to the point.

Recruiter general screening interview

Contingency recruiters, unlike retained recruiters, get paid only when they match up a candidate with a position. The more people they see, the larger their candidate pool from which to fill employers' job orders. Getting an interview with a contingency recruiter or employment agency consultant is easier than with a retained recruiter.

This doesn't mean you can waste a contingency recruiter's time. Hand over your resume and give your best performance to show a broad selection of work experiences. You're trying to make the contingency recruiter remember you for a variety of future job openings.

Make sure that you get high scores in the following qualities:

- ✔ Personality/likability
- ✔ Adept communication
- ✔ Enthusiasm and motivated interest in work
- ✔ Leadership and initiative

- ✔ Competence in skills and knowledge
- ✔ Experience (some job history)

Recruiter search interview

A recruiter may contact you about a specific job opening. Chances are that you've done or are doing a job similar to the one the client wants to fill, and that's why the recruiter called you. So you already know the basics of your industry, even though at first you might not know who the client is.

If you've been so busy doing your job that you're not up to date on industry trends, there's no time like the present for a cram review. Third-party executive and technical recruiters can't hire you, but you've got to get past them to see their clients.

To impress a recruiter in a search interview:

- ✔ Show that you have definite career goals and indicate how this position fits those goals.
- ✔ Ask probing, thoughtful questions about the company and position, showing you've done your homework.

Brainteaser job interview

If you were to eliminate one of the 50 United States, leaving only 49 states, which one would it be and why?

That's a question Microsoft interviewers like to ask, says John Kador, business writing consultant (www.jkador.com) and author of a smart book on logic-driven riddles and oxygen-sucking puzzles that job interviewers may spring on you without warning.

Brainteasers ("Why are manhole covers round?" or "How would you test a salt shaker?") ordinarily are reserved for very bright candidates as a challenge

to see who can rise and shine in professional and managerial positions in today's hypercompetitive work environment.

When you suspect that you're heading into interview combat, find guidance in Kador's book, *How to Ace the Brain Teaser Interview* (McGraw-Hill, 2004).

So what's the best answer if you are smacked upside the head with that Microsoft state-elimination haymaker? "Well, it's *not* the state of Washington," Kador says with a grin. (Microsoft is headquartered in Redmond, Wash.)

Use the 'Net to research recruiting firms that specialize in your industry or occupation. The gold standard is *Kennedy's Directory of Executive Recruiters* (with purchase of a print copy, you're entitled to a free online version): www. kennedyinfo.com. A good free resource is *Oya's Directory of Recruiters* at www.i-recruit.com/oya.

Second interview

Being called back is a good sign: You're a few steps closer to being offered the job you want.

To come out first in the second interview, be sure you understand the dynamics at play. (Actually, the second interview may turn out to be a series of interviews but the purpose is typically the same in all of them.)

I count three kinds of second interviews and suggest tips to come out ahead in each one:

- ✔ **The yours-to-lose selection interview:** The decision is virtually made in your favor. But the hiring manager is confirming it with endorsements and buy-in consensus from the team. Your qualifications aren't in question but your fit (how you fit in with the company culture) is being probed. Relax a little — these are your new colleagues. Keep your answers pleasant, straightforward, and brief but not terse.

- ✔ **The finalists' selection interview:** The decision has narrowed to two or three finalists. Keep selling your qualifications. Allude to cultural fit with subtle comments suggesting that you're one of them. ("I agree that we must build adequate electrical power into the infrastructure.") Ask intelligent questions, such as depth of support for stated missions and professional development opportunities.

- ✔ **The do-over screening interview:** Management still wonders whether you're underqualified and overpriced and wants to make another pass at you, perhaps with different screeners. Expect questions all over again about your job history, skills, salary history or requirements, resume gaps, and the kind of person you are. (You're reliable, honest, team-oriented and, overall, have laudable values.)

If you're working with a recruiter, ask the recruiter for tips and where you are in the selection process. If not, ask the same question of the interviewer who has shown you the greatest interest.

Mastering Interviews by Interviewer

You may have to face several pairs of measuring eyes — all at once. Or you may have to endure one interview after another, all with the same company.

In the upcoming sections, I outline the possibilities and your best bets for handling them.

One-to-one interview

The one interviewer, one interviewee format is the traditional and familiar style of job interview. You and the employer meet, usually at the employer's office, and discuss the job and your skills and other qualifications that relate to the job. You find suggestions on how to be bravo in the one-to-one interview throughout this book.

Group interview

The plot thickens. Also called a panel, board, team, collective, or committee interview, this style puts you stage center before a comparatively huge crowd — perhaps 5 to 12 questioners. Usually they are people from the department where you would work, or they may come from various departments throughout the organization.

You wouldn't be at this expensive meeting (think of all the salaries for the group's time) if you hadn't already been screened to be sure your qualifications are acceptable. These people are gathered to see whether they like you and whether you'll fit into their operation. Greet each person, handing out a fresh copy of your resume. Appear confident. Make a quick seating chart to help you remember names.

Before you answer a first question, smile, thank everyone for inviting you to meet with them, and then begin your answer, which will probably be "You asked me to tell you about myself. . . ."

Should you try to identify the leader and direct most of your remarks to that person? Not necessarily. The boss may be the quiet observer in the corner. Play it safe — maintain eye contact with all committee members. When your curtain goes up, play to a full house!

Group interviews highlight your interpersonal skills, leadership, and ability to think on your feet and deal with issues in a stressful setting. The purpose of a group interview is not only to hear what you say, but to see what behaviors and skills you display within a group.

When the interview is over, thank the group as though you just finished a speech.

> *Thank you for having me here today. I enjoyed being with you. This interview confirmed my research indicating that this company is a good place to work. I'll look forward to hearing from you, and hopefully, joining you.*

Ask questions. Periodically summarize important points to keep the group focused. Use a notebook to record several simultaneous questions, explaining that you don't want to omit responding to anyone's important concern.

Serial interview

A serial interview also involves a group of people, but not all at once. You are handed off from person to person. You typically are passed from screener to line manager to top manager — and perhaps a half-dozen people in between in the drawn-out process of the serial interview. You strengthen your chances each time you are passed onward.

Use your screening (plain vanilla personality) interview behavior with all interviewers you meet except those with whom you would work. Then go into your selection (full personality) mode.

Another type of serial interview is a prescheduled series of interviews, usually lasting one to two days, that each applicant must complete before the employer makes a hiring decision. The serial interview is almost always used when a candidate is flown in from a distant locale. Paste a smile on your face and hope that it doesn't fall off after a day of being "on stage."

When the initial interviewer says that you're being passed on to the second interviewer, try to find out a little about the second interviewer. Ask a question like "Does number two feel the same way about customer service as you do?" You'll get information you need to find common ground with your next interviewer. Continue the advance-tip technique all the way to the finish line.

When you're interviewed by one person after another, consistency counts. Don't tell a rainbow of stories about the same black-and-white topics. When interview team members later compare notes, they should be discussing the same person.

Mastering Interviews by Technique

One of the funniest movie reviews ever was for the 1960s film *Chitty Chitty, Bang Bang*.

The entire review read: "It went bang bang and it was chitty!"

The film's director, who here shall remain nameless, couldn't have been happy about that review. No happier than a job interviewer bearing responsibility for the hiring of a candidate who disappoints.

Much as a film director calls the shots on a movie set, placing actors and cameras to best advantage, a job interviewer sets the technique and tone of the interview, whether it be behavior-based, tightly or loosely controlled, intentionally stressful, or loaded with brain-crunching puzzles.

Behavior-based interview

Behavior-based interviewing relies on storytelling — examples of what you've done that support your claims. Premised on the belief that the past predicts the future, behavior-based interviewing techniques are used to ask the candidate how they have handled specific situations — what kinds of behaviors they used to solve problems.

The presumption is that if you were a good problem solver in the past, you'll be a good problem solver in the future. Behavior-based interviewing empha-sizes "What did you do when," not "What would you do if?"

Interview questions are designed to draw out clues to a candidate's work-place DNA. All candidates are asked virtually the same questions. The tip-off that you've just been handed a behavior-based question, which should be answered with a demonstrated skill or trait, is when the question begins with such words as these:

✔ Tell me about a time when —

✔ Give me an example of your skills in —

✔ Describe a time when you —

✔ Why did you —

A few fleshed-out examples illustrate the behavior-based technique more fully:

Think back to a time when you were on the verge of making a huge sale, and the customer balked at the last minute, promised to get back to you, but didn't. What action did you take?

Remember a time when you improved inventory turns; how big an improve-ment did you make?

Tell me about an on-the-job disaster that you turned around, making lemon-ade from lemons.

Describe the types of risks you have allowed your direct reports to take.

Can you give me an example of when you were able to implement a vision for your organization?

Why did you decide to major in sociology at the San Marcos State University rather than at a small private college?

Companies using behavior-based interviewing first must identify the behaviors important to the job. If leadership, for instance, is one of the valued behaviors, several questions asking for stories of demonstrated leadership will be asked:

Tell me about the last time you had to take charge of a project but were lacking in clear direction. How did you carry forward the project?

Because the behavioral style of interviewing attempts to measure predictable behavior rather than pure paid work experience, it can help level the playing field for rookies competing against seasoned candidates.

In mining your past for anecdotes, you can draw from virtually any part of your past behavior — education, school projects, paid work experience, volunteer work, activities, hobbies, family life.

As you sift through your memories, be on the lookout for a theme, the motif that runs through your choices of education, jobs, and activities. Put at least half a dozen anecdotes that illustrate your theme in your pocket and pull them out when you need them. Examples of themes are

- ✔ Leadership
- ✔ Problem solving
- ✔ Negotiating
- ✔ Initiative
- ✔ Overcoming adversity
- ✔ Succeeding
- ✔ Dealing with stress
- ✔ Sacrificing to achieve an important work goal
- ✔ Dealing with someone who disagrees with you
- ✔ Commitment
- ✔ Work ethic
- ✔ Task orientation
- ✔ Communications skills

Here are several more suggestions for best answering behavior-based questions:

- ✔ Tell a story with a beginning, a middle, and an end using the PAR technique — problem, action, result.

Here's an example: *Problem:* An e-commerce company was operating at a substantial loss. *Action:* I outsourced technical support and added seven new product lines. *Result:* We cut our expenses by 8 percent, increased our revenues by 14 percent, and had our first profitable year with expectations of higher profits next year.

✔ Rookies: Don't simply cite the subject of your classes — "I couldn't solve my accounting problem and so I asked my professor." No! Look back at your student class projects, previous work experience, and extra-curricular activities. Reach into real life for your success stories.

✔ Try not to sound as though you memorized every syllable and inflection, or like a machine with all the answers. Admitting that your example was a complex problem and that you experimented until you found its best solution humanizes you.

Realize that the interviewer is more interested in the process than in the details of your success stories. What was the reasoning behind your actions? Why did you behave the way you did? What skills did you use?

Behavior-based interviewing, which arrived more than 40 years ago, is popular today because employers are trying to snatch clues from history to project the future. The underlying rationale is that people tend to play the same roles in life over and over.

Theatrical insiders call this tendency "typecasting." In explaining a shift away from action films, film star Bruce Willis quipped, "I've saved the world so many times, they've given me an 800 number."

Directive interview

The *directive interview* is one in which the interviewer maintains complete control and walks you through the discussion to uncover what the interviewer wants to know. The *patterned interview* is similar except the interviewer works from a written list of questions asked of all candidates and writes down your answers.

A patterned interview is also called a *structured interview.* Although the structured interview has been around a long time, the format is finding new followers.

The argument in favor of structured interviews is that they promote fairness, uncover superior candidates, and eliminate the cloning effect (in which an interviewer essentially hires candidates in his or her own image — or one who the interviewer thinks will "fit in" merely because of shared values).

In structured interviews, the interviewer may throw out a *critical incident* and ask you to respond. A critical incident is a specific problem or challenge that was successfully handled by employees of the company. Like a quiz show, the host (the interviewer) has the "answer sheet" — the actual behavior that solved the problem or met the challenge.

Some critical incidents can be anticipated by researching industry trends and inferred by reading company press releases online.

Whether you are in a directive interview, or a patterned (structured) interview, expect interviewers to ask both closed- and open-ended questions.

A *closed-end question* can be answered yes or no:

> *Did you find my office easily?*

An open-ended question usually asks how or why:

> *How do you like this industry?*

This interviewer has an agenda and is intent on seeing that it's followed. Being too assertive in changing the topic is a mistake. The only safe way you can introduce one of your skills is to ask a question:

> *Would you like to hear about my experience in quality assessment?*

Nondirective interview

A *nondirective interview* rewards you for leading the discussion. It's often an approach of line managers who don't know much about professional interviewing.

Questions tend to be broad and general so that you can elaborate and tell all kinds of terrific stories about yourself. A few questions may reveal key areas of the employer's needs. These questions may sound at first as though they're critical incidents, but in this loose-limbed interview, the interviewer probably doesn't assume that he or she knows the answers. Examples of nondirective interview questions include

> *We had a problem employee last quarter who revealed information about our marketing strategies to a competitor — how would you handle this situation?*
>
> *You understand some of the difficulties this department faces — how would you approach these in your first four months?*
>
> *Tell me about your goals in the next five years and how this position fits in with them.*
>
> *Your resume shows you have a degree in Spanish and another in computer science — how do you plan to use both of these in this position?*

Carry agenda cards or a small notebook with a list of your qualifications and a list of questions about the company. When you have to carry the ball, working from notes can be a lifesaver if you have a leaky memory.

Stress interview

Recognizing the hazing that goes on in a stress interview is important; recognize it for what it is — either a genuine test of your ability to do the job or terminal pranksterism by a dumb jerk.

Don't take the horrors of a stress interview personally. Keep your cool and play the game if you want the job. Don't sweat. Don't cry. Your most reliable tactic is to speak with calm, unflagging confidence. You may have to practice remaining poised in the face of an interviewer's intimidation tactics.

Suppose that you're in sales. Asking you to sell the interviewer something — like the office chair — is fairly common. But having you face blinding sunlight while sitting in a chair with one short leg is, at best, childish.

Stress interviews often consist of

- Hour-long waits before the interview
- Long, uncomfortable silences
- Challenges of your beliefs
- A brusque interviewer or multiple curt interviewers
- Deliberate misinterpretation of your comments and outright insults

Typical questions run along these lines

Why weren't you working for so long?

Your resume shows that you were with your last company for a number of years without promotion and a virtually flat salary; why is that?

Can you describe a situation when your work was criticized or you disliked your boss?

Would you like to have my job?

What would you do if violence erupted in your workplace?

A famous admiral, now dead, used to nail the furniture to the floor and ask the applicant to pull up a chair. If an interviewer crosses your personal line of reasonable business behavior, you may want to make a speedy exit.

Storytelling your way to a job

Prepare for all your interviews — not just behavior-based interviews — by recalling anecdotes from your past experience that back up your claims of skills and other qualifications. Work on these stories as though you're going to present them in a speech before hundreds of people. Make them fun, interesting — even exciting! Few of us are natural-born storytellers, but do your best to tell a good story.

Experts claim the way to ace behavior-based interviews is to prepare, rehearse, and deliver one- to two-minute stories about your skills, experience, and accomplishments that relate directly to the job. Your commitment to meeting their interests shows as you recognize their goals and pay your respects in full with relevant stories.

Mastering Interviews at Remote Locations

A filming location is a place where some or all of a film or television series is produced, in addition to or instead of using sets built on a studio backlot or soundstage.

Going on location is not always a cushy assignment. Some years ago, while filming in a Philippines jungle, the movie's production chief warned star actor Michael Caine to beware of a poisonous serpent called the 1-2-3 snake.

Asking about the odd name, Caine was told it was because once bitten, after taking 1-2-3 steps, you're dead! Worse luck, the snake looked like a twig. The saving grace was that the film's native guides could smell the snake. Unsurprisingly, each morning Caine and the crew checked to be sure the guides hadn't caught colds.

While not every interview takes place across a desk at the company's home base, presumably you won't have to worry about snakes as you head out for an interview over a meal, in a campus interviewing room, at a job fair, or even at home where the whole family is inspected.

Mealtime interview

Just when you thought you'd been through all the interviewing hoops and assumed that landing the job was a done deal, you get a luncheon invitation from a higher-up in the company, perhaps your potential boss. Why?

Robin Jay, author of *The Art of the Business Lunch: Building Relationships Between 12 and 2* (Career Press, 2006) identifies the following reasons:

- ✔ To judge you on your social skills and manners
- ✔ To find out additional information about you that an employer may not legally be able to ask
- ✔ To get to know you better
- ✔ To compare your social behavior to that of other candidates

As an account executive, Jay ate her way through 3,000 business lunches (No, she's not fat.); she says that sharing a meal with someone reveals his or her personality faster and more effectively than all the office interviews in the world. "Many a job has been won or lost at the table," Jay observes.

So while a mealtime interview may seem more relaxed and social, stay as alert as you would in any other location. Mealtime interviewers are watching you with big eyes.

To avoid spilling precious job opportunities, mind your manners:

- ✔ Don't order entrees so hard to eat that you spend the entire interview lost in your plate with long pasta or saucy, messy, or bony food.
- ✔ Don't order alcohol unless you're at dinner — even then have only one drink. White wine is a good choice.
- ✔ Don't order the most expensive or the most inexpensive thing on the menu.
- ✔ Don't smoke (companies are becoming obsessed with employee health costs).
- ✔ Don't complain about the food, the service, or the restaurant.
- ✔ Don't over-order or leave too much food on your plate.

For savoir-fare in a mealtime interview, be sure to

- ✔ Order something that's easy to eat (like a club or veggie sandwich).
- ✔ Chew with your mouth closed, speak with your mouth empty.
- ✔ Order something similar to what the interviewer orders or ask the interviewer to suggest something.
- ✔ Show your appreciation for the treat — once hired, you may find yourself brown-bagging your lunch.

Practice a technique known as *mirroring* — what the boss or the interviewer does, you do. Take the interviewer's lead in resting arms on the table, holding forks, the speed of shoveling in the food. Subconsciously, you're establishing similarities, making the interviewer like you (See the sidebar "Bravo moves for all interviewing styles" later in this chapter.)

Always be polite to the food server. Even if the service or food is so bad you make a mental note never to set foot in the place again. Treating the server with disrespect is worse than spilling spaghetti sauce all over the interviewer's new suit.

No matter how much or how little the tab, the interviewer always pays, so don't reach for the bill when it comes, even if it's placed closer to you. Let it sit there unclaimed, unloved. Remember, this could be a test of your confidence or of your knowledge of protocol.

On-campus interview

Some employers recruit on campuses by setting up interviews through your college's career center. These are screening interviews conducted by company recruiters. (Check out the earlier section, "Screening interviews.")

Job market to college seniors: Snag the interviews you want by learning and using the system. Sign up for resume and job interviewing workshops; make friends with the career center counselors; ask for job leads.

Although the past few years have been favorable for new graduates, don't forget: Some jobs are better than others; why shouldn't you have the best?

When you don't get interview slots you want, check back for last-minute cancellations or additions to the interview schedules.

Job fair interview

Job fairs are brief but significant encounters in which you hand over documents — either your resume or a summary sheet of your qualifications (carry both types of documents). Your objective is to land an interview, not get a job at the fair. At best, you'll get a screening interview on the event site.

Try to preregister for the job fair, get a list of participating employers, and research those you plan to visit. Your edge is to be better prepared than the competition.

Fair lines are long, so accept the likelihood that you'll be standing in many lines. Make use of your time by writing up notes from one recruiter while standing in line to meet another.

Bravo moves for all interviewing styles

No matter what style of interview you're doing, some factors are all-purpose job winners.

- **Make them like you.** No matter how scientific the interviewing style, the quality of likability is a powerful influence in deciding who gets the job. And it's human nature to like people who like us, and who are like us in common interests and outlooks.

  Show your similarities with the interviewer and company culture. You need not be clones of each other, but do find areas of mutual interest: preferences in movies, methods of doing work, or favorite company products, for instance. When you successfully intimate that you and the decision-making interviewer share similar world views, values, or approaches to work, you create affinity that leads to job offers, as this true story shows:

  After trying for months, Julia Benz (not her real name) finally won an interview with a major Los Angeles company, and she was taking no chances on botching the interview. As a part of her preparation, Benz went to the office the evening before her appointment.

  She had merely intended to peek inside to see what the building was like but just as she looked in, a janitor cleaning the floor noticed her and asked if she needed help.

  Benz told the truth. She said, "I wanted to get a feel for the place where I'm having an important interview tomorrow." Probably against company policy, the janitor invited Benz into the interviewer's office and pointed out several meticulously detailed models of old ships mounted on a high shelf. The interviewer was clearly an avid collector. Later

that night, Benz read up on old ships at the library.

You know what happens next: When Benz met the interviewer, she pointed at one of the models and remarked — "Say, isn't that a Hudson sloop?" The affinity was instant. Benz got the job.

- **Listen well to interviewers' questions, statements, and feelings.** People like to be listened to more than they like to listen. Show your likability by summarizing, rephrasing, and playing back what interviewers say instead of concentrating just on what you have to say.

- **Don't drip honey by overdoing compliments or small talk.** Take cues from the interviewer's office mementos just long enough to break the ice. Most interviewers will cloy at such transparent, saccharin plays for empty approval. Rather, get to the point — the job.

- **Pause thoughtfully.** Show that you think as you talk. It's okay to pause in thoughtfulness during an in-person interview, where interviewers can tell you're contemplating, thinking things through before answering. Exception: Don't take a thinking pause in a telephone or video-conferencing interview, where any pause is dead airtime.

- **Take notes.** Have a small notebook handy and use it when the interviewer is talking, especially after you've asked a question or the interviewer has put special emphasis on a subject. Taking notes not only shows that you're paying attention, but it also flatters the interviewer. If you prefer using a laptop to take notes, ask first: "May I make a few notes as we talk? I don't want to forget any of your key points."

Everyone tries to arrive early, so think about arriving at half-time when the first flood has subsided. Dress professionally, whatever that means in your career field.

Work up a branding brief (see Chapter 18) with at least one strong memorable point to say to recruiters — *I am in the top 10 percent of my environmental engineering class.* If there's no immediate feedback inviting you for an interview, hand over your summary sheet and ask — *Do you have positions appropriate for my background?* If the answer is positive, your next question is *Could we set up an interview?* If you don't get a positive response, continue with *Could we talk on the phone next week?*

Whether or not you're able to schedule an interview on the spot, when you leave, hand over your resume. Think of your job fair interaction with recruiters as a major star's cameo performance in a film: Move in, make a high-profile impression through dress and preparedness, and move on to the next prospect.

What's Playing at the Roxy?

You may not know in advance the type of interview you'll encounter under the blinky lights, but at least you won't be caught off guard if you take seriously the message in the next chapter showing you how to research your way to a smooth interview.

Part II
Backstage Researching and Rehearsing

The 5th Wave   By Rich Tennant

"Well, so much for my lucky hat! I've worn it to five interviews and not ONE callback!"

In this part . . .

Anyone who tells you to be yourself in an interview is missing the point entirely. The self you present in a job interview is your best self, your fully prepared and ready for your close-up self. This part shows you how to step into that role.

I show you how to find out what you need to know about a job and company before you step into the interview room as well as how to rehearse so you're ready to market yourself powerfully. I tell you how to dress the part and how to handle salary talk.

Chapter 6

Research Is Your Ticket Inside

*W*hat do two Oscar-winning actors have in common? Al Pacino and Nicolas Cage understand that information is everything.

Al Pacino has performed more unforgettable gangster characters than just about any other actor. Even so, the superstar prepared for his role as an aging Mafia hitman in *Donnie Brasco* by chatting up actual New York wiseguys.

Nicolas Cage played a New York paramedic in *Bringing Out the Dead.* The paramedic, surrounded by the injured and the dying, nears the abyss of spiritual shutdown as his ambulance screams across city streets. To get a feel for what these health workers go through, Cage asked to do a ride-along with paramedics. He was told to put on a bulletproof vest and "just stay calm" because the real paramedics were going to the scene of a drive-by shooting, where Cage witnessed the reality of a young kid suffering with a bullet shot through his leg.

Information is everything — and everywhere. You may not want to go as far as traveling several thousand miles to eyeball gangsters, or holding back tears as you comfort a suffering gunshot victim. But don't pull up short in the opposite direction, either. That's one of the worst miscues job seekers can make. Too many have become nonchalant about research. (A single example: Late last night I received an e-mail that melted my servers. It was from a young woman who wanted me to immediately send her questions and answers for today's job interview!*)*

An indifferent attitude toward research won't devalue your candidacy during a screening interview (especially when a recruiter makes the initial contact), but it will badly bite you at an in-person selection interview. (Screening and selection interviews are described in Chapter 5.)

So even if you'd rather scrub morgue floors than do quiz-show-quality research on organizations and their people, go ahead and dig right in — or hire someone to do it for you. Here's why:

- ✔ You'll have the facts to demonstrate a convincing fit between your qualifications and the job's requirements.

- ✔ You can give brilliant answers when asked, "What do you know about our company?"

- ✔ You're better prepared to absorb and evaluate new facts the interviewer adds during the interview.

Here's What Computers Tell Us

Getting a ton of free information on most public — and some private — companies is as fast and as easy as "click here."

In just an hour or two, you can lay your eyes on

- ✔ Annual reports
- ✔ Financial data
- ✔ News releases
- ✔ Information about products and services
- ✔ Industry trends
- ✔ Competitor information

You may be able to find out about

- ✔ Employee views on a company
- ✔ Pending mergers and acquisitions
- ✔ Pending layoffs
- ✔ Shifts in management personnel
- ✔ Corporate culture
- ✔ Wall Street's outlook for the company

All the data you obtain on the "Big D" (big digital resource library) helps you make career moves that light up your eyes and boost your bank account.

Suppose you discover a company teetering on a legal edge or dumping employees like an out-of-control sociopath; take a pass. But when you discover no impending corporate collapse or toxic bosses running the show, and you want the job, research is a tiebreaker in a tight race with another candidate.

Asking Questions about Potential Employers

Use the following questions as a checklist to gather all the information you need. You probably won't be able to use information on all the factors that follow, and you may think of others as important for your specific search.

Here's the rule on how much research to do: The more responsible the job — or the more competitive the race — the greater amount of research you must do to pull ahead.

Size and growth patterns

The size of a company and the scope of its operations say a great deal about the company's ambitions and opportunities for advancement. Try to answer the following questions:

- ✔ What is the company's industry?
- ✔ Has the company expanded globally?
- ✔ Is it expanding or downsizing?
- ✔ What are its divisions and subsidiaries?
- ✔ How many employees does it have?
- ✔ How many clients does it serve?
- ✔ How many locations does it have?
- ✔ Does it have foreign satellites?

Direction and planning

Answers to questions about the company's plans may be difficult to find outside of the company's Web site, annual report, newspaper business pages, business magazines, or the industry's trade publications. The following information is worth pursuing as it lets you know some of the hot issues to address or avoid:

- ✔ What are the company's current priorities?
- ✔ What is its mission?
- ✔ What long-term contracts has it established?
- ✔ What are its prospects?

✔ What are its problems?

✔ Is it initiating any new products or projects?

Products or services

You shouldn't go into a job interview without at least knowing what products or services are the bedrock of the company's business. Find answers to these questions about any company you pursue:

✔ What services or products does the company provide?

✔ What are its areas of expertise?

✔ How does it innovate in the industry — by maintaining cutting edge products, cutting costs, or what?

Competitive profile

How the company is positioned within its industry and how hard competitors are nipping at its heels are measures of the company's long-term health and the relative stability of your prospective job there. Get to the bottom of these issues by asking

✔ Who are the company's competitors?

✔ What are the company's current projects?

✔ What setbacks has it experienced?

✔ What are its greatest accomplishments?

✔ Is the company in a growing industry?

✔ Will technology dim its future?

✔ Does it operate with updated technology?

✔ Can its jobs easily be moved to another country?

Culture and reputation

The answers to these questions are likely to be subjective, but they say a great deal about how well you'll be able to fit into the corporate culture. Look for clues especially on recruitment videos on the company's Web site. How fast is the pace — frantic? laid-back? formal? informal? aggressive? Tuning your performance to a company's cultural factors can make you look as though you'd fit in just fine. Answers to the following questions give you clues about a company's culture:

Private equity and job creation or loss

Private equity firms are all the rage in money circles these days. They've gobbled up many well-known companies.

Private equity firms are investment companies that pool big bucks from wealthy investors, pension plans and other institutional investors — and borrow a lot more money — to buy companies. Their aim is to squeeze more profit out of underperforming corporations. Equity firms have always been associated with job losses, despite claims by industry studies that buyouts create jobs.

When you're a potential employee of a company that's been taken over by a private equity firm, you want to know about the quality of jobs being created and the kinds of jobs that were sent to the dumpster. Is pay on the new positions going up or down, and do these jobs come with health insurance and retirement benefits?

✔ Does the company run lean on staffing?

✔ What's the picture on mergers and acquisitions?

✔ What is the company's business philosophy?

✔ What is its reputation?

✔ What kind of management structure does it have?

✔ What types of employees does it hire?

✔ Is it family-friendly?

✔ Is it woman-friendly?

✔ What is the buzz on its managers?

✔ How does it treat employees?

✔ Has it pushed out older workers?

Company history

Assess how the company's future may be influenced by its past. Was the company part of a hostile takeover? Has it been doing the same things the same way for years because its founder would have wanted it that way? Ask the following questions to find out:

✔ When and where was it established?

✔ Is it privately or publicly owned?

✔ Is it a subsidiary or a division?

    ✔ Has it changed much over time?

    ✔ How quickly has it grown?

Company financials

Collecting current and accurate information about financials is a long chase, but it's better to learn a company's shaky financial picture before you're hired than after you're laid off. Dig for the following nuggets:

    ✔ What are the company's sales?

    ✔ What are its earnings?

    ✔ What are its assets?

    ✔ How stable is its financial base?

    ✔ Is its profit trend up or down?

    ✔ How much of its earnings go to its employees?

    ✔ How far in debt is the company?

Ready, Aim, Fact-Find

As you begin to scope out and scoop up information for your job search, what curtains must you part?

Privately owned companies are harder to track than publicly owned companies. Local or regional companies are harder to check out than national companies. And discovering the details on a corporation's subsidiaries or divisions is harder than finding out about the corporation as a whole.

Ferreting out the financial and personnel scoop on small and mid-sized companies — where the great majority of jobs are found — is a still greater challenge. Unpeeling the onion on start-ups is a major sleuthing gig.

Ready to start your big dig? Here are basic questions paired with concise answers to speed you on your way.

Where can I find free guides and tutorials to researching companies?

The Riley Guide's *How to Research Employers* offers a collection of useful resources. Find it at `www.rileyguide.com`.

Quintessential Careers includes *Guide to Researching Companies, Industries, and Countries*. Find it at `www.quintcareers.com/researching_companies.html`.

Jobstar Central is a California library-sponsored Web site with organized research leads. The leads are useful almost anywhere in the United States. Find it at `http://jobstar.org/hidden/coinfo.php`.

Rutgers University Libraries in New Jersey has compiled an intensive 12-page guide to company research. It's stuffed with tons of resources you can sift through and follow up on, and you find it at `www.libraries.rutgers.edu/rul/rr_gateway/research_guides/busi/business.shtml`.

Where can I find a variety of free information about companies?

Company Web sites are the best place to begin. Run a Google search on the company name. Find Google at `www.google.com`. Don't miss the sidebar titled, "View recruitment videos with eyes wide open" in this chapter.

EDGAR is a government database that provides public access to corporate information, allowing you to quickly research a company's financial information and operations by reviewing documents filed on Forms 10-K and 10-Q with the Securities Exchange Commission. Find it at `www.sec.gov/edgar.shtml`.

Try these three Web sites to find annual reports:

- Annual Reports.com at `www.reportgallery.com`
- Annual Report Service at `www.annualreportservice.com`
- The Public Register's Annual Report Service at `www.prars.com`

Business.com is a directory of industry lists that you can use to identify competitors. Find it at `www.business.com`.

Manta Company Profiles makes available basic info on more than 13 million U.S. companies with such details as address, phone and fax numbers, year incorporated, annual sales, number of employees, and contact name and title. Find it at `www.manta.com`.

Yahoo Finance publishes a wide variety of business information you may find useful. Find it at `http://finance.yahoo.com`.

Large public and college libraries with business and reference departments inventory a number of resources priced for institutions but free for your use. (College and university libraries typically restrict subscription database access to students, alumni, and faculty.) For example, *Plunkett Research Online* is a terrific resource for easy-to-understand analysis of trends, challenges and opportunities in the most important industry sectors, from health care to InfoTech, from banking to energy.

Online social networks such as *LinkedIn* and *Jobster* allow you to find people who work at a company you're researching and ask them about it. Find them at `www.linkedin.com`, and `www.jobster.com`.

Members of a professional organization may be able to refer you to people who can give you advice. Find them on the site of the American Society of Association Executives, www.asaecenter.org.

Where do employees and others post what they really think about a company?

Search Google for "employee message board" and add the name of the company: "employee message board Bank of America," for example.

Check the following employee message boards:

- Vault at www.vault.com

- Monster.com at http://content.monster.com/

- HotJobs Yahoo! at http://hotjobs.yahoo.com/jobseeker/tools/messageboards.html

- WetFeet at www.wetfeet.com

View recruitment videos with eyes wide open

Companies are rushing to add videos picturing employees to their repertoires of recruiting tools. They often present these recruiting videos as a kind of day-in-the-life of a typical employee at ABC company. They can be very helpful when you watch for clues reflecting the people the company prefers to hire.

The videos are supposed to offer potential employees a glimpse of a company's work environment and culture. For example, a video may show employees seated in a cubicle farm. If you're an open-space type of person, you'll want to ask about the work-space assignment policy during your interview.

The workforce age mix is another inference you can draw from recruitment videos, according to Mark Mehler, a principal at CareerXroads, a recruiting technology consulting firm in Kendall Park, N.J. "Are all the people shown north of 40? Or does a mix of age groups offer a hint that experienced professionals are encouraged to apply?" Mehler asks.

The videos offer insights on how to dress for your interview and the kind of work wardrobe you'd need in the related job. When everyone in the video is dressed in casual attire and your grooming hallmark is a business suit — or vice versa — you're probably in the wrong theater.

In an abundance of caution, you may want to watch a company's recruiting videos twice. And when you see one that reminds you of an infomercial, put on your critical-thinking cap. Remember that happy talkers are chosen to appear on the company's silver screen instead of grousers who tell ugly little secrets. When you see employees shown merely talking about their jobs, rather than doing their jobs at their work stations, ask yourself why.

In fact, some of those smiling faces appearing in recruitment videos may belong to human relations professionals, says Todd Raphael, editorial chief at ERE Media (www.ere.net), a New York publisher of recruiting news. Raphael notes that a video may use an unfamiliar job title rather than a familiar version. A "sourcing manager" is actually a recruiter. "You want to hear from a person doing the job you want, not a company spokesperson," he advises.

How can I find out about smaller companies that aren't in the databases?

Jack Plunkett, who heads Plunkett Research Ltd. (www.plunkett research.com), a leading provider of business and industry information, says that most private companies will not divulge financial information to employees or to job seekers. "However, a few very entrepreneurial firms call themselves 'open companies,' meaning that they let all employees know about financial results each month," Plunkett explains.

What about a company that is not "open"? Plunkett advises that you politely ask such questions as: *What's the source of the company's backing? venture capital? partners? family-owned? angel investors? Is the company profitable?* When the company is funded by venture capital or angel investors, the business research expert warns job seekers to beware of potential financial instability.

Here are further ways to get the goods when information isn't readily available:

- For smaller firms, go online to *American Journalism Review* (www.newslink.org), where you can search news sites including hometown newspapers across the nation.

- Search local business newspapers published by American City Business Journals. Find them at www.bizjournals.com.

- Company Web sites won't tell you about financial stability, but you may get clues to the company's customers and suppliers. Call them and say you're doing a credit check (which is true) on the company you're investigating.

- Competitors often have a fair idea of a company's financials. Perhaps you can you find someone who knows someone who knows someone.

- When you really want reassurance, go to Hoover's, Inc. (www.hoovers.com) and use its links to order a credit report on the employer. These reports are compiled by D&B (formerly Dun & Bradstreet) or a credit bureau, such as Experian. Caveat: Business credit reports aren't cheap, so find out the cost before ordering. The reports can help you determine whether the company is paying its bills on time or has other problems that warn you off of accepting a job offer.

- Suppose you're dealing with a mini company, one with a half-dozen employees, for example. You can't find a shred of information written anywhere about the company. After the job offer, you might ask to speak privately with one or two employees "to get a sense of the company culture." Once alone, you can try to find out what, if anything, the employer doesn't want you to know. If you're replacing someone, ask to be put in touch with your predecessor.

- Notice the furnishings as you interview. Are you looking at cement blocks and boards for bookcases? The bare minimum in decor may be a clue to a serious operating capital problem.

How could I check out a start-up company?

When historical data on a company doesn't exist, you can ask questions of the interviewer: *How much capital is on hand? How fast is it being spent? Is additional funding in place?*

Additionally, if you can snare a copy of the company's business plan, review it for probability of success with an accountant, investment banker or SCORE consultant (a volunteer, free to you, of the U.S. Small Business Administration).

You also can make an informed guess about the competence of the principals of the firm by checking out the track record of the management team and financial backers. Try the free service of ZoomInfo. Find it at www. zoominfo.com.

Library copies of *Standard & Poor's Industry Surveys* and *Plunkett's Industry Almanacs* are other good places to poke around.

While no new venture is Oscar-certain, you're wise to avoid taking a part in a real-life production of *Frankenstein Meets Godzilla*.

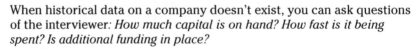

Preparation Makes You a Headliner

As you approach important job interviews, your research actually can change your life for the better.

That's because employers consider company research a reflection of your interest and enthusiasm, intelligence, and commitment. Research shows you are thorough, competent, and revved up to work. Every employer likes those traits.

And not so incidentally, finding out what you should know about a company may encourage you to make a decision to look elsewhere.

Extra! Extra! Print resources to the rescue!

When you need to pull out all the stops in preparing for a job you really, really want, turn to print publications. Study back-issue indexes and archives to major newspapers to see what journalists were and are reporting about a prospective employer. Many libraries have back issues of *The Wall Street Journal*, *The New York Times*, *The Financial Times*, and other important newspapers on microfilm. Try *BusinessWeek* and *Forbes* magazines, as well as industry-specific trade journals and newsletters.

Chapter 7

Your Close-Up: Personality Tests

*A*mong seemingly endless and entertaining online playgrounds designed to help you discover what kind of person you really are, you can gauge your similarities to your favorite Harry Potter character or your favorite James Bond villain. You can analyze your personality by your taste in music or your favorite colors. Alternatively, you can peek inside yourself based on quizzes featuring ink blots or superheros or Disney characters.

The online world offers all kinds of unscientific ways for you to plumb your depth. But flip that coin to the employment world, and personality testing becomes a serious assessment tool that helps decide who gets hired and who gets promoted.

One of the world's leading employment assessment authorities, Wendell Williams, Ph.D., Managing Director of ScientificSelection.com, offers this colorful thought: "While it's amusing to discover whether or not you have the personality of Air Bud or Seabiscuit, after the fun wears off and you decide you would rather bark than whinny at your co-workers, it's time to consider whether a bark or a whinny makes any real difference at work. Unless you're a budding Dr. Doolittle, help yourself by focusing on the specific personality factors that lead to job performance success or failure."

This chapter backlights employment personality tests, which have become familiar rites of passage into the corporate workplace as a condition of being hired.

Personality Testing Is Serious Business

Trying to anticipate why you do what you do at work is the reason that you may be required to take a *personality test* before being granted an interview. Or why you may have to take a personality test somewhere in the interviewing process before you're offered a job.

An *integrity test* may or may not be part of the personality assessment. Here's what each measures:

- ✔ Employment personality tests measure choice, preference, values, behavior, decisions, attitudes, and job-related interests.
- ✔ Integrity tests rate honesty, responsibility, and reliability for the job.

Test development expert Dr. Williams throws more light on the overall reason why personality tests are a favored business assessment tool: "Employers administer personality and integrity tests because they try to avoid making a bad hire which means they want to know as much about a potential employee as possible."

I asked test reviewer Ann Hart for still more reasons why employers use personality tests. Hart is the senior author of an insightful book she wrote with George Sheldon, *Employment Personality Tests Decoded* (Career Press, 2007). Hart says organizations give pre-employment tests for these reasons:

- ✔ To hire the employee who poses the least financial risk to the corporation.
- ✔ To hire people who can make good decisions under stress and who lead or work well within teams.
- ✔ To avoid hiring candidates who are dishonest, bullying, angry, disruptive, or a violence threat to the workplace.

How many companies require job candidates to take personality tests? Estimates are all over the place, topping out at 30 percent. Despite sketchy data, the personality-discovery star does seem to be rising. Don't be surprised if you face an employment personality test in your future. Will it be on paper or online?

Paper-and-pencil tests have been filtering out unsuitable candidates for years but Web-based personality tests have become important to the hiring process only within the past decade or so. In the foreseeable future, the relentless push of computer power and 'Net connection speeds will change the nature of work, but those advancements can't change human nature. Personality tests open a window on human nature.

What You Might Not Know about Personality Tests

To borrow from an anonymous saying, here's my observation: "If you can stay calm while all around you is chaos in the pressure of a pre-employment personality test, then you probably haven't completely understood the seriousness of the situation." Personality tests, love 'em or loath 'em, guard the gateways to your future.

A rundown of six important things to understand about your future encounters with personality tests follows.

Asking questions before the test

Although you can't blow off a request to sit for an employment test and get hired, you can ask a few questions to spread a small safety net under your candidacy. Try these feelers:

- ✔ I read about a rash of lawsuits over hyper-intrusive personality tests that originally were developed to spot mental illness, such as The Minnesota Multiphasic Personality Inventory, and its knock-offs. Can you tell me the name of the test I'll be taking, whether the test provider has been involved in any legal challenges of the test, and if so, what was the outcome?

- ✔ I sometimes get nervous and uptight about tests. Can I take the test again if I don't do too well today, or is this take final?

- ✔ What kind of test(s) are you asking me to take? Personality, integrity, performance . . . ? What is the title of the test?

- ✔ Can I get any feedback regarding test results? How about areas I didn't do well in . . . at least I'll know what areas need improvement.

- ✔ Will I still be considered for the job if I don't do well on the test?

Expect to hear "no" more often than "yes" to these questions, but any one of them is worth a try. If the interviewer is dismissive, at least you know the kind of company you're dealing with — if you think they're tough now, wait until you're hired and the honeymoon is over.

Anyone can write a personality test, but is it validated?

Would you be surprised to learn that literally anyone can author a personality test? It's true, and virtually anyone does, from creative homemaker and college psych major, to advertising writer and company hiring manager. From their fertile minds come questions such as these:

- ✔ Do you prefer riding in a car to riding a motorcycle?
- ✔ Can a white drummer kick with a black band?
- ✔ Do you sometimes get bored or always find life interesting?

Yes, anyone can write the questions, add up the answers, and declare statements about what they mean. The problem is that without validation research, the statements are virtually meaningless.

To prove valuable, psychometric tests must be *statistically validated* with enough people over enough time to give users confidence that the tests actually predict what the test-makers claim — that they work as advertised.

"Once a company knows what it wants to measure and has chosen a legitimate hiring test, the company studies its own employees to prove test scores are associated with job performance, turnover, training, or other essentials of a successful organization before judging the test to be validated," Dr. Williams explains.

That's why psychometrically-trained professionals are assigned to identify the kinds of psychological traits that lead to the selection of an achieving, profitable workforce. These professionals develop a test that measures human traits and then verify the test by proven methods. Statistically supportable personality tests typically are written by experienced professionals with doctorates in some aspect of psychology.

Finding out what a test measures

If you can discover the title of the personality test that you'll be taking, you may be able to identify the traits measured by the test. In pursuing a test chase, look for test reviews published by the Buros Institute of Mental Measurements at the University of Nebraska-Lincoln, a gateway for serious and validated testing information.

Be sure to read the FAQs on the Buros Web site (www.unl.edu/buros) to learn about

✔ Locating tests in Buros's *Mental Measurements Yearbook,* a regularly updated reference containing test reviews; it is available to read free in many large public and university libraries.

✔ Accessing *Tests in Print,* a bibliography of commercially available tests in the English language.

✔ Using *Test Reviews Online*, a service that provides access to the same test reviews that appear in the Mental Measurement Yearbook series; each test can be downloaded for a modest fee.

When you have no inclination or time to do a test chase, don't give up — Dr. Williams has your back. The widely-quoted industrial psychologist reports university research showing that only about five traits are associated with job performance:

✔ Conscientiousness about the job

✔ Agreeability and flexibility

✔ Extroverted behavior

✔ Inquiring mind

✔ Non-neurotic

Of the Big Five (which may go by different names, depending on whom you talk to), Dr. Williams says the three traits most commonly associated with good job performance are conscientiousness, agreeability, and not being neurotic. Expressed another way, good workers care about their work, get along with others, and are emotionally stable.

Who's most likely to use tests

High-level executives in any industry rarely are asked to undergo a personality test, with or without an integrity component. Government agencies typically use their own tests and assessments.

Non-manufacturing businesses tend to use personality tests more than do manufacturing industries. Examples of non-manufacturing businesses include retailers, banks, utilities, insurance companies, staffing agencies, and communications corporations. Integrity tests are prevalent in jobs involving money, public safety, or merchandise, especially in entry-level positions.

Your civil rights in testing

Using personality tests to gauge job candidates that weren't specifically designed for hiring has led to lawsuits. Usually employers have been on the losing end because the tests were ruled invalid, invasive, or discriminatory. You have the following rights when it comes to testing:

- ✔ You have a right not to be subjected to wanton invasion of privacy with intrusions into non-job-related areas such as your sex life, religious beliefs, and political views.

- ✔ You have a right to expect compliance with the Americans with Disabilities law, which prohibits requiring medical examinations before you get a job offer.

- ✔ You have a right not to be subjected to a test that has a "disparate impact" on a protected class of people, such as certain racial or ethnic groups.

If you think your rights may have been violated by a personality or integrity test, research the topic online (Run a Google search for personality test civil rights.) or consult an employment lawyer.

Peeking into privacy issues

"Personality tests need to be handled like confidential medical records," observes Anne Hart, senior author of *Employment Personality Tests Decoded* (Career Press, 2007). "Find out whether test results are given to your health insurance company along with medical information. Psychological testing, like medical exams, should be confidential and not stored in open-ended databases in your employer's human resources department," Hart adds.

What if you're not hired — how long will your records be kept at both the employer's office and/or at the vendor testing company? I asked a legal expert in pre-employment testing about that issue.

"Testing companies should be willing to discuss their records and security procedures with candidates," noted eminent employment attorney Joseph Schmitt at the Halleland Lewis Nilan & Johnson firm in Minneapolis. "Reputable testing firms won't be offended if you ask about confidentiality, and should be able to detail their security procedures upon request."

But Schmitt explains that the tests legally can't be destroyed overnight: "Candidates should be aware that their records will be retained for a minimum of one year (two years in California) under federal and state regulations regarding retention of hiring records. You may wish to ask when records are destroyed, and for a confirmation that your records are deleted after the records retention period has expired."

You certainly don't want your test results whizzing around the Internet. Underscoring the serious need to protect test score privacy, reports of irreparable damage to someone's reputation surface too often. The reports are caused by accidental or malicious posting of another person's personal information online. Even if your records are online for just minutes, they can be copied and distributed around the world for employers to read. You can never be 100% certain that an online image has been killed off.

Making the Grade on Job Tests

Conventional wisdom advises that you get a good night's sleep, be truthful in all your answers, and relax and enjoy a personality test that the interviewer says is standard operating procedure.

About the kicked-back mindset, at least, conventional wisdom is wrong. Instead, consider the flower vendor who sells her basket of posies by arranging the freshest pieces on the top. If you want cash for your flowers, learn how to display your best blooms.

In the following sections, I give you tips for displaying your best blooms (traits) in a personality test, tips that I gathered from the four corners of the testing industry.

Visualize yourself fitting in

Based on your research of the company, imagine the ideal candidate. How would that paragon of virtue think? When you hit a wall with a weird question, your fallback position is to try to answer as the ideal candidate/perfect employee.

Obviously, answering as the ideal candidate/perfect employee is not easy. You need to guess what the paragon is like. (Hint: Review video clips featuring employees on the company Web site.) How much and what kind of personality characteristics are you being compared to?

When in doubt, position yourself as a person of moderation in the mainstream of contemporary thought. Test administrators tend to grade unconventional beliefs as potential trouble.

Company managers prefer to hire people like themselves. Although similarly minded employees don't always do better, a personality kinship gives managers a warm, fuzzy feeling by knowing that everyone looks and talks alike. At least in spirit.

Watch for combination tests

Many tests are combinations of several types of test questions. Even if the first 10 questions ask about your personality traits, stay alert for questions about your aptitudes (such as potential for leadership or creativity) or abilities or your integrity (such as lying). These questions may require greater concentration to answer in ways that will help you.

Beware of absolutes

Watch out for absolutes like *always, ever,* and *never.* For example, saying you never took more than your share of things in your life may paint you as a goody-two-shoes who can't be trusted. Unless it's an honesty question, answer in the middle of the range; middling answers tend to confuse hiring managers who aren't sure what they're looking for.

Choose answers suggesting positive traits

Try to select answers that put you in the most positive light. Examples of favored characteristics include

- ✔ Achievement-oriented
- ✔ Agreeable
- ✔ Assertive
- ✔ Conscientious
- ✔ Dependable
- ✔ Emotionally stable
- ✔ Good communicator
- ✔ Imaginative
- ✔ Intellectually curious
- ✔ Open to new experiences
- ✔ Optimistic
- ✔ Responsible
- ✔ Sociable
- ✔ Tolerant
- ✔ Trustworthy

Avoid answers suggesting negative traits

Stay away from answers that show you in a less-than-stellar light. Examples of negative characteristics to avoid implying include

- Inability to function under stressful conditions
- Dishonesty
- Emotional dysfunction
- Acceptance of fraud, as in filing a fraudulent worker's compensation claim
- No opposition to stirring up legal trouble
- Poor impulse control
- Propensity for interpersonal conflicts
- Thievery
- Tendency toward time theft (sick leave abuse, tardiness)
- Illegal drug use
- Disregard for rules
- Tendency to be tense or suspicious
- Rigidity
- Prejudice
- Predisposition for negative interpersonal relationships
- Lack of self-worth

Be alert to replayed questions

Some tests ask virtually the same question on page one, page three, and page ten. The test is trying to catch inconsistencies — figuring you forgot a lie you told 30 questions ago. If possible, read through the test before you start. Consistency counts.

Anticipate integrity test questions

Integrity questioning may be part of a personality test or a separate test.

A lie scale measures the position of a test answer on a gamut from lie to truth. The scale functions as a kind of lie detector.

Special tips for salespeople

The sales representative who maintains long-term relationships selling ongoing telecom services to a company has a different kind of job than does a sales representative who sells an automobile to a customer in a one-time transaction. Personality tests for salespeople differ as well. Even so, any test administered for the sales industry probably measures such core characteristics as the following:

✔ Empathy — the capacity to identify or sympathize with another individual's feelings

✔ High energy — the force to stay with a challenge until you meet it

✔ Achievement orientation — a drive for learning new abilities and impatiently accomplishing goals

✔ Intellect — qualities showing culture and imagination

✔ Self-control — a feeling of being in personal control of your destiny

✔ Self-efficacy — the belief that you can meet your expectations if you try hard enough

✔ Self-monitoring — the tendency to use social cues (not only your personal convictions) about what is expected

✔ Positive resilience — the ability to not take sales failure personally but also to bounce back for the next sales call

But even if you're as truthful as Honest Abe, people under pressure of testing sometimes give questionable answers. For example, if you're asked to estimate the percentage of workers who steal from their employer, make a low guess. A high guess may be interpreted to mean you think employee theft is common, and therefore, acceptable.

Most integrity questions are fashioned for entry-level or mid-level workers who have access to merchandise or trade secrets, or for financial workers who handle money.

Take a lot of practice personality tests

Ready yourself for employment personality tests by working through as many practice questions and tests as time permits. Find practice tests online at such test publisher Web sites as

✔ eTest (www.etest.net)

✔ SHL Group (www.shldirect.com)

✔ Kogan Page, UK (www.profilingforsuccess.com/kogan-page)

Additionally, find practice tests — and leads to others — in a number of books, including the following:

- *Employment Personality Tests Decoded* by Anne Hart with George Sheldon (Career Press, 2007)

- *How to Master Psychometric Tests* by Mark Parkinson (Kogan Page, UK, 2004)

- *Ace the Corporate Personality Test* by Edward Hoffman (McGraw-Hill, 2002)

Sample Personality Questions

Questions on all types of tests may require uncomfortable yes/no answers. (Following the questions, I explain their meaning in parentheses.) Here are some examples:

- *Do you believe that children or spouses are far more important than anything?*

    (Will your family life interfere with your job?)

- *Do you exercise regularly?*

    (Are you likely to be a high risk for health insurance?)

- *I would like to be a florist.*

    (Are your interests suited to this field?)

- *I still maintain close contact with friends from high school.*

    (Do you get along with people for long periods of time?)

- *I have thought of trying to get even with someone who hurt me.*

    (Are you vindictive, or can you put hurts behind you?)

Some questions require specific answers, rather than *yes* or *no:*

- *How often do you make your bed?*

    (Do you clean up after yourself? Are you obsessive about it?)

- *On average, how often during the week do you go to parties?*

    (Will you frequently come to work hungover?)

- *Describe how you see work.*

    (Do you see work as mandatory or as a way to obtain rewards?)

Concerned that you didn't do well?

The stark truth is that you can't really do much about a test score when you mess up. Busy employers are focused on finding the right people to hire, not on helping those who are among the unchosen.

"Do-overs are rare," explains Dr. Williams. "Regardless of what you say or do, most hiring managers have a die-hard perception of their favorite personality profiles. If you don't fit their molds, you seldom get a second chance. In the final analysis, testing is a roll of the dice for the unwary and quicksand for the uneducated."

Keep On Keeping On

When you've taken a personality test but you weren't invited to an interview, soldier on to your next opportunity. Although you'll probably never learn your test scores or even hear anything back from the employer, your results may have hurt your chances of being hired for the position. If so, the only return you'll get on your investment of 50 minutes or more of your time is experience gained. The way to win employment is to keep applying for more jobs.

Chapter 8

Showing You the Money

. . . .

In This Chapter

▶ Recognizing sales pitches for you to accept less cash

▶ Finding out what the position is worth

▶ Updating thoughts on how to duck premature money talk

▶ Avoiding tipping your hand in a negotiation

▶ Gracefully addressing your less-than-stellar salary history

▶ Scripting the best deals for your negotiation

. . . .

*I*magine this uncomfortable scenario: After accepting and starting a new job, you discover that you're paid 20 percent under market and that instead of climbing what an enthusiastic recruiter called a stairway to the stars, you're on a road to nowhere.

Fiascos like this can happen when you fall hook, line, and sinker for a recruitment pitch that deflects a position's cheapo cash compensation. The pitch distracts you by spotlighting non-monetary aspects of the position — growth opportunity, latest technology, fabulous coworkers, super company — you name it.

Although this chapter shows you how to deal with under-market offers in general, there are a few justifiable exceptions when you will and should seriously consider making cash secondary to opportunity or lifestyle in a job you accept. A few examples:

 ✔ You're a new graduate or career changer with scant experience and you need good breaks and helping hands in a nourishing environment.

 ✔ You're taking a lower rung on a ladder that positions you to compete for a higher rung.

 ✔ You're a parent who needs home time with the kids.

Special concerns aside, most of the time thee and me are zeroed in on the legal tender we want to earn for the rent of our brains and labor, to maximize cold cash and monetary-based employee benefits. We usually begin our pursuit for fair compensation through salary negotiations with recruiters.

Recruiters are employers' personal shoppers, tasked with going into the marketplace and bringing back the best qualified candidates for the thriftiest prices. In this chapter, I list the types of recruiters you're likely to encounter, the siren songs they may sing to snag the best bargains, and the ways you can get the best employment deal for yourself.

Recruiters and Their Talking Points

REMEMBER

Recruiters are sales professionals, not your new best friends. This is true when

- The recruiter (a.k.a. headhunter) is an external recruiter (a.k.a. third-party recruiter or independent recruiter).
- An external recruiter is employed as a retained recruiter on an ongoing basis and is paid a set fee — much like a retained lawyer or accountant.
- An external recruiter is employed on a transaction basis as a contingency recruiter and is paid only when a submitted candidate submitted is hired.
- The recruiter is an internal recruiter (a.k.a. company recruiter), who is staffed in a company's human resource department and paid a salary.

All recruiters are engaged by employers to find people for jobs — not jobs for people. And they do it by being superb sales professionals.

Recruiters who deem you qualified for a position pass you up to a hiring decision-maker, often the individual to whom you would report.

How can you tell when you're being recruited with a song-and-dance to divert your attention from a chintzy salary? Look out for yourself by discovering the insider secrets straight ahead.

Tactics meant to sell low offers

When a company gives a recruiter a limited compensation budget to offer candidates, the recruiter's job and livelihood depend upon convincing you, a qualified candidate, to take the "downpay" job offer by pointing out collateral benefits the job may or may not truly offer.

It's a tough sell. So tough that employment consultants write industry articles for recruiters advising them on how to increase their offer acceptance rate, when, in the words of one prominent consultant, "your company pays crummy wages."

The consultants' suggestions include the following sales techniques and talking points:

- ✔ Offer "exploding bonuses" that shrink in amount the longer you take to consider the offer. (Don't give candidates too long to think about accepting a job that pays under market.)

- ✔ For a management job, invite comradeship with the company CEO, who calls asking you to accept the offer, commenting that "You and I can build this company together." In a variation, a potential coworker calls urging you to "Join the team — it's great." (This too refocuses your attention from legal tender.)

- ✔ Make a great "higher-calling" offer. This includes such rewards as a title, telecommuting, training options, a socially responsible and environmentally friendly employer, working with new technology, and the opportunity to make a difference in people's lives rather than "just making money."

- ✔ Reframe the discussion by speaking less of cash compensation and benefits and more of job stretch and growth opportunity.

  Job stretch describes an environment in which you show what you can do on a larger stage — heftier operating budget, bigger challenges, and supervision of more employees. In baseball, a job stretch move is from the minors to the majors.

  Growth opportunity is the lure of future raises, promotions, and company growth. In entertainment, a growth opportunity move could be from stunt double to featured player.

In a funny kind of arithmetic, a recruiter may speak the language of "an overall increase of 30 percent" if you take the offered position. Here's a typical break-down of what the recruiter may really mean by that 30-percent figure: perhaps 15 percent for stretch in the job, plus likely long-term growth of 10 percent, and 5 percent for a cash compensation boost over your last job. Do the arithmetic. And do due diligence before you buy that reasoning.

You're not yet finished with the give-and-take of sophisticated salary negotiation. The recruiter has plenty of arguments in reserve, as the next section reveals.

Recruiter comebacks when you stick up for yourself

When you're hot on the track of treasure and refuse to budge from your "show me the money" stance ("If this is such a great job opportunity, I need greater money."), experienced recruiters may balk. They, who practically live in the salary negotiation space that you infrequently visit, are famous for classic comebacks. Here are five golden oldies with suggestions for countering their rejoinders.

- *Don't make the mistake of overvaluing compensation and undervaluing opportunity.* (I appreciate your calling that important point to my attention and I'll bear it in mind.)

- *If I succeed in getting the cash compensation increased, the company will probably want me to produce other candidates with more experience.* (I hope not. But you have a fiduciary responsibility to your client to produce the best candidate for a fair price — and I'm that person hands down.)

- *We're looking at other candidates who don't share the level of expectations you express. Why should we consider raising the bar so high in your case?* (I have the same level of performance expectations for the work I produce. I'm sure the other candidates know what they're worth better than I do. Are you looking for an outstanding or a mediocre hire? If it's talent you want, you should choose me because of my proven record in —.)

- *Prove your ability. Do a great job and you could get a sizeable raise next year.* (I appreciate that and I admire your line of thinking about rewarding performance, provided promises for the future build on a fair market rate going in. I have done a lot of salary research and believe that a starting salary of $___ would be attractive to me because my performance with previous employers has been exceptional. Do you think your client could confirm your progressive thinking about a future raise based on a starting salary of $___ and include that promise in the offer letter?)

- *If I can get the cash increased, will you sign an iron-clad guarantee to take the position with no further haggling?* (Yes, I am very interested in this position, but we need to clarify figures. How much of a cash increase and what benefits are included?)

The lesson: To avoid walking away wishing you had come up with a better answer to recruiter comebacks than you did, plan your responses ahead.

New thinking for new times

Perhaps the hour has come for a rethinking of conventional wisdom extolling job seekers to take the long view. The 21st-century rate of company upheavals, mergers, downsizings, and other job-busters may mean that you won't be around long enough to fully benefit from job stretch and growth opportunity.

Whether you choose to take the money and run or to put your faith in blue-sky projections of a rosy future, invest the necessary time learning the ropes of salary negotiation to avoid being snookered on future offers.

A first step toward being shown the money is discovering what the market will pay someone with your qualifications. The upcoming section, "Discovering Market Pay Rates," shows you how to find out.

Discovering Market Pay Rates

Knowing your market value — the going rate for people in your industry with skills and a job description similar to yours — is the centerpiece for negotiating the compensation you deserve.

Finding salary information online

Discovering the market rate for the kind of work you do has never been easier than it is today. Two companies — Salary.com (www.salary.com) and Payscale (www.payscale.com) — dominate the online salary research services now available to job seekers. A third service, SalarySearch (www.salarysearch.com), launched as I wrote this book.

All three services offer free basic data and informative salary negotiation articles; a custom report for your specific situation costs between $25 and $150. Why would you want to pay for something you presumably can get for free? Generalized averages produced by online salary calculators aren't always spot-on for specific companies and jobs.

Be certain to benchmark the job you're applying for by *job content* — not just by job title. The same job title can mean different things to different people in different companies.

Handling salary boxes in online applications

Recently I was asked for a practical way to handle the *salary requirement* and *salary history* (two different things) questions when either or both are embedded as required fields in an online application. B.I. (before Internet), you could write "Negotiable" for salary expectation to keep from under- or over-pricing yourself. But most online applications won't accept "Negotiable" (or "Open" or "Will discuss in an interview") for expected salary as a viable answer, so that tactic is out history's window. What now?

Jack Chapman (www.salarynegotiations.com) rides to the rescue. Salary consultant and workshop leader, Chapman is the author of the best-selling guide *Negotiating Your Salary: How to Make $1,000 a Minute* (Ten Speed Press, 2006), my favorite book in the genre. Here's what Chapman told me about working those windows:

"Your self-interest is best served by putting whatever number in the salary-requirement box that you think won't get you screened out. The employer is essentially asking, 'Can we afford you?' Since you won't require anything other than a competitive salary, your answer, by putting in a competitive number, is 'Yes, you can afford me.'

"This strategy works nicely when the box is entitled 'Salary Requirements' or 'Expected Salary,' but requires an additional step if it is labeled 'Current Salary,'" Chapman says. "Once you're in the interview, you'll need to explain that you interpreted 'Current Salary' to mean 'Current Salary Requirements,' and if they want a 'Salary History,' you'll be glad to provide it later as needed."

Background on the bucks

WorldatWork (www.worldatwork.org), an international association of human resource practitioners, is a recognized authority on compensation matters. Here's a selected glossary of WorldatWork terminology:

Cash Compensation

Pay provided by an employer to an employee for services rendered (time, effort, and skill). Compensation includes four core elements:

- ✔ **Fixed pay:** Also known as "base pay," fixed pay is nondiscretionary compensation that doesn't vary according to performance or results achieved.

- ✔ **Variable pay:** Also known as "pay at risk," variable pay changes directly with the level of performance or results achieved. It's a one-time payment that must be re-established and re-earned each performance period.

- ✔ **Short-term incentive pay:** A form of variable pay, short-term incentive pay is designed to focus and reward performance over a period of one year or less.

- ✔ **Long-term incentive pay:** A form of variable pay, long-term incentive pay is designed to focus and reward performance over a period longer than one year. Typical forms include stock options, restricted stock, performance shares, performance units, and cash.

Benefits

Programs an employer uses to supplement the cash compensation that employees receive. Some are legally mandated, such as Social Security and Workers' compensation. Others are awarded at the discretion of the employer, such as health and life insurance, vacations, holidays, personal days, tuition assistance, automobiles, and professional group and club memberships.

Who wins, who loses on a lowball offer

When you're working with a contingency recruiter who encourages you to take less than the going rate for a job, the recruiter may have your best interests at heart. Or the recruiter may just want to close the job order quickly.

A contingency recruiter's fee is based on your first-year earnings. Follow this admittedly over-simplified example: Say the recruiter is to be paid 25% of the job's first-year salary. If the job's market rate is $100,000, the recruiter would earn a $25,000 fee. But when the job's budget figure is under market — say, only $90,000 — the recruiter takes a hit of $2,500, compared to your loss of $10,000.

From the contingency recruiter's viewpoint, most of a loaf is better than none. And the recruiter hopes for future assignments from the employer that can more than compensate for losing a relatively few dollars on a single transaction.

Negotiating in the Moment

After all your salary prep, the time has arrived to reap your rewards: You're in the interview room, and the back-and-forth begins.

But just when the interview is starting to fly, *bam!* — the interviewer lets go with a dangerous question that could severely clip your wings: *How much money are you looking for?* Should you name your price right then and there? Not if you can help it.

As salary request that's too low devalues your abilities; a salary request that's too high looks like you're too big for the company budget. Both bids leave you out of luck. Be aware that some employers have already budgeted for the position, and the first offer is their best offer. They ask what you want merely to confirm that the money's enough to interest you in the job.

Your compensation should be based on the value of the job someone wants to pay you to do, not on the value of the job someone has paid you to do in the past.

Giving and taking at the right times

Sure, you have a pretty good idea going in about the remuneration you're shooting for, but you may discover wild cards while you're in the interview. You knew, for instance, that the job requires travel and you figured maybe 25 percent of your time would be spent on the road, but now the interviewer reveals the true travel requirement — 75 percent. Would that revelation cause you to rethink the money or re-evaluate whether you should accept the job at any salary?

Moreover, if you have to talk salary too early in the interviewing process, a decision-maker may not yet be sufficiently smitten with you to make the company's best offer.

In the previous edition of this book, I posed a key question for salary negotiation: What is the best single thing you can do to receive a higher pay offer when you're interviewing for a job? My answer:

> *Delay discussing salary until you're offered (or nearly offered) a specific position.*

Until you have the offer, the employer holds all the weight. Once you have the offer, the scales shift. You have something the employer wants, and you become equals negotiating a business proposition. From outsider, you have become poised to become the newest insider — a good place to be.

Learning to deflect salary questions until the timing shifts to your advantage can greatly influence the amount of money that you take from the bargaining table.

But although the advice to sit tight until the timing is right is still on the mark, doing so is easier said than done these days, says salary negotiation pro Jack Chapman. He explains:

"In the 1980s, it was easy to postpone the salary talk. That has changed over the years. Employers are more demanding or inquisitive or something. Yet, the principle is the same — postpone when and if you can."

But when you're pressured to talk money sooner rather than later, Chapman warns that digging in your heels and flat-out refusing to comply is a mistake. By being hard-nosed, you set up a power struggle that you can't win. You'll be seen as obstinate and hard to work with. A power struggle can cost you the job.

Nor should you move to the other extreme in which you meekly cave-in, tell all and let it go at that. As a dogmatic refusal earns you a label of being too strong, a roll-over and-scratch-my-belly response may make you seem too weak.

Sometimes you can just ask

To make certain your salary research is on target, network in professional groups. At association meetings, speak to people in a position to hire you. Work the conversation around to asking a question: "What could someone with my skill set expect to earn in your organization?"

Another take on pre-interview salary talk

"There's more than one way to avoid being boxed in by the salary boxes in online applications," says Jim Lemke, director of organizational development for Opportunity International, as well as technical reviewer for this book and a much-lauded HR consultant. Here's Lemke's recommendation:

"When you're asked to fill in salary requirements in an online application, I suggest that you write the absolute minimum salary for which you're willing to work. Do this to avoid any chance of being seen as too pricey to consider inviting in for an interview. The negotiation begins in the interview when you make the assumption that the pay quoted is base cash salary only and then negotiate for additional compensation such as bonuses, perks and benefits.

"Here's an example: Suppose you're searching for a job that pays a salary of $90,000. The interviewer remarks that the job pays $80,000. You respond that the figure is below your last job, which was worth $125,000. The interviewer says 'Wait a minute — that doesn't reflect your application statement that quoted your salary as $75,000.' Now you say: 'What I said is true — *my last base cash salary was $75,000. But with additional performance bonuses and benefits, my total compensation was $125,000.*' From there you continue to negotiate." (See Chapter 14 for more information on negotiation in an interview.)

Moreover, when you're too low or too high for the company's budget, you hand the employer's interviewing screener information to judge you by your price, not by your whole package of qualifications. Even in the final interview round, premature dollars talk may lead a decision-maker to see you as too expensive without your being given an opportunity to justify your worth and negotiate.

Fortunately, there's a better way to connect when you're giving away your bargaining leverage too soon: get a quid pro quo. I think of this kind of fair exchange as Chapman's rule:

When you comply with an early request for your salary numbers, get markers in return. Something for something.

What markers do you want as IOUs for your upfront compliance? You want agreement that your early money talk won't screen you out of further interview opportunities. And you want agreement that your salary discussion will focus on the market value of the position and not on your salary history.

To side-step the negative consequences of early revelation as much as possible, you want fair consideration. Here are Chapman's illustrations of what you can say to get fair consideration in three interviewing situations (Find out about the differences between screening and selection interviews in Chapter 5.):

✔ **Phone Screening:** *Before I give you all that information, can I ask a question? (Yes) I don't know who you'll hire, but from what I've seen so far, you should definitely at least interview me. If I'm forthright about all my compensation factors, can I be assured of an interview?*

✔ **Interview Screening:** *Before I give you all that information, can I ask a question? (Yes) I don't know who you'll hire, but from what I've seen so far, I would definitely like to participate in the second round of interviews. If I'm forthright about all my compensation factors, can I be assured of that?*

✔ **Selection Interviewing:** *Before I give you all that information, can I ask a question? (Yes) I'm a little concerned that we could lose a perfectly good match over salary expectations. And I'm confident that you'll pay a competitive salary — which is all I need. Can you, first, give me your rough range, your ballpark compensation, and I'll be candid and tell you how that compares?*

If you're too high or too low, Chapman's approach gives you the opportunity to address the discrepancy in the interview process instead of having the employer decide behind closed doors with no input from you.

Why salary questions come early

Some interviewers know exactly what they're doing by front-loading the salary question, others may just be feeling their way through the process. The salary question comes up quickly when the interviewer

✔ Is trying to instantly determine your professional level, or is slyly probing to see whether you'll be happy with the low side of an offer.

✔ Wants to test the market. The interviewer may not even have an idea of the position's market value and is shopping candidates to simplify budgeting.

✔ Is open to paying whatever is necessary to get the right person and just wants to know what he's in for.

Whatever the interviewer's motivation for prying a salary disclosure from you, without a job offer, salary disclosures put too much power in the employer's hands. That point was confirmed to me by an HR executive (who understandably wishes to remain anonymous): "While I may request salary histories from others, I never comply with that demand when I'm in the job market. Why not? I know a guillotine when I see one — I design them."

So what should you do when the salary question comes at you too soon? What can you gracefully say to hold off a precipitate discussion? The following section, "Stalling Money Talk with Smart Replies" gives you a number of script lines to use in response to premature questions about your salary

Tell recruiters your salary history

Should you ever disclose your salary history or salary expectations before a job offer? Yes. Tell all when you're asked by third-party employment specialists — chiefly executive recruiters and employment consultants who find people for jobs.

These professionals are specialists at their work and are paid for their time, either on a retained or contingency basis. They get paid to find good talent, and so they won't let salary deter them from presenting you when your skills are a match for a job opening. Recruiters are far too busy with the matchmaking task to waste time with you if you make their work difficult. Time is money.

expectations. They're followed by lines useful in sidestepping a salary history so low that interviewers will wonder why — if you're such a standout candidate — you've been so grossly underpaid in the past.

Stalling Money Talk with Smart Replies

Don't let a frog clog your throat when an interviewer presses for the salary discussion before you've established your value. Instead, answer along the following lines:

I'm sure that money won't be a problem after I'm able to show you how my qualifications can work to your advantage because they closely match your requirements.

My salary requirements are open to discussion. Your company has a reputation of being fair with employees, and I trust you would do the same in my case. I don't think salary will be a problem if I'm the right person for the job.

I'm aware of the general range for my kind of work, but I'd feel better talking about pay once we've established what specific performance goals the job calls for.

I'd be kidding if I said money isn't important to me — sure it is! But the job itself and the work environment are also very important to me. I wonder if we can hold the pay issue for a bit?

I'm a great believer in matching pay with performance, so I can't speak with any certainty about the kind of money I'm looking for until I know more about what you need.

Money is not my only priority; I'd really like to discuss my contributions to the company first — if that's okay with you.

I can't answer that question until I know more about this job.

The amount of my starting compensation is not as much of an issue to me as how satisfying my filling the position will be for both of us. Can we talk more about what the position entails?

Before we get into the compensation issue, can you tell me more about the kind of skills and the type of individual you're looking for to help you reach your goals? What do you expect the person you hire to accomplish within the first three months?

All I need is fair market value for the job's demands, which I'm sure you'll pay, so is it okay if we talk about the details of the job first?

As far as I can tell, the position seems like a perfect fit for me — tit for tat on your requirements and my qualifications. So as long as you pay in the industry ballpark, I'm sure that we won't have a problem coming up with a figure we're both happy with.

Before we can come to an agreement, I need to know more about your strategy for compensation, as well as confirm my understanding of the results you're looking for. Can we hold that question for a bit?

Since pay includes so many possibilities for compensation, I'd like to first know more about your compensation plan overall and how it relates to the position.

I'm sure that you have a fair salary structure, and if I'm the best candidate for the position, we can work something out that we'll all like.

I'm not used to talking money before a job offer; are you making me an offer?

My requirement is market within the area — shouldn't be a problem. Can we put that off to the side until we decide if there's any need to go further down the money road?

I will consider any reasonable offer. Should we talk about it after we've wrapped up the details of the job, and I've been able to show you what I bring to your company?

I'm paid roughly the market value of a (occupational title) with (number of years') experience and the ability to (manage, or do something special). If you're competitive with the market, there won't be a problem with salary.

Downplaying a Low Salary History

You know that disclosing an under-market salary history can jeopardize your negotiating power. Try out these scripts to lessen the impact of having worked for too little money:

> *I'm uncertain how my salary history will help you, because salaries are affected by geography, benefits packages, and company priorities. Maybe I'm wrong, but it seems to me that the going market value for the position will be more useful. According to my research, that's a range of $X to $Y.*

> *A biting-the-bullet answer: My salary history won't bring us to any conclusive figures. I've been working under market value, and that's one more reason I want to make a change. This job seems perfect for me. I wonder whether we could price the position on the basis of its worth to you?*

> *I don't feel comfortable limiting the discussion to my salary history because a large portion of my compensation has been in variable and indirect pay. I've received bonuses regularly based on my performance. What I think you're really asking is how I plan to do the job you need done — can we talk about that?*

> *If we discuss my salary history, can I say up front that I view this position as a new challenge that will require higher performance than my last? I'd like to think I'm worth more to you than to previous employers.*

To get the best return on your negotiation when you've been working for less than market value, repeat after me: *Focus on my worth, not on my past. Focus on my worth, not on my past. Focus on my worth, not on my past.* Get it? Got it? Good!

Considering More Factors That Affect Job Pay

In addition to the timing of the offer, the size of the company influences how high the interviewer will bid for you. Although large companies typically pay more, small companies without formal pay structures are easier to negotiate with than corporate titans.

But even at huge companies where pay scales are cut-and-dried, your potential boss may have the latitude to cut you a better deal. In fact, some interviewers see your negotiation attempts at improving your compensation as a desirable trait — yet another indicator that they've made the right choice. Their reasoning: *If you can look after your own best interests, you can look after ours.*

Other factors identified by negotiation authority Jack Chapman that influence the size of pay offers include the following:

- **Supply and demand:** In employee-driven markets, salary offers tend to rise; in employer-driven markets, salary offers don't rise and may even fall.
- **Special skills:** Skills in short supply may merit premium pay.
- **Urgency:** A company losing revenue because a job goes unfilled may offer higher pay.
- **Recruiting fatigue:** A company weary of failure in filling a position may ease salary limits.
- **Salary compression:** Concern that paying you a higher wage may lead to revolt by current employees can cause a company to stick rigidly to a certain salary.

Getting Your Worth's Money

Oh happy day. Your interviewer looks you straight in the eye and says, "We'd like you to join our team; I'm offering you a job, but before we go any further, we should talk about how much you'd like to be paid." The moment of truth has arrived. You've got the offer. No more dodging the money issue.

To nab the best offers, follow the guidelines in the sections that follow.

Find a home in the range

The market rate that big companies typically pay for a job is often stated in a range with a minimum, midpoint, and maximum salary. Smaller companies may not operate on such a formal spectrum.

Negotiating doctrine has long insisted that he who goes first in a price negotiation loses. To follow classic counsel, when you're offered (or virtually offered) a job and are asked to name your price, bounce the ball back into the interviewer's court: *Can I ask you to take the lead on this question — can you tell me your range for this position?* (If you did your homework, you already know the range. You're merely asking for confirmation.)

Most often the interviewer who doesn't mind tossing the first figure on the table will respond with a straightforward answer. But anecdotes abound in recruiting circles about interviewers who try to save the company a few dollars by purposely misrepresenting the midpoint to be the maximum salary.

For example, suppose you're applying for a job that through research you've learned is budgeted at between $50,000 and $60,000. To your surprise, the interviewer claims that $55,000 is the maximum wage. And you know it's really the midpoint. Hmmm.

Polite probing is one way to respond: *I'm not sure I heard you correctly, or perhaps my research is wrong. Did you say that $55,000 (midpoint figure) is the high end of the range for this position? I thought it was $60,000, which fits in my range.*

But when the interviewer bounces the ball right back into your court and you have to go first or look like a sock puppet, express your salary requirements in a range based on the going rate for the job: *I'd be expecting salary in the range of ($58,000 to $65,000). I think that's a range we can work with, don't you?*

Citing a range is good because it gives you haggling room and shows that you're economically aware.

Not sure where you realistically should land in the range? Match your request to your experience level. The following guidelines show you how:

- ✔ Don't ask for bottom of the range unless you're a rookie. Even then, if you've worked while in school, ask for a two-striped corporal's pay rather than a one-striped private's. You're positioning yourself as a top rookie candidate.

- ✔ A conservative school of thought recommends that experienced people ask for a pay point just above midrange — not only to show that you're above average, but also that you understand the need to leave room for raises.

- ✔ Highly qualified candidates head toward the top of the company's projected range where they belong.

Plot your salary history carefully

Bear in mind that salary is a cash figure; total compensation includes benefits and such variable pay as potential annual bonuses, stock options, and expected merit raises. Example: *Last year I earned $42,000 to $45,000 compensation, based on a salary of $30,000.* (Review the sidebar titled "Background on the bucks" earlier in this chapter.)

When your salary history ranks you at the top or above the range of market value, you can afford to discuss that history verbatim.

When your history is less impressive, be less specific. State your figures in wide ranges so that you're more likely to stay in the game for positions for which you're qualified. Include figures slightly above and below the market value to cover all your bases. Usually this approach requires bundling your income figures for multiple years: *For the past three years, I have earned total annual compensation ranging from $95,000 to $125,000 for my work in this field.*

Some job seekers feel they should inflate their salary history. That's a risky idea — the odds of discovery are stacked in the employer's favor.

Instead of misrepresenting your history to try to improve your lot in salary negotiations, try the following:

- ✔ Show compensation modules. List base pay and variable pay in one figure; give another figure for benefits; then add the figures together for the total compensation package.
- ✔ At executive levels, list compensation items line by line.

You might be asked to back up your salary claims. Decide in advance what you will do if your interviewer asks you for tax forms or pay stubs. The request isn't illegal, but you should anticipate whether you will comply.

Some job seekers adamantly refuse to supply a salary history and give a middle-finger salute to requests for one. They look at their pay records as a supreme privacy issue and may feel that they're grossly underpaid or wouldn't be looking for another job. As one job seeker anonymously commented online: "I don't want to work for a company that demands to know my salary. I want to work for a company that wants me and will do whatever it takes to get me." I applaud that sentiment but know that a dogged flat refusal is unlikely to produce the most invitations to audition.

Stonewalled? Try to upgrade the job

Once you've established what the position entails and you're told you've received the best offer and that the job isn't worth more, try to make the position more important in the scheme of things:

- ✔ Point out that the job requires more than the standard duties suggested by the job title — that the job's content fits into a job description that merits a higher pay bracket. Clarify how you plan to minimize company costs through your performance. Explain how you'll pay for yourself. By using this tactic, you more firmly establish your worth to the company and justify your performance-based reason for asking a higher price.
- ✔ Beef up the job. I once became one of the highest-paid managers in an organization by combining two positions and creating a new job title. An employer may be interested in considering a "two-for-one" who is paid a "one-and-a-half" salary.

Even if you don't succeed in your upgrade move, you'll have put your new boss on notice that you're ready to see the money.

Use dramatic silences

What should you do when the interviewer offers you a salary on a lower level of the salary range for the position? Two words: Keep quiet!

As the interviewer finishes the offer and waits for your reply, let the interviewer wait for enough time to notice your silence. Everyone has trouble outwaiting 30 seconds of silence. Look at the floor. Keep your face glum.

These moments of nonverbal communication show your dissatisfaction with the offer, without a word to incriminate you as overly hungry for money. The interviewer may feel compelled by this uncomfortable silence to improve the offer. Or at least open a dialogue in which you can campaign for other kinds of rewards.

Don't try this technique on video interviews; see Chapter 3 to find out how to handle these unique interview situations.

Words of last resort

When it seems as though the right numbers just aren't on your radar, you have little to lose by trying a straightforward response:

> *It pains me to say this. While I'm very attracted to what we've been discussing, the figure you named is just not an incentive for me to join your group. The good news is that we're both interested, so let's keep talking. What do you think?*

Finding Web-based negotiation help

Continue learning all you can about the ins and outs of getting employers to show you the money. Here are two suggestions:

✔ Jack Chapman's Web site, Salary Negotiations, (www.salarynegotiations.com).

✔ Online salary calculators noted earlier in this chapter under the headline "Where to find salary information online" provide a number of responsible how-to articles.

No flexibility? Make creative suggestions

In negotiating with a small company, you're less likely to encounter fixed pay policies, permitting you to get creative about your compensation package. If a small company can't afford you on a cash basis, what else do you want?

You have a wide range of options for sweetening an offer. Ask for some combination of the following:

- A company car
- Stock options
- Extra-generous mileage reimbursement
- Parking privileges
- Additional paid vacations
- Dental plan
- Tuition reimbursement
- Recreational or daycare facilities
- An expense account
- An early salary review

If you're negotiating for a job that pays below $30,000 and you know the company's salary cap can't be raised right now, try to get a shorter work week or flexible work hours, and take a second job to keep a roof over your head. If your spouse can cover you with health benefits, maybe you can trade health insurance for cash.

The Magic of Market Value

You researched the fair market value of your work before negotiating a price. Slip those exact words into the discussion whenever you can — *fair* and *market value* are terms that people like. Remember, too, that you can always come down on your price — but coming up is almost impossible after you name a low figure.

Most of us want to get the most we can in return for the parts of our lives that we sell. Negotiating pay with skill and savvy can mean that you gain hundreds of thousands of extra dollars throughout your career.

How's your imagination?

In the iconic movie *Star Wars,* do you remember the part where Han Solo (Harrison Ford) asks Luke Skywalker (Mark Hamill) how much the reward would be to rescue rich Princess Leia (Carrie Fisher)? Luke tells him it would be more wealth than he could imagine. Han's knockout answer: "I don't know, I can imagine quite a bit!"

Chapter 9

Costuming Yourself for a Starring Role

A pair of Judy Garland's ruby slippers from *The Wizard of Oz* sold at auction for $666,000.

John Travolta's white suit from *Saturday Night Fever* fetched $145,000.

Darth Vader's helmet from *The Empire Strikes Back* brought in $115,000.

Pricey collectibles! They'd cause quite a sensation if you wore any of them to a job interview. But you wouldn't dream of wearing such attention-grabbing memorabilia because you want to be remembered for what you say in that scene — not for what you wear.

When you want to begin your career — or take it up a notch, or pull it back from the edge — you need the right clothes, accessories, and grooming to make a boffo first impression. How you're dressed impacts the tone of the interview and enshrines the first visual of you as a candidate.

By making your appearance appropriate for the job you seek, you set the stage for the *halo effect.* That is, when the interviewer likes you right away, the interviewer may assume that if you excel in one area (image), you excel in others. Some potential employers make a subconscious hiring decision within seconds of meeting a candidate and spend the rest of the interview validating their initial impression. With these stakes in mind, be sure your appearance is a real curtain raiser.

This chapter tells you how to impress the hiring squad by selecting interviewing attire that boosts your confidence because you look, act, and feel good.

Three Commandments of Style

By dressing appropriately, you signal employers that you respect their company's culture and that you care enough to expend the effort to make the right impression.

Begin your mastery of interviewing impressions with these three key principals of presenting yourself in the right team uniform.

Dress to fit the job and the job's culture

Social DNA draws people to others who are like them. When extending a welcome to a newcomer, you pay compliments that indicate "You're one of us."

Companies and organizations are made of people working as a group to accomplish common goals. An anthropologist might think of such a group as a kind of workplace tribe.

When your choice of clothing or your grooming keeps you from looking like you're a member of the tribe, you create an image of an outsider, perhaps causing the interviewer to perceive you as "not one of us." That's why you should make the effort to look as though you absolutely belong on the company's tribal land.

How can you find out about the company's dress code and grooming conventions? You have several options:

- Visit the company's Web site and search for videos of employees. Check for beards, mustaches and long, loose hair. Notice whether the men are wearing sport jackets or suits, or simply shirts with or without a tie. Observe whether the women are in pants or skirts, and if the latter, how short they are.

- Call the human resources office and ask about the company's dress code.

- Use your personal network — or an online social network — to find an employee whom you can quiz.

- Loiter near the workplace and observe employees coming and going. Just don't wear a raincoat, show up in a white van, or watch through binoculars.

Correctly interpreting the company dress code is the Number One Commandment to follow in dressing for job interviews.

Think of interviewing attire as a costume

The Number Two Commandment in interview dressing is to understand that your attire is a work-related costume. With a few exceptions, which I discuss later in this chapter under "Heading for Fashion Frontiers," the job interview isn't an outlet for unconventional self-expression.

On that point, a rookie job seeker once asserted to me her right to wear to an interview whatever she chose to wear: "My personal style and how I look is my business," she petulantly insisted. "True," I agreed, "and the person an interviewer hires is the interviewer's business."

Treating an interview as a chance to show off a free-spirited or eccentric personality is a big mistake. To drive home the point, here are several extreme examples of the do-your-own-thing-no-matter-what error:

- Imagine a woman of 50 trying to look nifty in a sparkly, hand-painted T-shirt, or wearing a baby-doll mini dress floating above a pair of tights.

- Imagine a man of 25 making a Tony Soprano statement with a black shirt and white tie, or channeling *Indiana Jones* in a beat-up leather jacket.

- Imagine a woman of 35 whose nails are so long she looks like *Edward Scissorhands* in a skirt, or as if she's preparing to duel with Cruella De Vil in *101 Dalmatians*.

Okay, you get it: Keep far-out personal image statements safely locked in the closet when you're out on job patrol. Otherwise, some interviewers will think you're outlandish, maybe even weird, and they'll want you gone.

When you're not sure whether your interview wardrobe borders on bizarre or is more appropriate for after-hours wear, ask yourself the ultimate litmus question:

> *Would my favorite film director cast me as a person who would be hired if I auditioned wearing this get-up?*

By wearing an interview-appropriate costume, you're not selling out your authentic self, you're moving on. And, if fortune and preparation smile, you're moving on to a better place: making the short list and then being hired.

"Look the part, and the part plays itself"

This old theater adage is the Number Three Commandment in constructing your interview image, says Jack D. Stewart of Abilene, Texas.

A retired recruiter, Stewart once accepted a recruiting search for an industrial sales rep. The job order came from a new client. Stewart's firm began referring quality candidates, recommending to the candidates that they dress conservatively for their interviews, meaning business suits, well-pressed shirts, and silk ties.

Six interviews with different individuals brought the same puzzling response from the new client, who said: "Each candidate was basically qualified, but not what we're looking for."

Stewart's firm had a policy of re-evaluating a client's assignment when six candidates were referred and none received a job offer. A recruiter was sent to the client's offices to uncover the problem.

Imagine the recruiter's astonishment when he entered an office filled with people dressed in very casual slacks and sport shirts sans ties. "Well," the recruiter thought, "these must be the foot soldiers. What does the captain wear?" The recruiter found out soon enough when the sales manager arrived to greet him in a pair of black work shoes topped by white socks.

"From that day forward," Stewart explains, "we dressed down our candidates for their interviews with that client — but we couldn't bring ourselves to tell them to wear white socks. Finally, one of our referrals was hired. The experience is a good reminder for job interviewees — *When in Rome, wear a toga.*"

Following Today's More-Relaxed Dress Code

Is the following statement true or false? "You can never be overdressed. Even if they say to wear business casual, it's appropriate for you to be in a suit and tie."

If you guessed "true," you may have guessed wrong. A sea change has floated into American workplaces defining what constitutes acceptable clothing to wear on the job. And to a certain extent, the lightening up on dress codes has spilled over into job interviewing.

First, a little background: I can't remember a time when virtually every job interviewing expert hasn't hammered home the basic tenet that dressing conservatively is the safest route. Period. That advice retains validity but here's the thing: For many people, the notion of what dressing conservatively means has changed. Traditional suit-and-tie wisdom is no longer universally and automatically correct. Conservative in many cases now means nicely pulled-together business casual apparel.

Who says so? A number of studies over the past decade confirm that workplace dress codes have become more liberal than they were back in the starchier twentieth-century days:

- ✔ A 2001 poll by the Society for Human Resource Management reported that 87 percent of U.S. companies allow some form of casual dress in the workplace.

- ✔ A 2003 survey by the Business Research Lab, a research and management consulting firm, noted that about half of respondents said the dress code where they work had changed in the previous two years, and by three to one, they said the code had become more casual.

- ✔ A 2006 tally of employers conducted by the National Association of Colleges and Employers revealed that companies seem to be considerably more relaxed about appearance these days. Just 12 percent said that a male job candidate wearing an earring would be a negative and only 28 percent said they'd frown at weird hair color (like blue, green, violet). Two-thirds of employers surveyed said that body piercing would not strongly influence a hiring decision.

The casual and laid-back dressing trend working its way across the country has moved beyond workers who work alone or in creative groups. Even sales and other professionals who interact with the public have jumped on the casual fashion runway.

Dressing for a job interview isn't a foregone decision these days. Consider your options in the next section, "Running Down Four Basic Categories of Work Wear."

Running Down Four Basic Categories of Work Wear

Both women and men should expect every nuance of their appearance to be noted and interpreted at a job interview. As Mark Twain supposedly said, "Clothes make the man. Naked people have little or no influence on society."

When you're getting ready for the big days, choose your attire from these four basic fashion categories:

- ✔ **Conservative:** Examples of conservative dressing environments include banks, accounting firms, management offices — especially in big corporations, law firms, and offices of elected officials. Formal and conservative Donald Trump is a poster boy for this work category.

Should you dress 10% above your level?

When you go job interviewing, the classic advice is, "Dress one step up from what you'd typically wear to work in that position." Other lines you may hear are "Dress 10 percent better than you ordinarily would," or "Dress for the position you'd like to have, not for the one you do have, so you'll be seen as promotable."

My take on upscaling for interview days is to "Dress the best you're ever going to look in the job you want."

- ✔ **Business casual:** Business casual environments and career fields include information technology, sales, government agencies, education, retail, real estate, engineering, small companies, and certain dot-coms. Poster nominees: classic Oprah Winfrey and relaxed Ellen DeGeneres.

- ✔ **Casual:** Casual environments are those such as construction, trucking, maintenance, repair, landscaping, and other jobs where work clothes may end the day stained and sweaty. Home improvement icon Bob Villa has dibs on the poster honors for this job lot.

- ✔ **Creative fashion:** Examples of creative career fields include entertainment, fashion, graphic design, interior design, and popular music and other arts. Poster people: trendy Jessica Simpson, and offbeat Johnny Depp.

A discussion of each category follows.

Taking the conservative approach

Conservative dressing means no surprises. Your look is traditional or restrained in style. You avoid showiness. You aren't flamboyant. Conservative dressing means you not only wear the established team uniform, you wear it well from the tip of your white collar to the closed toe of your dark shoes.

For *women*, a conservative checklist includes the following:

- ✔ **Suit:** Wear a two-piece suit or a simple dress with a jacket. Good colors are navy blue, gray, dark green, dark red, burgundy, or black. Make sure your skirt length is a bit below the knee or not shorter than just above the knee.

  In a dark color, a pantsuit is a tasteful choice. Accessorize it with a simple shell and silk scarf. Caveat: If your research shows you're interviewing with a super-traditionalist, stick to skirts.

✔ **Shirt:** A white, off-white, or neutral-colored blouse is a safe choice.

✔ **Shoes:** Closed-toe pumps with low or mid-heels suggest that you're work-minded.

✔ **Accessories:** Briefcases look more serious than purses, but a handsome leather purse is fine. Avoid distracting jewelry or watches, and make sure you wear stockings.

✔ **Make-up:** Moderate makeup for daytime wear is appropriate. No looking like a Britney Spears stunt double.

✔ **Hair:** Simply styled hair looks contemporary; observe styles on TV anchors, for whom maintaining a professional image is essential.

For *men,* the following conservative checklist applies:

✔ **Suit:** Power suit colors are navy or charcoal gray. (Black on men is seen as somber.) Tans and medium-tone colors work well if your research shows they're included in the company's color chart for team uniforms. Suits should be well-tailored.

✔ **Shirt:** White is the first choice for shirts; blue is second. In either case, wear only long sleeves.

✔ **Tie:** Dark or low-key (blue, black, navy, blue, or gray) or power red colors look executive-like. Geometric patterns are okay, but only if they're minimal. Be sure your necktie knot is neat and centered on your neck; the bottom of the tie should just reach your belt. Don't don a bowtie.

✔ **Shoes:** Wear lace-up shoes in the same color as your belt. Wear black shoes if your suit is gray or navy; dark brown shoes for tans or medium-toned colors — polished and clean shoes that are in good condition, of course. Rubber-soled shoes are a bad match for a professional suit and tie, as are alligator shoes or sandals.

✔ **Socks:** Wear dark socks in mid-calf length so no skin shows when you sit down.

✔ **Accessories:** Limit jewelry to a wristwatch and, if you wear them, cufflinks. No surprise earrings, necklaces, or body piercings.

About that fragrance

Perfumes and after-shave scents should be minimal or missing. Some people are allergic and others may be reminded by the fragrance of someone they didn't enjoy knowing.

Online wardrobe mistresses and masters

When you're trying to scope out the latest fashion scene — what's hot and what's not — the World Wide Web is your oyster. Here are several sites to get you started:

✔ Fashion.About.com (fashion.about.com): A guide to women's fashion, including fashion trends.

✔ MensFashion.About.com (mensfashion.about.com): A men's fashion and grooming guide for today and tomorrow.

✔ Ask Andy About Clothes (www.askandyaboutclothes.com): A popular and comprehensive site devoted to men's wear, which includes a feature enabling you to ask questions of an expert.

Choosing business casual

The nation's work attire has morphed from Casual Friday to Casual Every Day and, in sync, the trend has moved to the interview outfit, too. An increasing numbers of recruiters say that a business suit is too formal for an interview at their company.

The interpretation of *business casual* varies too widely for universally accepted rules but mainstream opinion nixes casual clothing you might wear to a picnic or ball game, such as sweatsuits, spandex, shorts, T-shirts with slogans or commercial logos, bared midriffs, halter tops, and tank tops.

For *women,* a business casual checklist includes the following:

✔ **Clothing:** Guidelines here are looser than for conservative dress. Sticking with the following points is a safe bet:

- A casual jacket or blazer with well-pressed trousers or a skirt is a top option.

- A jacketed tailored dress is a fine choice.

- Tailored knit sweaters and sweater sets are appropriate.

- A knee-length, or longer, skirt with a blouse works well for support jobs.

- Pastel overload (pink, baby blue) is fine in a nursery but not in your outfit.

- Provocative clothing (see-through tops, uncovered cleavage, second-skin pants, festive shimmering-fabric, super-short skirts) isn't your best option.

- **Shoes:** Shoes should look business-like and be dark colored — no strappy shoes, sandals, or mile-high stilettos.

- **Stockings:** You can skip them for a business casual look.

- **Make-up:** Avoid wearing heavy makeup — on you or your collar line.

- **Accessories:** Leave flashy or distracting jewelry — dangly earrings, clunky bracelets, giant, spiky rings that bruise fingers when shaking hands — at home in your jewelry box. If you wear it, make sure your nail polish is fresh, unchipped, and in a classic color.

For *men*, a business casual checklist includes the following:

- **Clothing:** Don a sport jacket or blazer, especially navy blue, back or gray, with color-coordinated long trousers or pressed khakis. Shirts must have collars, be long-sleeved and tucked into pants; button-down shirts are good but not mandatory.

- **Shoes:** Choose dress shoes and matching belt; loafers are acceptable.

- **Socks:** Wear dark socks that are mid-calf length.

- **Ties:** Choose simple (not too busy) ties for job interviews unless you know from your research that a tie isn't part of the uniform where you're interviewing.

- **Accessories:** Limit jewelry to a conservative wristwatch. Removing earrings is safest but check for the company culture.

Any interviewee, male or female, is better off steering clear of the following:

- Dark tinted glasses; sunglasses atop your head or front of collar

- Electronic devices (even on vibrate mode — the buzzing sound is annoying)

- Joke or fad watches

The Internet has been given a large chunk of credit/blame for shifting workplace wear to more comfortable, less formal wardrobes, and I believe it. As *BusinessWeek Magazine* says, "All those YouTube videos and MySpace pages zipping back and forth on the 'Net have revived the (moribund) telecom industry" and brought it back from the dead. If so, the 'Net certainly has the power to spread the popularity of relaxed workplace dress codes.

Advance research is the only way to be on sure footing. You're gambling if you assume that you know what business casual means in your interview setting — or even whether you should dress in business casual. When in doubt, scout it out.

Don't let them smell you first

Grooming has a strong influence on hiring decisions. Who hasn't nearly passed out after smelling someone's "salami" breath? Who hasn't been revolted by rank body odor? Who hasn't been turned off by spinach flecks on teeth?

A recent survey of employers by the National Association of Colleges and Employers fingered being slovenly as an unacceptable sin. In fact, 73 percent of respondents said they don't want slovenly, smelly, dirt-ridden employees working on the premises.

Shower. Brush. Comb. Don't make the interviewer send out for a hazmat suit.

Aiming for casual wear

Casual work attire is suitable for hands-on working men and women. Often a company uniform is required when you're on the job, but when you're in job interview mode, the main thing to remember is to look neat and clean with no holes or tears in your clothing. Colors and style don't matter as much as they do in conservative and business casual interview dressing, but your overall appearance still counts a great deal.

Here's a short checklist for men and women:

- ✔ **Clothing:** Shirts or knit tops and well-pressed pants are appropriate. Avoid wrinkled or soiled clothing, and don't wear t-shirts with writing on them.

- ✔ **Shoes:** Polished leather shoes or rubber-soled athletic shoes are fine. Don't choose grungy sneakers.

- ✔ **Grooming:** Make sure your hair and fingernails are neat and clean.

Heading for Fashion Frontiers

Most job-seekers interview in attire suggesting that they're serious and centered in a business culture. But if you work in a creative environment, take fashion risks and go for artistry, design consciousness, innovation, trendiness, new styles and, yes, even whimsy.

You probably are way ahead of me and already follow high- and low-fashion statements in magazines like *Vogue* and *Marie Claire, GQ* and *Details.* You know what they say about fashion: in one year and out the other. So although

I won't attempt to compile a fashion checklist for either sex, here are two classic possibilities for what *men* might wear when interviewing for a position in a fashion-forward office:

- ✔ Turtlenecks and flat-front pants.
- ✔ A blazer or cashmere V-neck sweater and a shirt (or all three) atop denim jeans.

Women? Plenty of fashion magazines show you what's new in the fashion world if you don't already know.

In offices where employees are encouraged to show originality, a reasonably creative look (not too far over the top) beats out conservative dress, and maybe business casual as well. It's all in the eye of the culture.

Guessing at Tomorrow's Styles

As this chapter fades to black, I share a few forecasts gleaned from America's fashion observers:

- ✔ The era of the traditional suit is nearing an end.
- ✔ Business casual will become the new traditional dress in the workplace.
- ✔ Americans are moving toward a standard where there's virtually no difference between what you wear during work and after hours.

These predictions hint at a developing new paradigm in work wear.

No worse for wear

When you've no budget to burn but need quality-looking interview wardrobe items, why not treasure hunt in resale shops? I checked out several such emporiums in Southern California and found great bargains. And as soon as I lose a few pounds....

When you've no budget at all, seek free donated workplace clothing, which is available to help economically disadvantaged women acquire and keep jobs. Dress for Success (www.dress forsuccess.org) is a worldwide nonprofit organization with chapters in many American cities.

The Women's Alliance (www.thewomens alliance.org) is another national organization whose members provide professional clothing and other services to low-income women seeking employment.

Men seeking free gently used work clothing can check for local "clothes closets," usually church-sponsored, by inquiring at public job service offices.

Chapter 10

Overcoming Stage Fright: Rehearse, Rehearse, and Rehearse

*Y*ou're nervous. You have a queasy feeling, a mouthful of "ah" and "um" cotton, and a rabbit pulse. You're feeling jittery — from your shaking knees and clammy palms to the tummy butterflies eroding your confidence as you enter an interview.

In short, you have a galloping case of stage fright. Sound familiar? As Walter Cronkite remarked, "It's natural to have butterflies. The secret is to get them to fly in formation."

Beating Stage Fright to Pitch Better, Sell Faster, and Ace More Interviews

You're not alone in your nervousness. Most people start out with a case of the shakes when interviewing or making a speech, including me. When I began giving speeches, I could feel my throat drying up as panic fried my memory banks. I knew I had to go out and orate to promote my media careers column, but doing so was not fun.

One day I was in Florida addressing a group of career counselors when a teacher with whom I shared a podium watched me shake my way through my remarks. The teacher, herself an accomplished speaker, took me aside after the program and delivered one of the best pieces of advice I've ever heard. The teacher explained that nervousness is caused by the fear of looking ridiculous to others:

"When you are nervous, you are focusing on yourself. Try to focus on how you are helping other people by sharing with them the knowledge you've acquired. You've been privileged to gather information not many people have. Think about serving others, not about yourself when you're up there on stage."

Those words of wisdom were like a lifetime speech-making tranquilizer for me. Thanks, Teach, for putting nervousness in perspective. How can *you* use that perspective? Preparing for a job interview is not unlike preparing for a speech or theatrical performance. The trick is to first get the kinks out of your basic self-presentation, which you accomplish with plenty of rehearsals — plenty of them.

After you get your basic act down pat, you will, of course, polish it with new words before each interview — words you find by researching the interviewing company (see Chapter 6).

After you know your material cold — and how the skills you're selling benefit the potential employer — the outward-looking perspective kicks in. Divert your attention to the needs of your audience. Concentrate on fulfilling the interviewer's needs.

Focus on your audience, not on yourself. Just as I found that focusing on the audience is a giant step toward eliminating nervousness, so will you.

Here's a recap of the three critical steps you can take to deliver a compelling and poised interview performance:

1. **Polish your basic message.**

   Get your skills, competencies, and other qualifications down pat. Rehearse until you're comfortable answering questions and have practiced your basic presentation techniques.

2. **Personalize each sales pitch.**

   Research each potential employer to customize your basic presentation for each job.

3. **Spotlight your audience.**

   Focus on how your talents can benefit your audience. Don't focus on yourself or worry about how imperfect you may appear.

More Techniques to Stop Stressing Out

When stars of the theater walk on stage, they claim the stage from wing to wing, backdrop to footlights. With confidence and charisma, they win the audience's undivided interest. In a phrase, stars have stage presence. They are comfortable on stage.

Performance advisers offer numerous suggestions to get your butterflies flying like Air Force Blue Angels, ranging from relaxation techniques to visualization exercises. Here's a list of ideas that may be just what you need:

✔ Deep breaths are an instant stress reliever: Take a deep breath, breathing from your toes all the way through your body, and then slowly exhale. Repeat twice more for three deep breaths in all.

✔ Another simple technique: Clench your fists and hold for three to five seconds. Release. Releasing your hands relaxes your shoulders and jaw. Repeat three times.

✔ Push away anxiety: Go into a nearby restroom and lean into a wall like a suspect being frisked in a cop show. Push hard, as though you would like to push the wall down. Grunt as you push. It sounds funny, but try it — it works. Speech coaches say that when you push a wall and grunt, you contract certain muscles, which in turn reduces anxiety. Don't let anyone see you do this exercise, though — heaven knows what an observer might think other than you're loony tunes.

✔ Visualize the outcome you want: Top athletes often use visualization techniques to calm jitters, improve concentration and boost athletic performance. They picture in their mind opponents' actions and strategy, and then picture to counter their maneuver. A golfer may run a movie in his head of where he wants the ball to go before he takes a swing. For an interview, you can visualize meeting the interviewer, answering and asking questions, closing the interview well (see Chapter13) or even being offered the job on the spot (See Chapter 14).

✔ Combine relaxation with visualization: Visualize a quiet beautiful scene, such as a green valley filled with wild flowers, or a soothing garden with a waterfall. Inhale, thinking "I am." Exhale, thinking "calm." Breathe at least 12 times. Next, recall a successful interview experience.

Free your mind of personal worries to concentrate on the subject of your job interview. If your personal concerns can't be handled immediately — and most can't — write them down and promise yourself that you'll deal with them after your job interview.

Rehearsing out loud

Practice speaking aloud the messages you plan to deliver at your job interview — such as a listing of your five top skills, how you will answer questions (Chapters 18 through 24), and how you will ask questions (Chapter 11).

Why not just silently read your message statements over and over? Coaching experts say *rehearsing* information helps fix content in your mind. Rehearsing your statements at least five times makes them yours.

Yes, that's a lot of repetition, but remember this: Rehearsing five times beats the time frame of a famous orator in ancient Greece. Demosthenes

worked to improve his elocution by talking with pebbles in his mouth and reciting verses while running along the seashore over the roar of the waves. Supposedly Demosthenes also went into a cave to learn oratory skills. Not having a watch or calendar (and unable to use a sundial in a cave) Demosthenes shaved off the hair on half of his head and didn't come out until it grew back three months later. When he finally came out, listeners gladly lent him their ears because he was the man with the golden tonsils. (Brad Pitt is rumored to be first choice to play Demosthenes.)

Practicing with a Video Camera

Discover yourself through an employer's eyes. With a friend feeding you practice questions, work with a video camera. An audio tape recorder is useful, but isn't in the same league as being able to see as well as hear yourself in interviewing action.

Taping a practice session enables you to see how— with image improvement and mannerism modification — you can look alert, competent, and confident. You can refine actions that turn hiring on and eliminate those that turn hiring off. Rehearse nonverbal as well as spoken messages, and keep an eye out for the following image-detracting actions:

- ✔ Leg swinging
- ✔ Foot tapping
- ✔ Rocking from side to side
- ✔ Fiddling with your hair
- ✔ Waving around nervous hands
- ✔ Leaning back
- ✔ Crossing your arms
- ✔ Bowing your head frequently
- ✔ Darting your eyes
- ✔ Blinking slowly (comes across as disinterest or slow thinking)

✔ Touching your mouth constantly

✔ Forgetting to smile

Use the following techniques to put your readiest foot forward:

✔ Look interested when you're seated by leaning slightly forward with the small of your back against the chair.

✔ Look the interviewer squarely in the nose, and you appear to be making eye contact. You look open and honest. More earnest honesty is communicated by upturned, open palms.

✔ Pause and think before answering a question to seem thoughtful and unflappable.

✔ Refer to your notes, and you're seen as one who covers all the bases. Just don't make the mistake of holding onto your notes like they're a life preserver.

✔ If you find your voice sounds tight and creaky on tape, try warming up before an interview or your next practice run: Sing in the shower or in your car on the way to the interview. La la la la. . . . Maybe you shouldn't sing on the bus.

Stage Directions for All Players

As you rehearse your interviewing presentation, aim for the A-list of candidates by heeding the following hints:

✔ Practice focusing your discussion on the employer's needs; show that you understand those needs, that you possess the specific skills to handle the job, and that you are in sync with the company culture.

✔ Don't discuss previous rejections — you come off as a constant audition reject.

✔ Make eye contact, but don't try for a laser lock on the interviewer. Imagine two cats in a staring contest — in the animal kingdom, nobody moves until somebody swats. Break the tension — periodically look away.

✔ Develop and practice justifiably proud statements of your accomplishments that relate to the job you want.

✔ Practice descriptions of your leadership qualities and initiative.

✔ If pressed, you can admit you've made a mistake in your career (when was it — 3:48 p.m. on June 14, 2003?), but rehearse satisfying explanations of how you learned from your one mistake — or two or three.

✔ Don't practice long monologues — be fair: Split air time with your interviewer.

Anticipating Interview Trapdoors

No matter how well you're doing as you sail through an interview, certain things can throw you off balance if you're not forewarned. Rehearse handling the situations in the upcoming sections.

Disruptions

As you rehearse, keep in mind that not everything that happens during the interview is related to you. Your meeting may be interrupted by a ringing telephone, the interviewer's coworkers, or even the interviewer's needs. Add some interference to your mock interviews. Because the show must go on, find methods to politely overlook these interruptions with patient concentration. Practice keeping a tab on what you're discussing between disruptions in case the interviewer doesn't.

Silent treatment

Interviewers sometimes use silence strategically. Moments of silence are intended to get candidates to answer questions more fully — and even to get them to blurt out harmful information they had no intention of revealing.

Instead of concentrating on your discomfort during these silences, recognize the technique. Either wait out the silence until the interviewer speaks, or fill it with a well-chosen question (see Chapter 11) that you have tucked up your sleeve. Don't bite on the silent treatment ploy, panic, and spill information that doesn't advance your cause.

Turning the tables, you can use your own silence strategy to encourage the interviewer to elaborate or to show that you're carefully considering issues under discussion.

Never should the unnecessary be volunteered by the unwary for the unforgiving.

Take One . . . Take Two . . . Take Three . . .

Practice your scenes until they feel right, until they feel spontaneous. Rehearsing gives you the power to become a confident communicator with the gift of presence. No more nervousness, no more zoning out. Your butterflies fly in formation.

Not a pretty picture

Watch videos of your mock interviews with these lists of don'ts in mind:

Don't say

- Um
- Uh
- Yeah or Yup (instead of yes)
- Y'know
- Like
- Okay
- I guess
- Pretty good

Don't

- Jingle pocket change
- Tap feet, fingers
- Twirl, pull, or rearrange hair
- Fold arms
- Sit with arms or legs far apart
- Offer a limp handshake
- Fidget
- Maintain unbroken eye contact
- Display shy eyes
- Have gum or anything else in or near your mouth
- Mumble
- Interrupt
- Speak too fast
- Slump
- Twiddle props — pens, paper, or desk items

Chapter 11

Looking Good with Questions You Ask

So you just finished answering a seemingly endless line of questions about your work history and your education, and you're pretty confident that you held your own. Now the interviewer turns to you and asks, "Do you have any questions?" This question is your cue to ask how much money you're gonna make at this outfit anyway, right? Wrong!

The types of questions you ask and when you ask them are the least understood parts of the interview. Your questions offer major chances for garnering curtain calls or being booed off the stage. Sort your question opportunities into two categories:

✔ **Questions that sell you:** These questions help you get an offer; they're a way to sell without selling.

✔ **Questions that address your personal agenda:** These questions about pay, benefits, and other self-interest items should be asked only after you receive an offer — or at least a heavy hint of an offer.

Asking Selling Questions before the Offer

For all jobs, asking about anything other than work issues before a hiring offer comes your way is a serious strategic error. The interviewer, particularly a hiring manager who resents the time "diverted" to an interview, doesn't give two figs about your needs at this point.

What's important to the interviewer is solving the hiring problem. *First we decide, then we deal* — that's the thinking.

To talk about your needs before an offer turns the interviewer's mind to negative thoughts: All you want is money, insurance, and a nice vacation on the company. You're not interested in doing the job.

As an Applause candidate, you're not going to make that mistake. Keep your focus on the employer's needs and how you can meet them. Sell yourself by asking questions that are

- ✔ Work-focused
- ✔ Task-focused
- ✔ Function-focused

Ask about the position's duties and challenges. Ask what outcomes you're expected to produce. Ask how the position fits into the department, and the department into the company. Ask about typical assignments. Here are examples of work-related questions:

- ✔ *What would be my first three goals if I were hired for this position?*
- ✔ *What would my key responsibilities be?*
- ✔ *How many and whom would I supervise? To whom would I report?*
- ✔ *Will I be working as a member of a team?*
- ✔ *What percentage of time will I spend communicating with customers, coworkers, and managers?*
- ✔ *Will on-job training be required for a new product?*
- ✔ *Can you describe a typical day?*
- ✔ *If I produce double my quota will you double my base pay?*
- ✔ *Was the last person in this job promoted? What's the potential for promotion?*
- ✔ *How would you describe the atmosphere here? Formal and traditional? Energetically informal?*
- ✔ *Where is the company headed? Merger? Growth?*
- ✔ *What would my first project be?*
- ✔ *What type of training would I receive?*
- ✔ *What resources would I have to do the job?*

✔ *How much would I travel, if any?*

✔ *(If a contract job) Do you anticipate extensive overtime to finish the project on schedule?*

✔ *Where does this position fit into the company's organizational structure?*

✔ *What results would you expect from my efforts and on what timetable? What improvements need to be made on how the job has been done until now?*

How much time should you invest in asking selling questions? Five to ten minutes is not too much. Gregory J. Walling, a top executive recruiter in Alexandria, Va., says he's never heard an employer complain about a candidate being too interested in work.

Don't ask questions about information you can glean from research. And don't ask questions that could cause the interviewer to wonder when you were melted from a glacier, such as quizzing an interviewer from Google, "Do you make money from anything other than your search engine?"

Asking Self-Interest Questions after the Offer

When you have the offer, you're ready to make the switch from giving to receiving information. I discuss negotiating salary and benefits in Chapter 8, but you'll also want to know about things like leave time, overtime, flextime, frequency of performance reviews, and (if it's a contract job) how long the job will last. Asking personal agenda questions in advance of an offer is dangerous, but after the offer, let fly with questions such as these eight examples:

✔ *Your company culture seems fairly unstructured. Is my impression correct?*

✔ *What problems might I face in this job?*

✔ *Is my future relocation a possibility?*

✔ *Is my employee parking included in the offer?*

✔ *Does management delegate decision-making to others, or does it micro-manage — requiring that I get approval of even the tiniest details?*

✔ *Where would I work in the building? Could I take a look at the location for a minute?*

✔ *Is the schedule fixed (such as 9 a.m. to 5 p.m.) or is it flexible (my choice of hours)?*

✔ *Would I have an exempt (from overtime pay) or non-exempt position?*

Ask with confidence

Be aware of how you phrase questions. Ask "what would" questions that presume you'll be offered the job ("What would my key responsibilities be?" Not, "What are the job's key responsibilities?").

Presumption-phrasing shows self-confidence and subtly encourages the interviewer to visualize you in the position.

Drawing Out Hidden Objections

The questions you ask have one more mission in the interview: They're a good way to bring concerns or objections to the table that the interviewer may not want to verbalize.

Why doesn't the interviewer want to raise certain issues?

Reasons that employers hang back with unspoken anxieties usually relate to legal vulnerability (see Chapter 24 on inappropriate questions), or the interviewer may simply be uncomfortable asking about them.

Whatever the reason, silent concerns are hurdles standing in the way of your getting the job. Before the interview is over, you need to find a way to address the thorny issues and overcome them.

Good salespeople call techniques that do this *drawing out objections*. Once you know the issues you're dealing with, try to calm anxieties that keep you from being hired.

Ask the interviewer questions that create openings for her to find the answers she wants but can't figure out how to find without getting hauled into an inquiry by the Equal Employment Opportunity Commission.

Here are a pair of examples of easing an interviewer's hidden concerns by bringing up a legally risky topic:

> *In your place, I'd probably be wondering how my children are cared for during the day. I may be concerned that I'd miss work should they become ill. Let me explain my very reliable child care arrangements to you . . .*

> *If I were you, seeing on my resume that I have spent a great deal of time in Paris, I may be questioning my legal residency and, green card or no green card, whether I plan to stay in Chicago long enough to complete this project. Let me assure you . . .*

Critics pan showoffs

I noticed in subsection 3.a of the government defense contractor's manual I.2.A, concerning future plans, that you squared the round table, using your supercomputer's component play box, and found your sandbox is 95 percent superior to the market's; does this mean you plan to circle an outer galaxy and return to earth on Greenwich mean time?

Huh? Research is essential, but guard against flaunting your newly found knowledge with questions that might give Einstein a little trouble. Interviewers interpret these questions as a transparent bid to look smart.

But, you ask, shouldn't you look "smart" at an interview? Yes, just don't cross the fine line that exists between being well researched and fully prepared for an interview, and trying to be a *nouveau omniscient.* (Don't you love that term? It means newly informed know-it-all.)

Showing off is a quality that causes otherwise charming, bright, gregarious, and attractive people to be turned down. It's just not a likable trait. If you don't have a good handle on what is and what isn't showing off, maybe a friend can help you work on that distinction.

As I see it, your basic choices are to allow an employer to make assumptions about you or to control the unspoken problem by telling the employer what you want known about the situation.

After hidden objections see daylight, you have a chance to shoo away elephants in the room that are standing between you and a job offer.

Asking Certain Questions Very Carefully

Handle questions to potential employers about their own performance with great tact — especially when a millennium generation candidate asks them of a boomer generation boss. Proceed with caution into territory like the following:

- *How would you describe your management style?*
- *Do your employees admire you as a boss?*

Although you need as much information as possible to make good job choices, asking a potential boss these kinds of questions in the wrong tone of voice may make you seem way too audacious. Moreover, direct questions about personal characteristics and values tend to elicit pure topspin.

Instead, ask questions designed to draw out companywide anecdotal answers:

> ✔ *How did the company handle a recent downsizing?*
>
> ✔ *How did managers react to someone who took a stand on principle?*
>
> ✔ *Who are the company's heroes?*

This approach encourages conversation that can be very informative. Questions are tools. Use them wisely.

Ending Suspense by Asking the Right Question

Page ahead to Chapter 13 and you see a lineup of fundamental questions to ask at the end of each interview. Want another option for immediate feedback? When your meeting has sailed smoothly along and you'd like to know your odds right now but don't want to appear overconfident or too anxious, ask the right question:

> *Should I assume you'd like me to continue in the interviewing process?*
>
> [yes] *What would the next step be?*
>
> [no] *I'm sorry to hear that. Could you tell me why I won't be in the running?* (If you can overcome the objections, give it a try; if not, thank the interviewer for the time spent with you and move on.)

When you don't hear the *yes* word, at least you won't be holding your breath to know whether this particular work opportunity is a lost cause. If the *no* word sparks a serious state of doldrums, break out an effective mood elevator — hot fudge sundae? funny movie? upbeat music?

Chapter 12

Outlining Interview Scenarios You Can Expect

*I*t's showtime! This chapter contrasts the choices made by two contenders for a middle management job in a conservative establishment. (The same kinds of interview scenario choices apply for virtually any type of job.)

For this tale of two job seekers, I've created a pair of characters, loser Cory and winner Chris. Visualize Cory's inept interview tactics and Chris's spectacular moves.

The Day Before

The day before an important interview is the day to prepare. You have a choice. You can let the jitters send you into a tailspin, or you can take steps to turn your nervousness into excitement and energy.

ShowStoppers

Chris begins the day before to prep for an interview at 11 o'clock the next morning. Chris visits the employer's Web site, paying special attention to the recruitment videos, noting how employees dress. After getting a handle on the company's costuming culture, Chris decides on a charcoal suit and rushes it to the neighborhood cleaners for a quick press. He polishes his black shoes. Next, Chris double-checks the requisite briefcase for five copies of his targeted resume that won the interview. (See my book, *Resumes For Dummies,* 5th Edition.)

Then Chris verifies routing and parking directions. He carefully reviews lists of job-related questions he will ask and scopes out questions the interviewer can be expected to ask. Finally, Chris goes over how his qualifications — including skills and accomplishments — match the position's requirements. He's ready to engage the interviewer. Finally, Chris gets a full night's sleep.

Clunkers and bloopers

Cory's interview is set for ten o'clock the next morning. A nervous wreck the night before showtime, Cory decides a few drinks at the local bar would be calming. Tomorrow morning is soon enough to get his interviewing act together — he thinks.

Critic's review

To give yourself the best shot at a ShowStopper interview

- ✔ Get everything ready the day before.
- ✔ Become familiar in advance with the route you will travel to the interview.
- ✔ As you travel to the interview, visualize yourself as someone about to be hired. As though you were starring in a movie, run interviewing images through your mind. Imagine the stories you'll tell and the impressed look on your interviewer's face as you ask your own questions and present your own commercial of qualifications. Float pictures through your head about the scenario as you wish it to be.
- ✔ Imagine yourself being at ease, radiating sincerity, credibility, energy, enthusiasm, and competence. You act the way you think.

Opening the Interview

As the actors find their places on the job-interview scene, all the building blocks of the actor's preparation come together. Lights . . . camera . . . action!

ShowStoppers

Chris arrives 10 minutes before show time and makes polite small talk with the receptionist. The receptionist buzzes the interviewer, who comes to the lobby to greet Chris. As they walk through a hallway toward the interviewer's office, Chris breaks the ice by saying nice things about the pictures on the wall.

Once inside the interviewer's office, Chris smiles and returns a firm hand-shake to the interviewer. Chris's eyes sweep the room, looking for some mutual interest (sports, colleges, or travel mementos) and spots a baseball picture of the Yankees on the wall. Chris doesn't sit until invited.

For a moment, Chris feels jittery. Then Chris thinks about CNN's John Roberts and CBS's Katie Couric, who always seem to have everything under control. Chris takes a deep breath and feels poise return.

The interviewer is distracted with Chris's resume, but to keep the momentum going, asks a few questions. Chris glides right into strong answers — stressing the good fit between his skills and the job's requirements. Chris makes a mental note to repeat that information as soon as the interviewer's full spot-light is away from the resume and on him in the flesh.

Clunkers and bloopers

Cory scrambles into the office wearing a super-trendy outfit topped by hair stiff with mousse. Conservative managers see Cory as being "too much" — "not one of us."

Arriving late after losing the way to the interview, an unsmiling Cory rushes to the receptionist's desk and, without bothering to greet the receptionist, asks for the interviewer. The receptionist hurries Cory to the interviewing office.

The interviewer glances up and calmly asks, *Do you know that you're 25 min-utes late?* Nervously, Cory sits down, uninvited, and mutters, *Yeah, sorry. I got stuck in that stupid traffic jam that always happens on the bridge, and then I got totally lost. I guess I should have started earlier.*

The interviewer responds, *Uh-huh. Well, before we begin, I seem to have mis-placed your resume — do you have an extra copy?* Flustered, Cory says, *Sorry, no. Because you already had a copy, I didn't bring another.*

Critic's review

When making your entrance, keep these tips in mind:

- ✔ Dress as though you belong where you're interviewing.
- ✔ Be friendly to all office staffers — they'll discuss you openly after you leave.
- ✔ Wait for the interviewer to initiate a handshake and then make your handshake a firm one.

> ✔ Make several copies of your resume in case you're asked for a copy. More likely, you'll be introduced to others who have a say in the hiring decision — leave one with each important person you meet.
>
> ✔ Stand until invited to sit.
>
> ✔ When you feel a sudden case of nerves, learn from the dramatic arts. Think of yourself as a favorite media personality who is cool, calm, collected, and confident.

During the Interview

Research and rehearsal grow confidence in actors and job interviewees. R&R ensures that they know their lines and moves. It turns interviews into fairly predictable auditions.

ShowStoppers

As the busy interviewer skims Chris's resume, Chris comments on the Yankees' baseball picture — the interviewer and Chris are "alike," which results in a bonding experience. Right away, the interviewer subliminally thinks — I like this person! Let's see what else Chris has to offer.

As soon as Chris has the interviewer's attention, Chris asks

> *I wonder if you can confirm my understanding of this position. What are the job's most important duties, and what kind of person do you see as being best suited for it?*

The interviewer begins the questioning portion of the interview with — *Could you tell me about yourself?* After a thinking pause, Chris skillfully builds into his one-minute memorized commercial (see Chapter 18) that shows he's the company's ideal employee for the target position. Chris focuses on skills and accomplishments.

Chris can smell a job offer coming when suddenly the interviewer falls deathly silent — the kind of silence that makes most people uncomfortable enough to blabber and say silly things. But when Chris is satisfied with the information delivered, he falls silent, too, and waits for the interviewer to respond. But the interviewer, an old hand at playing the silence card, remains mute. Finally, Chris asks — *Would you like me to tell you more about my skills in working with other people?*

Secretly impressed that Chris is nobody's fool, the interviewer asks what Chris knows about the company's products and organization. The question session turns into a kind of fact-trading mini-workshop. Chris successfully engaged the interviewer. Both participants feel good about the meeting.

Clunkers and bloopers

After finding and studying Cory's resume while Cory sits quietly, the interviewer asks — *What can you tell me about yourself?*

Cory begins to ramble — *Um . . . I mean, like it says on my resume, I just got my degree from UTC . . . Um . . . I graduated summa cum laude . . . and . . . well, you know, I'm looking for a job. I was born in Kansas City, Missouri . . . but, my mother was in the Marines, and so we traveled a lot . . . I like tennis . . . I know I can do this job . . . what else would you like to know?*

Cory picks up a letter opener from the interviewer's desk and begins to fiddle with it.

Critic's review

Use these tips to give an award-winning performance:

- ✔ Anticipate, prepare for, and rehearse challenging questions.

- ✔ Take note of the interviewer's personal items in the office as you try to establish rapport, but never touch anything.

- ✔ Ask the question that reveals the key to the entire interview — *What is the scope of the position and what are the qualifications of the ideal person for it?* And then work it into your answer, starting with your personal commercial.

- ✔ Recognize that an interviewer's silence can move you to speak before you think. When things become too tense, ask a job-related question to parade your skills.

Sizing Up Audience Reaction

If an actor is doing comedy and no one's laughing, the actor needs to change the lines or the delivery. Similarly, if you notice your audience (a potential employer) is disinterested, try to switch the subject and save the show.

How can you tell how your act is going over? Watch for obvious signs of inattention: The interviewer's eyes are glazed over, or the interviewer fiddles with desk objects, for example.

ShowStoppers

Following the main question segment of the interview, Chris's interviewer lapses into lengthy praise of the company and the job. But, unlike Cory's experience, the body of the interview had gone wonderfully well, and Chris realizes that an offer is imminent. The interviewer isn't just filling time talking about the company — the interviewer is selling Chris!

Chris smiles and listens attentively.

The interviewer does have a few concerns — Will Chris be able to handle the travel the job requires? This job calls for about two days of travel a week, but the requirement is flexible. Will that be a problem?

Chris overcomes the concern by expressing a genuine interest in traveling and then re-encapsulates the other strengths that point toward a perfect job-applicant match. The interviewer's relief shows — *Then the commute won't be a problem for you?*

Absolutely not! Chris confirms.

Clunkers and bloopers

Cory's interviewer spends a lot of time discussing the company and the job and asks very few questions — the interviewer is filling time until Cory can be decently dumped; the interviewer has already lost interest. Cory still has a slim chance of putting the interview back on track, but Cory doesn't notice the warning signals of disinterest.

Cory misses nonverbal clues, too: When the bored interviewer begins tapping fingers on the desk, Cory doesn't say — *Would you rather hear more about my computer programming work or my international marketing studies?* Cory doesn't notice two more negative body-language signals when the interviewer crosses arms and leans back.

To top it off, Cory fails to observe how the interviewer is phrasing judgments, clearly implying that Cory is not under consideration. The interviewer says — *Many people have a problem handling all the travel required; frankly, the traveling is too heavy a burden.*

Cory nixes all chances at salvaging the job opportunity by agreeing — *Yeah, I'm really not much for travel. I like to stick around home with my friends and family.* Cory has never understood that once you're in a hole, it's time to stop digging.

Critic's review

Follow these tips to keep your interviewer's attention:

✔ Pay close attention to your audience. Observe body language. Note subject matter and how comments are phrased.

✔ When you think the decision on you is thumbs down, try a last-chance statement:

Because I'm very interested in this job, I want to be sure that you have all the information you need to make a positive decision on my candidacy. Would you be interested in hearing more about my — ?

✔ Note how interviewers ask touchy questions. The interviewers phrased the question about travel negatively in Cory's interview and positively in Chris's interview. The negative shading implied that Cory just didn't fit the job. Take a hint or move to overcome objections.

✔ Avoid money talk until you have a job offer. Money wasn't a factor in the examples of Cory and Chris because the interviewer didn't raise the issue. (See Chapter 8.)

Ending the Interview

Put the finishing touches on your ShowStopper routine as the interview curtain begins to fall. Find out about the coming attractions of future contacts and prop open the stage door for your return.

ShowStoppers

Chris notices the interviewer glancing occasionally at the office clock before saying — *Thanks for coming in, I'll notify you when we make a decision.*

Chris refuses to fade into the sunset and grabs for a follow-up interview:

I'm sure you have a busy schedule, and I appreciate your time. Thank you. But before we close today, could I make sure I understand what you're looking for?

Chris wraps up with a superb 60-second recap of the job's description and requirements, matching them directly. The theme is "you want, I deliver." After this short monologue, Chris offers the interviewer the floor:

Do you see any gaps between what you need and what I'm offering?

The interviewer mentions one deficiency in Chris's skills profile — a lack of supervisory experience. Chris immediately counters with two stories of managing huge special events for a church organization and a campus club, both of which required supervisory duties. Chris hadn't had paid supervisory experience, but the compensatory answer beat no answer at all.

As Chris and the interviewer shake hands, the interviewer implies that Chris is well-suited for the position, but that there's a pool of candidates yet to be interviewed. Chris asks: *When do you expect to make a decision or to schedule follow-up interviews?*

As the interviewer answers and shakes hands, Chris has a final question — *Can I get back to you to get an update on your timeline?*

Feel free to call me, the interviewer responds, thinking — *This candidate has plenty on the ball.*

Clunkers and bloopers

Cory tries to stretch the interview with small talk — chiefly personal information not related to the job — while the interviewer is making an obvious effort to leave by gathering papers, rising, and walking toward the door. Cory finally gets the picture and anxiously asks — *So, do I get the job?*

Cory's desperation adds to the interviewer's doubts. The interviewer decides to end the misery — *Sorry, you don't really fit the needs of this job.*

Hurt and offended, Cory demands to know why — *Hey, I've got the right college degree. What's wrong with me?*

Critic's review

To end the interview on the right note, follow these tips:

- ✔ Interviewers get the message that a desperate candidate is a bottom-of-the-barrel candidate.
- ✔ Learn sales closing techniques; those who don't learn to close a sale don't get job offers. (And make no mistake about it, you're selling yourself in an interview.)
- ✔ Watch the interviewer's body language closely for signs that the interview should end. Take the hint. Arguing wastes everyone's time.

  ✔ Expecting that an educational or experience credential is all you need to get the job is a mistake.

  ✔ Summarize your best-selling points one last time for the interviewer.

  ✔ Leave the door open for a follow-up contact.

After the Interview

You get one last chance to make the interview memorable. Your follow-up work is an opportunity to write a happy ending to your job-search scenario.

ShowStoppers

After leaving the interviewer's office, Chris immediately writes down everything that happened, including the main points Chris made, the interviewer's name, line of questioning, areas of interest, and the timelines of the hiring process.

Then Chris writes the interviewer a thank-you letter. Chapter 13 tells you more about marketing yourself in a thank-you letter.

Clunkers and bloopers

Cory promptly writes off the interviewing company as unfair and erases from memory all that happened during the interview.

Because Cory hasn't learned from these mistakes, Cory's other interviews won't go much better.

Critic's review

To make the most of every interview, follow these tips:

  ✔ Turn every interview into a learning experience.

  ✔ Note what you learned in the interview (such as names and additional aspects of the company new to you) for your next contact with the interviewer.

  ✔ Note points discussed. Did you leave out significant selling points? Add them to your thank-you letter.

Pre-Interview Checklist

Want to be sure that you'll do everything you can to stop the show? Use this pre-interview checklist to get yourself prepped for a ShowStopper performance.

❑ Have you reviewed the requirements for this position? Can you identify which of your qualifications are most relevant for this position?

❑ Did you research the position, company, and industry? (See Chapter 6.)

❑ Do you know how people dress where you're interviewing? (See Chapter 9, and the section "The Day Before" in this chapter.)

❑ Is your interviewing costume clean, pressed, and ready to go?

❑ Do you know where the interviewing site is located and how long it takes to get there?

❑ Have you memorized a short commercial to highlight your best selling points? (See Chapters 18.)

❑ Have you rehearsed everything, from small talk to answering potentially dangerous questions? (See Chapter 10.)

❑ Have you practiced answers to anticipated questions? (See Part IV.)

❑ Have you prepared and memorized a list of questions to ask? (See Chapter 11.)

❑ Have you researched the market salary for the position? (See Chapter 8.)

❑ Did you gather everything you need? (Five copies of your resume, list of references, and samples of your work, if necessary.)

Once you knock each question off this checklist, stop cramming and relax. Otherwise, you'll suffer stage fright. Enter your interview with confidence. You've done ShowStopper preparation for a ShowStopper interview!

Chapter 13

Closing the Show

You sense it's almost time to go. The interview seems to be winding down. In most instances, a job offer doesn't come at this point.

How can you be sure the interview is almost over? Watch for these nonverbal clues: The interviewer may begin shuffling papers, glancing at a wall clock or watch, and, perhaps, standing up. Then you hear words that confirm your hunch:

✔ *Thanks for coming in. We'll be interviewing more candidates through the next week or so. After that, I'll probably get back to you about a second interview.*

✔ *Thanks for talking with me. I think your qualifications make you a definite candidate for this position. Once I'm done with all the initial interviews, I'll get back to you.*

✔ *All your input has been really helpful. Now that I know everything I need to know about you, do you have any questions about the company or the position?* (Careful — ask only job-related questions — you don't have the offer; see Chapter 11.)

In this chapter, I show you how to walk out of the interview without walking out of the race.

Making a Strategic Exit

Don't go away from a job interview empty-handed. Rather than quietly fading into history, remember what you found out in this book:

- Never leave a job interview with a zipped lip. Immerse your departure in verbal persuaders and *interactive selling*. The latter is a term that sales professionals use to mean a great deal of back and forth, give and take, and questions and answers. (See Chapters 11 and 18—23.)

- Never leave a job interview without reprising your qualifications and the benefits you bring to the job. You're a great match, a wonderful fit!

- Never leave a job interview without knowing what happens next.

- Never leave a job interview without propping open the door for your follow-up.

Your parting sales pitch

Haven't you sold yourself enough during this ShowStopper interview? Yes and no. People — including interviewers — often forget what they hear. Start your close with another chorus of your five best skills. (See Chapter 18 for answers to the question, "Why should I hire you?") Then ask

Do you see any gaps between my qualifications and the requirements for the job?

Based on what we've discussed today, do you have any concerns about my ability to do well in this job? Any reservations about hiring me?

You're looking for gaps and hidden objections so that you can make them seem insignificant. But if the gaps aren't wide and the objections not lethal to your candidacy, attempt to overcome stated shortcomings. You can make this attempt based on what you found out in your earlier research. Here's an effective formula you can use to *engage the interviewer* (see Chapter 2):

1. **Sell your qualifications (benefits — chiefly skills).**

2. **Ask for objections.**

3. **Listen carefully.**

4. **Overcome objections.**

5. **Restate your qualifications (using different words).**

After you restate your benefits, you may find the time is ripe to reaffirm your interest in the job. Here's one way:

I hope I've answered your concerns on the X issue. Do you have further questions or issues about my background, qualifications, or anything else at this point? This job and I sound like a terrific match.

If it seems appropriate, try to lead subtly toward an offer.

I hope you agree that this position has my name on it. As I understand, your position requires X, and I can deliver X; your position requires Y, and I can deliver Y; your position requires Z, and I can deliver Z.

So there seems to be a good match here! Don't you think so?

I'm really glad I had the chance to talk with you. I know that with what I learned at Violet Tech when I established its Internet Web site, I could set up an excellent Web site for you, too.

Leaving the door open

How can you tape the door open for a follow-up? You seek the interviewer's permission to call back; with permission, you won't seem intrusive. Use these statements as models to gain the permission:

What is the next step in the hiring process, and when do you expect to make a decision? (You're trying to get a sense of the timetable.)

I'm quite enthusiastic about this position. When and how do we take the next step?

May I feel free to call if I have further questions?

I know you're not done reviewing candidates; when can I reach you to check up on the progress of your search?

I understand you'll call me back after you've seen every candidate for this position; would you mind if I call you for an update or if I have more questions?

I appreciate the time you spent with me; I know you're going to be really busy recruiting, so when can I call you?

I look forward to that second interview you mentioned — can I call you later to schedule it after my work hours so I don't have to throw off my current employer's schedule?

In the final moments, be certain to express thanks to the interviewer for the time spent with you. Say it with a smile, eye-to-nose, and a firm but gentle handshake: *It looks like a terrific opportunity — I look forward to hearing from you.* Don't linger.

Recruiters follow up for you

You don't have to follow up with the employer when you were introduced to the company by a recruiter or employment consultant — the recruiter or consultant follows up for you, negotiating the offer or turndown. Usually, you can get a report card from your recruiter or consultant fairly quickly.

As soon as you're alone at a place where you can make notes, write a summary of the meeting. Concentrate especially on material for your follow-up moves, described later in this chapter.

How Aggressive Should You Be?

How hard you should sell and how eager you should be depends on such things as age, critical experience, and the level of the job you're seeking. No behavior is perfect for every person and every situation.

If you're in a sales field, just starting out, lack experience in a job's requirements, or aren't obviously superior to your competition, don't hold back on selling your advantages or showing your enthusiasm.

If you have relevant experience and offer in-demand skills or are being considered for a senior-level job, allow yourself to be wooed a bit. You don't want to be seen as jumping at every opportunity. It's the old story: The more anxious you seem, the less money you're offered.

When the gap between your qualifications and the job's requirements is the size of the Grand Canyon, accept the fact that the job will go to someone else. Suppose, for instance, that the position requires five years' experience, including two years of supervisory experience. You thought you could talk your way through the gap with your three years of total experience and no years of supervisory experience. Fat chance!

 When you just don't have the chops for the position, salvage your time and effort by acknowledging that although you may not be ideal for this particular position, interviewing for it has caused you to admire the company and you'd appreciate being contacted if a better match comes along.

Follow Up or Fall Behind

What takes place after the first interview — when candidates are ranked — decides who has the inside track on winning the job.

Your follow-up may be the tiebreaker that gives you the win over other promising candidates. And even if the employer already planned to offer you the job, your follow-up creates goodwill that kick-starts your success when you join the company.

Follow up vigorously. It's your caring that counts.

Your basic tools are

- Letters
- E-mails
- Telephone calls
- References

Letters

How much do post-interview thank-you letters really impact hiring decisions? When they're canned, flat, and "Dear-Aunt-Martha-thanks-for-the-graduation-gift" boring, interviewers may see them as a snore.

But when you're in a classy field of candidates, each trying to race through the stretch for the win, skipping a dynamic marketing-tool-of-a-thanks-letter is unwise.

In constructing a thank-you letter that actually does you some good, use the same powerful concepts that you would for a targeted resume that directly matches your qualifications with the job's requirements (Read my book, *Resumes For Dummies,* 5th Edition; Wiley, 2007.)

The resume and the thank-you letter are book-ends for your interview: The resume is the "before" communicator of your high-value qualifications and the thank-you letter is the "after" chance to market yourself for the win.

Your resume content and interview performance sold you as being a great fit for the job with tit for tat in qualifications and interest, punctuated with true and lively tales of accomplishments. Don't stop the winning streak that got you this far — build on it! Here are sales pointers for your thank-you letter aimed at converting your candidacy into a job offer:

- Express appreciation for the interviewer's time and for giving you a fresh update on the organization's immediate direction.

- Remind the interviewer of what specifically you can do for a company, not what a company can do for you. As you did in closing your interview, draw verbal links between a company's immediate needs and your qualifications: "You want X, I offer X; you want Y, I offer Y; you want Z, I offer Z."

- Repeat your experience in handling concerns that were discussed during the interview. Write very brief paragraphs about how you solved problems of interest to the company.

- After researching an issue that the company is wrestling with, include a concise statement of your findings, perhaps even enclosing a relevant news clip about the matter.

- Tie up loose ends by adding information to a question you didn't handle well during the interview.

- Overcome objections the interviewer expressed about offering you the job. For example, if the job has an international component and the interviewer was concerned that you have never worked in Europe or Asia, explain in your letter that you have worked in the Caribbean and in Mexico and that you are proven to be productive in other cultures.

- Reaffirm your interest in the position and respect for the company.

Content is not the only aspect you need to consider when preparing a follow-up letter. The following are tips for presenting and delivering a letter that gets you noticed:

- For an important job, a typed dead-tree-industry letter is impressive and memorable; send it by postal mail, or if time is short, via an overnight delivery service.

- The letter can run two, even three pages, if it is flush with white space and easy to read.

- Some very savvy people swear by handwritten notes. But here's my take: Even when your penmanship is good, a note doesn't readily lend itself to heavy-duty service as a marketing tool when you're going for the win.

- Write a thank-you letter for the interview within 24 hours to strengthen the good impression you made in person.

- When an employer leaves you twisting in the wind waiting for a hiring decision, try to think of new facts to add in a second or even third letter (send by postal mail, fax, courier, or e-mail).

- After the third letter, switch to sending a note with a relevant news clipping or even an appropriate cartoon. The interviewer will know what's going on, but at least you're keeping your name where it can be seen; remember the truth of the adage, "Out of sight, out of mind."

Figure 13-1 shows you a sample letter for postal mail. You can find a lot more sample thanks letters on the Web; search for "job interview thank-you letters." But before adapting any sample for your own use, make sure that it carries a marketing punch and won't be mistaken for a bread-and-butter "Aunt Martha" letter.

[Date]

Mr. A.J. Cortes, Vice President
21st Century Developments
[Address]

Dear Mr. Cortes:

Thank you for the opportunity to interview for a subcontractor coordinator position. I would very much like to be on the respected 21st Century Developments team. I'm appreciative of your genuine interest in acquainting me with your staff and company goals. In summary, here's a review of what I offer as a potential colleague:

I have delivered on building working relationships with key vendors:

- Beginning 11 years ago [date], when I became a subcontractor coordinator, I have consistently achieved high-quality results by keeping abreast of the quality of materials used by various companies. Among my favorite suppliers, you may recognize the following names: Namath Re-bar, Drywall By-the-Mile, and Lionel Fixtures.
- Two years ago, [date] I eliminated one whole clerical position by implementing a new software package to manage daily progress reports from subs, making the work competition intelligence faster and cheaper.

I have delivered on facilitating the control of subcontractor costs:

- I have carefully monitored signs of cost run-ups, strategizing with project managers on cost control. On the previous three projects alone, my notifications saved my employer $X dollars, an amount equal to 13 percent of the total cost.

I have delivered on first-class scheduling strategies:

- Because I have solid competencies, skills and experience in construction requirements, I have been able to reverse errors made by my predecessors at several organizations where I have been employed. For example, at Bogart Industries, I was able to turn around a looming fiasco due to improper scheduling of subs (more than $2 million) and bring the project in nearly on time. Bogart's CEO said that my extreme scheduling turnaround kept the company from losing the project to creditors.

High standards have always been central in my work. Now, as an accomplished professional, I feel ready to join such a demanding company as yours. Thanks again for the interview. I look forward to speaking with you soon.

Sincerely,

Max Hong

[Contact information]

Figure 13-1: Use a thank-you letter as a marketing tool.

E-mail

In this digital age, most people send e-mail thank-you letters. This medium is usually fine for most jobs. Consider these observations on communicating after an interview by e-mail:

- ✔ Use e-mail when you hope to start or continue a dialogue with an interviewer. E-mail is more conversational and easier for a quick reply. On the other hand, it's also easier to say *no* in an e-mail message than on the telephone.

- ✔ Use e-mail when quick action matters. The job could be filled while you're waiting for postal mail to be delivered or a phone call to be answered.

- ✔ Use e-mail if that's the way you sent your resume and especially if the employer requested electronic communication in a job ad.

- ✔ Use e-mail when you are dealing with a high-tech firm; the firm's hiring authority probably doesn't remember what paper is and may think voicemail is a bother.

Don't make blanket assumptions about whether spam filters will prevent your message from reaching the interviewer; ask the interviewer or a receptionist in advance about the best way to send an e-mail message.

The content for a thank-you e-mail need not differ much, if at all, from that of a paper thank-you letter (see Figure 13-1). You can write a couple of lines in your e-mail referring to your attached letter:

> *I was impressed with the warmth and efficiency of your offices, as I explain in my attached letter.*

Telephone calls

Once upon a time, all that job seekers calling about potential employment had to worry about was getting past human gatekeeper assistants. They solved that problem in various ways, by adopting a pleasant and honest manner and making an ally of the assistant by revealing the refreshing truth about why they're calling, for example. Or by trying to reach the interviewer before 8:30 a.m. or after 5:30 p.m., when the assistant isn't likely to be on duty and the interviewer fields phone calls alone.

Those were the good old days. Now, voicemail has joined human gatekeepers in throwing roadblocks in front of job seekers who try to follow up on interviews.

The big voicemail question for job seekers is whether to leave a message on voicemail. Opinions vary, but, as a practical matter, you may have to leave a message if you don't connect after the first few calls. All your calls won't be returned, but your chances improve when you say something interesting in a 30-second sound bite:

This is _____. I'm calling about the (job title or department) opening. After reflecting on some of the issues you mentioned during our meeting, I thought of a facet of one problem you might like to know. My number is _____.

Opening the conversation

Here's a sprinkling of conversation starters:

- ✔ *Is this a good time to talk?*
- ✔ *I think you'll be interested to know _____.*
- ✔ *I understand you're still reviewing many applications, but . . .*
- ✔ *I forgot to go into the key details of (something mentioned during the interview) that might be important to you.*
- ✔ *While listening to you, I neglected to mention my experience in (function). It was too important for me to leave out, since the position calls for substantial background in that area.*
- ✔ *I was impressed with your _____.*
- ✔ *I appreciate your emphasis on _____.*

Keeping the conversational ball rolling

Try these approaches to maintain the conversation:

- ✔ Remind the interviewer why you're so special, what makes you unique (exceptional work in a specific situation, innovating).

  Let me review what I'm offering you that's special.

- ✔ Establish a common denominator — a work or business philosophy.

  It seems like we both approach work in the (name of) industry from the same angle.

- ✔ Note a shared interest that benefits the employer.

  I found a new Web site that may interest you — it's XYZ. It reports on the news items we discussed . . . Would you like the URL?

Reminding your references

References can make all the difference. Spend adequate time choosing and preparing the people who give you glowing testimonials. What they say about you is more convincing than what you say about yourself.

Call your references and fill them in on your interview:

> *I had an interview today with (person, company). We talked about the position, and it sounds like a perfect match for me. They wanted (give a list of key requirements), and that's just what I can supply.*
>
> *For instance, I have all this experience (match five key requirements with five of your qualifications) from when I worked with (name of company).*
>
> *Would you like me to fax you those points I just mentioned? . . . I was so happy about the interview I just wanted to thank you once more for all your help and support. I couldn't have done it without you.*

Your After-Interview Checklist

Experts in any field become experts because they've made more mistakes than the rest of us. After your interview, take a few minutes to rate your performance. The following checklist can help you curb bad habits and become an expert at job interviewing:

- ✔ Were you on time?
- ✔ Did you use storytelling, examples, results, and measurement of achievements to back up your claims and convince the questioner that you have the skills to do the job?
- ✔ Did you display high energy? Flexibility? Interest in learning new things?
- ✔ Did the opening of the interview go smoothly?
- ✔ Did you frequently make a strong connection between the job's requirements and your qualifications?
- ✔ Was your personal grooming immaculate? Were you dressed like company employees?
- ✔ Did you forget any important selling points? If so, did you put them in a follow-up e-mail, letter, or call-back?
- ✔ Did you smile? Did you make eye contact?
- ✔ Did you convey at least five major qualities the interviewer should remember about you?
- ✔ Did you make clear your understanding of the work involved in the job?
- ✔ Did you show your understanding of the strategies required to reach company goals?
- ✔ Did you use enthusiasm and motivation to indicate that you're willing to do the job?

When you get a job offer at the interview

Once an offer is on the table, bring up your self-interest (vacation, benefits, lunch hours) requests for information. Whip out a note pad and say

I'm excited and grateful for your interest. I'd like to clear up just a few issues. Can you tell me about — ?

Unless the circumstances are unusual, accepting or rejecting a job offer on the spot is not in your best interest. You're likely to think of something later that you forgot to negotiate. Improving an offer after you have accepted is difficult.

Even if you have survived multiple interviews and have long known the likely outline of the offer, think about it overnight at least (see Chapter 14).

✔ Did you find some common ground to establish that you'll fit well into the company?

✔ Did you take the interviewer's clues to wrap it up?

✔ Did you find out the next step and leave the door open for your follow-up?

✔ After the interview, did you write down names and points discussed?

Think about the following questions to help you clearly identify your strengths and weaknesses on the job interview stage:

✔ What did you do or say that the interviewer obviously liked?

✔ Did you hijack the interview by grabbing control or speaking too much (more than half the time)?

✔ Would you have done something differently if you could replay the interview?

Onward and Upward

You've done it all — turned in a ShowStopper performance at your interview and followed up like a pro. Keep following up until you get another job or until you're told you aren't a good match for the position — or that while your qualifications were good, another candidate's were better.

Even then, write yet one more thank-you note, expressing your hope that you may work together in the future. Sometimes the first choice declines the job offer, and the employer moves on to the next name — perhaps yours.

Chapter 14

When You're Offered the Part

Congratulations! You've been offered the part you auditioned for. A few small things may curb your unbridled enthusiasm: Your salary's so low you have to rent your toothbrush. Your hours are so late that even the cable channels are running test patterns when you get home. Your health benefits consist of your giving up only one of your kidneys. Otherwise, the job is great.

Failing to think through the pros and cons of a job offer is how people become cemented in a routine of disappointing work. This chapter deals with issues to consider in your decision.

Don't Say Yes Right Away

When you hear those sweet words, "We're offering you the job," anticipate your reaction. It probably proceeds through the following stages:

1. **Enthusiasm.**

   Act as though you've just won a lottery.

2. **Thoughtfulness.**

   Ask for a day or two to "sleep on it."

3. **Enthusiasm.**

   Act as though you've just won a lottery.

Why should you be so enthusiastic when you're not certain you want the job? Because it's more fun to turn down than to be turned down.

New grads can ask for three weeks to accept job

Although job changers normally are expected to give a *yea* or *nay* to job offers within a few days, college seniors who're trying to figure out where they want to work after graduation should be given plenty of time to explore all their employment options, says the National Association of Colleges and Employers. NACE recommends that employers give graduating students a minimum of three weeks to choose among job offers.

Some employers use a competitive tactic called the "exploding offer," which means the student is given too little time, sometimes only a few days, to accept before the offer is withdrawn. This rush of decision-making backfires on all parties when students make poor, pressured decisions and then renege or resign early. If you're a rookie, quote the NACE policy recommendation when asking for enough time to think clearly and thoroughly. Choosing a first job is a major life decision.

You need a little time to get over the excitement of being chosen and calmly consider whether accepting the offer is in your best interest.

The employer probably expects you to take a day or two to decide. After all, you're making a choice that impacts many facets of your existence. An immediate response could be seen as impulsiveness or failure to take the job seriously.

Even when the job's the only game in town and everyone wants it, your interests are best served by reflecting a bit before giving your answer. This is especially true when relocation is involved. Ask for overnight, a few days, or, at most, a week to think over a job offer.

Before saying *yes,* you may still be able to extract one last benefit that didn't come with the original offer. Or the additional facts provided by the interview may have opened your eyes to aspects of the job you hadn't considered — pro or con.

Stick to Your Career Script?

Not so long ago, a key consideration in choosing a job was the opportunity to stay in your career field to follow your personal goals. Zigzagging from career field to career field rather than changing jobs within the same career field wasn't a smart strategy. The situation has changed. Turning down a job today because it doesn't "fit into your long-term career goals" is still a desirable policy but not always a practical choice.

Analyzing who you are and what you want to do will always be relevant. Staying within the boundaries of the work you love and are prepared to do is always more satisfying — and always better for your career.

Please stay. We're not kidding.

With good labor tight, employers have rediscovered counteroffers when a useful employee quits to take a better job. If you find yourself being wooed back, it's usually best to leave the counteroffer on the table, say thanks, and move on. Here's why:

✔ When substantial financial considerations aren't in the mix, most people leave a job because of a personality rift, blocked advancement, or boring work. A generous counteroffer doesn't fix any of these things.

✔ After you've announced a departure, count yourself out of the inner circle. You won't be trusted as before.

✔ Renewing your enthusiasm will be challenging: You already know why you want to find the exit. If your current employer wouldn't promote you or give you a decent raise before you put on your walking shoes, don't expect anything different when it's time to move up to your next career level.

✔ If a recruiter connected you with the new offer, and you say *yes* and then *no,* your credibility goes up in smoke — a negative that could come back to haunt you.

Ask yourself whether you'd join the company that now employs you if you were looking for a good job. (This exercise can help you make the right decision.)

Economic realities may sometimes mean that to earn a living, you have to do what you *can* do rather than what you *love* to do. Should you find yourself in this situation, try to identify new skills and knowledge you will gain that enhance your original career direction if you return to it.

What's most important to you is that any job you take must allow you to develop and tweak portable skills that you can use in your next job.

To Accept or Not to Accept

Once you stop dancing around and whooping it up after finally getting the job offer, think about the particulars of whether the job is right for you. The following sections outline the kinds of questions you need to ask yourself.

Is the job itself a good one?

Is this job worth one half of your waking hours? Only you can decide. When considering the worthiness of the job itself, ask yourself the following questions:

✔ Does this job allow me to strengthen my marketable skills? Does it offer career mobility?

✔ Do I like the people I would be working with day to day?

Feedback when you're not offered the part

If you aren't ready for this chapter yet — that is, if you lost the part to another candidate — you may be wondering where you went wrong. Disappointed job seekers often ask interviewers for reasons why they weren't selected and for tips on how to do better in the future.

Don't waste your time: You almost never will be given the real reason. Employers have no legal or ethical obligation to explain why you weren't the one. Instead, they're likely to offer these kinds of innocuous rationales: "We didn't feel you were the best fit for this job" or "We chose another candidate who had more experience" or "Company policy won't allow me to comment."

Why won't interviewers take you behind the scenes and share the truth? Here are some of the reasons they give:

✔ **Legal exposure:** Companies are extremely wary of lawsuits accusing them of discrimination. The less said, the less to be sued about.

✔ **Fast-paced world:** There's no profit in wasting prime hours on a dead end.

✔ **Discomfort factor:** Managers dislike giving negative feedback.

✔ **Scant information:** HR (human resources) interviewers may not have enough details from hiring managers to give helpful answers, even if they were inclined to do so.

When you're not offered the part, review the After-Interview Checklist in Chapter 13. If you have the requisite qualifications and your performance doesn't need pumping up, the reason you didn't get an offer may have nothing to do with you. Square your shoulders and get ready for the next interview.

✔ Will the boss(es) and I get along?

✔ Will this work hold my attention?

✔ Does the job use the best of my talents, skills, and abilities?

✔ Will this work give me a sense of enjoyment?

✔ Is this a job that "makes a difference?" Do I care?

✔ Do I get to make the important decisions about how I do the job?

✔ Will I have to travel? How much? Is that okay with me?

✔ Will I have to work hours when my friends play? Is that okay with me?

✔ Will this job allow me to add to my personal network?

✔ Will I be visible to people who make decisions?

✔ Could this job be a stepping stone to something better?

✔ Do I need a whole new wardrobe for this job? Is that okay with me?

Is the company a good choice?

Is this a company you admire? When considering the kind of company you may be joining, ask yourself the following questions:

Employers expect you to negotiate

When you get a job offer in a tight labor market, your compensation may be more negotiable than you think. For example, when you can't bump up the pay, the following compensation may be open to change:

☞ Relocation costs reimbursement

☞ Early reviews with the option for salary increases

☞ Signing bonuses

☞ Vacation leave

See Chapter 8 to cop a compensation attitude and become a more confident negotiator.

☞ Does the company culture fit my personality?

☞ Does the company have room for advancement?

☞ Are the company policies in writing?

☞ Can I live with these policies?

☞ Is the company in a good position to survive and grow in a competitive market?

☞ What's the company's reputation for consideration of employees? Severance policies?

☞ Is the company's industry growing or shrinking?

☞ Can I handle the commute?

Is the pay enough?

You can be just as happy with a lot of money as a little. For most of us, getting our hands on any money means working at paid jobs for our material things — home, food, transportation, clothing, entertainment, and education. As I note in Chapter 8, compensation comes in a package of base pay, variable pay (such as bonuses), and indirect pay (employee benefits such as health insurance). Weigh each of these factors when considering the company's compensation package. Ask yourself these questions:

☞ Am I being offered my fair market value in base pay?

☞ How valuable are any variable pay opportunities — bonuses, commissions, stock options?

☞ What good are the benefits? Health insurance (what percentage do I pay; can I choose coverage plans)? Retirement plan? Company car? Vacation time? Sick days? What else?

☞ What is the basis for raises?

Pre-Employment Contracts Promise Protection for Everyone

Although your verbal job offer covers such specifics as the term of employment, duties, and compensation, what happens if disputes arise in the future and memories fade? It's your word against theirs. He said–she said. That's why getting your offer in writing is to your advantage. (Would you buy a house or an insurance plan without a written contract?)

A written pre-employment contract, or its little brother, the job offer letter, also benefits an employer because you as an employee agree to provide specific work benefits and make certain promises (like you promise not to reveal company secrets or steal company customers).

Legally, no iron-clad contract rules apply in every state, and each employment contract is different.

Fifty years ago employment contracts were reserved for theatrical royalty and big-shot corporate executives. That's changing. Employment relationships are increasingly contract-oriented for professional, managerial, technical, and administrative positions.

So when you're asked to sign a pre-employment contract, you know that the company considers you an investment it wants to protect. But what should you do when a contract's provisions include factors that you don't like and have not verbally agreed to? Can you negotiate the boilerplate? In most cases, the answer is *yes* — to a degree. You have more leverage to negotiate a contract to get what you want in tight labor markets; you have less leverage in surplus labor markets when ten people are standing behind you ready to grab the job.

What do pre-employment agreements cover? Usually they regulate one or more of the following issues:

- ✔ The position being offered and accepted.
- ✔ The compensation that will be paid.
- ✔ Whether the job is for a specified length of time or at will. (You or the employer can call it quits at any time for any reason.)
- ✔ Specific benefits regarding paid leave time (like vacation and sick days) and whether such time accrues from year to year.
- ✔ Responsibilities of both parties concerning the work to be done.

Danger points for you to recognize and investigate fully before signing your acceptance include the following:

✔ Repayments of training cost or relocation expense that are required under certain conditions.

✔ Non-compete clauses that prevent you from working elsewhere in a given locale for a specified period of time.

✔ A statement that the terms of the agreement are subject to change in the future.

✔ A statement that you are to be bound by the terms of the company's employee handbook, which you may not yet have seen. (The handbook itself usually notes that it is subject to change at any time by the company.)

✔ Agreement to arbitration and other alternate dispute resolutions that come with a muzzle clause prohibiting you from discussing settlement details of disputes. Arbitration is a contentious issue with employees often feeling that arbitrators (wishing to be hired again) may side with companies because they're more likely to be repeat customers. St. Louis employment attorney Sheldon Weinhaus comments: "Companies keep track of previous awards. It is much harder for a worker to know the history of any arbitrator."

If you're required to sign a pre-employment agreement that mandates arbitration, ask that language be inserted requiring that the arbitrator be chosen from a list maintained by the American Arbitration Association or another selection organization that operates with a code of ethics.

A *job offer letter* is the minimum promise protection you should have in any work opportunity requiring you to resign your current job or to relocate out of your residence. A job offer letter is a condensed pre-employment contract outlining the basics of your employment. In small companies a job offer letter may be written without a lawyer's help. Details and samples of offer letters are available on an About.com Web site, `http://jobsearchtech.about.com`; scroll past ads to Job Offer Letters.

Pre-employment agreements and job offer letters are generally legal and enforceable — but not always. If you can't afford to consult an employment lawyer before signing a pre-employment contract, bulk up your knowledge; run a Google search for "pre-employment contracts" and "employment contracts."

Last Chance to Back Out

Maybe you've decided to accept the offer. Before popping a Champagne cork, make sure that you have the salary, benefits, and starting date in writing. Assurance that you correctly understand this information is critical when you're being asked to relocate or give up a job.

If you received the offer over the telephone, ask whether the company can mail you a job offer letter; if not, you write one, perhaps calling it a "letter of understanding."

Sometimes you decide the job isn't for you. Don't feel obligated to accept it merely because you've been dickering over your potential employment for weeks. If you ultimately decide to pass on it, send an amiable letter that reveals no details. Say that while you greatly appreciate the offer and the interviewer's time, you have made a difficult decision and that you have accepted a position with another employer (or that you have ultimately determined that you aren't a good fit with the company).

When the job offers the breakout role you've been searching for, throw a wrap party. Pop the Champagne. Cheers all around!

Part III

Actors' Studio: Casting Your Character

The 5th Wave   By Rich Tennant

"Other than that, what would you say are your special skills and competencies?"

In this part . . .

*B*eing typecast is a real danger in an interview situation. You're a recent graduate? *Bam* — you're inexperienced and ill-equipped for the responsibility of the position. You're 55 years old? Set in your ways and expensive to insure.

This part shows you ways to overcome preconceived notions about who you might be, whether you're looking to change careers or have a history of short-term work.

Chapter 15

From iPods and Texting to Jobs and Paychecks

*H*ello new or recent college graduate! Remember that I'm on your side as you read the first part of this chapter and reach for the anxiety meds. Stay tuned. I show you later in this chapter how to use interview settings to counter criticism of your generation that sometimes lurks but remains unspoken. As you know, you have to recognize a problem to fix it. So please bear with me for a couple of pages while I lay out common negative presumptions you may have to cope with. Now, on with the show. . . .

First, I share with you some of the stereotypical presumptions that I've gathered from media reports and personal conversations with recruiters about new and recent graduates in the workplace, and then I tell you how to deck them.

Peering into the Eye of the Inter-Generational Storm

Four generations are hanging out together in the workplace for the first time in U.S. history. The sheer range of ages and values-shaping experiences makes for some dramatic days at the office as intergenerational tension bubbles up.

The four generations now rubbing elbows in conference rooms include the following, more or less. (There's much argument as to the exact range of birth years that describe each generation.)

- *Radio Babies* (a.k.a. The Silent Generation) were born between 1930 and 1945, and they lived through World War II.

- *Baby Boomers* came into the world between 1946 and 1969. Because there were so many of them, they've impacted society like a pig moving through a python.

- *Generation X* (or *Baby Busters*) were born between 1970 and 1979 and were once slammed by earlier generations as slackers, cynics, and underachievers.

- *Millennials* (or *Generation Y*) were born after 1980. They have the dumb luck of being criticized by the three older generations as coddled, praise-needy whiners who only want to work on their own terms.

The three older generations of workers have largely made peace among themselves, but their members may experience culture shock when they see new and recent college graduates showing up for work with exposed midriffs that display a belly ring, or find them audaciously text-messaging senior managers with requests about issues that should be handled with an immediate supervisor.

Employers pass their dissatisfactions onto their recruiters, who also accuse Millennials of not getting the seller mentality that grows job offers. Twenty-somethings are said to interview with unrealistic expectations of how employers should accommodate their desire to have a life outside the workplace. Unlike their parents who worked killer hours in a single-minded drive to achieve, members of the youngest generation insist that while they sure do want to make a difference, they work to live, not live to work.

Inspired by printed reports of actual exchanges between recruiters and Millennials, I illustrate with a fictional but representative snippet of an interview to illustrate the take-it-or-leave-it attitude that leaves employers speechless:

> Management consulting firm interviewer: *Would you like to know more about our company's quantitative analysis group?*
>
> Millennial professional: *Who would I be working for? I am not interested if I can't choose my boss. Would I start as a senior analyst? What is the salary? How soon would I be eligible for a raise? When would I be considered for a promotion? Would I have to work past 5 pm? I need a vacation the first two weeks of every June because I have a time-share in Costa Rica. And to be upfront with you, I will need a half-day on Fridays because I have a cabin in the mountains and my friends count on me being there.*

Finding Yourself in Demand Despite Shortcomings

Even as charges that Millennials too aggressively demand work/life balance, demographics are working in your favor. As the workforce's youngest begin replacing retiring Boomers, many top corporations cite a "War for Talent" imperative and go all out to recruit twenty-somethings. These companies are willing to make whatever concessions they must to recruit you. Benefits at some major organizations include these perks:

- ✔ Free lunches
- ✔ On-site massage
- ✔ A bonus for hitting the gym
- ✔ The full tab for grad school for some hires
- ✔ Summer office closures at 3 p.m. on Fridays

Clearly, the world is your oyster at prestigious corporations if you have a good education from a recognized college or university. But here's the reality: Top-of-the line workplace bounty is not universal. Most companies aren't willing to bend to what they consider excessive demands of Millennial candidates.

As a huge generation, Millennials will eventually have the last word. As your numbers pour into the job market, Millennials seeking less grueling tours of duty than your parents' long and rigid workweeks eventually will liberalize the workplace.

But my sources tell me that the vast majority of bosses, especially those in smaller companies who bootstrapped themselves to a corner office, continue to seek hungrier and more easily moldable rookies. That's why this chapter speaks directly to you in the stadium crowd, more so than to you in the opera-house elites.

Facing Presumptions of Millennials' Work Ethic

As a new or recent college graduate, your *ability* to do the work that a job requires isn't so much in question. The iffy factor is your *willingness* to do the work in a manner an employer prefers. While the work-ethic question isn't singular to 20-somethings (Gen X members used to hear the same gripes when they were younger.), it does hit your generation hardest. Here's what critics say about Millennials:

✔ You have an attitude toward work that looks like laziness and impatience.

✔ You had to overachieve to get through the most competitive college admissions process in history, so you don't feel particularly inclined to pay your dues.

✔ You make up the most pampered generation in history; you were expected to spend your spare time making the varsity team, not working part-time. You're like Gen X on steroids.

✔ You're likely to look at a job interview in the way one 20-year-old candidate defined it to a recruiter: "a two-way conversation where the company puts out what they want and expect from me, and I put out what I want and expect from the company." Not!

✔ You're more demanding than previous generations and dismiss as hopelessly old-fashioned the traditional work ethic that people should work hard and do the best job possible, regardless of the reward.

✔ You can't think on your feet. You don't work well alone, maybe because you grew up on a steady stream of organized sports and other team activities. You're comfortable only when pursuing well-defined goals as part of a team and can't solve problems independently. (Mom, help!)

Today's rookies are too often stereotyped as lazy and impatient to take a seat at the table, refusing to pay dues, slacking off, holding galling expectations, being unwilling to work hard or long, and being limited in the ability to make independent decisions and solve problems. No generation is of one mind. Nevertheless, if you don't meet the generalization head-on, it can cause you to miss out on a job you want.

The positive performance you give during an interview dispelling the poor-work-ethic stereotyping can erase doubts about your willingness to do a job.

Tips for Millennial Rookies

Concentrating on the skills and accomplishments you provide and on what you bring to the employer — not what you want from the job — go a long way toward wiping out unspoken concerns that chill job offers. Here are other tips for combating perceptions:

✔ Don't get sandbagged by generational myths. Every generation believes that it's substantially different from those who have gone before and therefore deserves a pass to rewrite the rules. That's true only in the methods and technology used to make one's way in life. As scholar and publisher Dr. Ron Krannich (www.impactpublications.com) says: "Despite a trendy Generation Y designation, today's college graduates still must learn to connect with the right people who can hire them for good jobs, showing they can add value to the organizations they want to join."

✔ Don't be a prancing pony in your interviewing persona, confusing attitude with confidence. Try to come across as able but eager to learn. Radiating arrogance that implies the workplace rules must bend to accommodate your preferences because you're young and tech-savvy won't play well with older bosses who have the power to choose someone else.

✔ Bring a notepad and take notes during the interview. This shows you're interested and paying attention. Think *respect.*

✔ Don't be shocked if an employer refuses to negotiate entry-level salaries. But after you've presented your value, do ask about the timing of performance reviews, as well as performance bonuses and how they're calculated. (See Chapter 8 for salary talk.)

✔ Storytell. Prepare detailed true examples of all your skills, with as many examples from off-campus as on-campus. But stay away from personal stories that may work on Facebook but are more than interviewers want to know.

✔ Don't apologize for a lack of workplace experience beyond internships and student jobs. The employer already knows that you're starting out. Instead, explain how your experience at your summer job waiting tables helped you hone your customer-service skills. This is a golden oldie but especially important to young graduates.

Scripts for Millennial Newbies

You find suggested scripts to answer a large number of interviewing questions elsewhere in this book; especially in Chapters 18–24. In addition, the script examples below suggest strategies for smacking down bad press aimed specifically at Gen Y candidates. Here goes:

✔ *You should hire me because I'm the best person for this job. I am not only a hard worker and a fast learner but I bring a passion for excellence. I won't disappoint you. For example —.*

✔ *Yes, I'm an experienced team player. I've had opportunities in my internships, college, and athletics to maximize my skills as a team player. On a recent project, for example, —. But being on a team doesn't mean I can't lead a team. I was elected president of the Environmental Action Club at my college. I enjoy making well-reasoned, well-thought-out decisions. For instance, when I —.*

✔ *You asked how I handle conflict on a team. Basically, I try to make dispassionate judgments about what's best for the group and our goal and then use good communications techniques to make my point. Let me tell you how I mediated a flap over —.*

✔ *I am excited to learn that your company encourages volunteering for service work. I believe that people who do not give back to their community make a misjudgment both personally and in their career development. Based on my volunteer stints in college, I find that service work adds another dimension to my understanding of what people really want and how to satisfy those longings. I hope you'll select me for this position because we're on the same page here.*

✔ *You asked me where I would like to be in five years. I would like to become the best marketing representative you have in the company. At the same time, I'll be preparing to take on greater responsibilities. For example, I've enrolled in an advanced level marketing course online to be ready for future challenges. I love creative challenges, and I'm comfortable making decisions.*

✔ *You asked how well I work with people who are considerably older than me. That's great. In my work with the Batiquitos Lagoon Foundation, which I've done for three years, all the volunteers have a mutual respect for each other. Obviously I look to the older crowd for their experience and I think they like what I bring in the way of my newer education and experience that maybe they don't have. So you could say it's a mutual admiration society.*

✔ *I have no problem working the hours you require. In fact, I would look forward to the opportunity to move around and see different areas of the company relatively early in my career to get a better feel for what I can contribute down the line and where I want to go within the company. I'll work very hard to make a difference for this company and for the company's customers. I think my professors will back me up on that — would you like to see some of their letters of recommendation?*

✔ *Although I don't have experience doing this exact kind of work, my education has given me a considerable background in this area. With a combination of my educational background and my internship job experience, I know that I will be a productive new addition to your team and I will go all out to make that happen.*

✔ *I know that many employers consider my generation, the Y generation, to be somewhat difficult to manage and inspire. The joke I've heard is, "You're in the Why generation — Why aren't you more interested in your career prospects?" Mr. Clemons, that's not me. I've been focused on joining a team such as this one all during my senior year. And I've worked diligently to succeed at this goal, as I hope some of my earlier statements have conveyed. Do you think I'm the committed addition to your team whom you hope to hire?*

Gird for a competitive search

Although current prospects for new graduates are encouraging, employers receive many applications for each available starter-employee position. When you aren't snapped up by an on-campus recruiter, pull together a wish list of places you'd like to work and use online networking sites to connect with employees inside the prospective employer companies. Get more tips online from such Millennial-friendly Web sites as

✔ www.collegegrad.com

✔ www.collegerecruiter.com

✔ www.erecruiting.com

✔ www.nacelink.com

✔ www.experience.com

✔ www.jobsearch.about.com

✔ www.monstertrak.com

Good Times and Your Future

The intergenerational shift in the workplace puts today's new and recent college graduates on the job market's red carpet. If that's you, enjoy your edge. But recognize that the hiring picture could change in a few years:

✔ Consider the flip-flop rhythm of the economy (remember Econ 101?). Cyclical recessions and hiring slowdowns force younger as well as older people to stalk jobs for months on end.

✔ As workforce ranks repopulate — until the year 2020 or so — with other Millennials who, like you, are tech-savvy, you'll compete for jobs within your own age group.

✔ By far the biggest question mark for your future is how worldwide competition for the best jobs will impact Americans of all ages. The end of communism and capital's chase for cheap labor across the planet has unleashed hundreds of millions of workers on global markets. A number of these competitors have a bachelor's or an advanced degree.

On a cheerier note, a rising job market for new college graduates has been a long-running show. Over the past half-decade, employers have consistently projected double-digit annual hiring increases, according to the National Association of Colleges and Employers.

And as you gear up to begin an awesome and magnificent trip toward an award-winning work/life-balanced career, remember this one last tip: Some days you're the bug, some days you're the windshield.

Chapter 16

Tips and Scripts That Sell a Switch

*P*eople change careers for many variations of two reasons: They leave their career or their career leaves them. Either way, employment challenges are much the same when it comes to marketing yourself in places where you haven't been before.

Even when you think you can easily transition from one career field or industry to another (the manager-can-manage-anything syndrome), employers can be a hard sell when it comes to greenlighting career changers for a payroll. Except when they're filling entry level jobs, hiring authorities have a frustrating habit of preferring candidates who, on someone else's dime, have proven that they can do the work a job requires.

American poet Henry Wadsworth Longfellow's summary of the two views — yours and an employer's — leaps to mind:

> *We judge ourselves by what we feel capable of doing; others judge us by what we have done.*

When you're trying to swim in new ponds, you have to figure out ways to get past an employer's inner voice, the one that says you're a fish out of water.

Remembering Career Change Basics

How does that new cliché I just made up go — this isn't your father's interviewing market? Truer words were never spoken. Global trade is changing life for all of us. Technology is automating human processes. Computer modeling is trumping gut feeling. Teleconference marketing is replacing sales trips. Highly qualified candidates are being hired on temp contracts and cut loose when the project is over or the job is shipped offshore to cheaper labor nations.

Keep your dreams alive as you assume the role of career changer in a new era, but be clear-eyed about the challenges you face when you set out to interview yourself into places where you're a stranger. Mull over the following points of practical straight talk about career-changing:

- ✔ **Career change is not job change.** A career change involves a marked shift in jobs requiring new primary skills or knowledge, or a totally different work environment — or both. For example, when a manager in the telecom industry leaves one company for another managerial position in the same industry, he makes a job change; when he leaves the telecom industry to become a museum curator he makes a career change to a different job and different industry.

- ✔ **Retraining may be unavoidable.** When you attempt to make a clear change to a different kind of job (for instance, engineer to sales rep) in the same industry, you may well be able to pitch your way into an employer's graces without investing in additional formal education or training. Your challenge is more difficult when you try to change both your job and industry at the same time, but you may be able to pull it off without immediately spending additional time and money in school. However, you won't be able to get out of educational renewal to satisfy credibility and licensing requirements in such careers as law, public accounting, and nursing.

- ✔ **Employers worry most about risk.** Managers are concerned whether the crossover skills (which I tell you about in the upcoming section "Leveraging Crossover Skills for Change") you acquired in your former career will translate to your new career. When your skills don't convert and you can't do the work, the business suffers a negative impact and — if you're canned — a risk of being sued for wrongful discharge. Another worry is whether you'll suffer changer's remorse, quickly becoming dissatisfied and turning into a "bad hire." These risks drive employers to seek out directly applicable skills in proven performers.

- ✔ **Your competitors are new graduates.** When you're starting over, you compete with new graduates who are starting out. Expect to be paid entry-level money; an employer is unlikely to compensate you for your 15 years' experience in another field (unless you can show that your experience can save or earn money for the new employer). Even so, you have an ace up your sleeve: You bring judgment, commitment, high motivation, proven good work habits, and real-world lessons.

Eyeing the Best Career-Change Tips

The hilarious misadventures of characters in *A Funny Thing Happened on the Way to the Forum,* the Broadway show megahit and subsequent movie, spawned an echo chamber of knock-off media — books, articles, videos. A Google exploration shows a half-million hits on the funny-thing phrasing.

The send-ups start with the first part of the title (A Funny Thing Happened on the Way to . . .), and end with whatever topic is being skewered. Among my favorites: *A Funny Thing Happened on the Way to the White House,* a book, and *A Funny Thing Happened on the Way to the Moon,* a video.

The phrasing formula has become shorthand for what happens when foolhardiness and folly lead a perfectly good journey into unexpected and unintended consequences. If you don't read the pointers that follow, you could be nominated for a lead role in *A Funny Thing Happened on the Way to My Career Change.*

- ✔ **Connect with others in your intended field.** When your change is voluntary, at least six months in advance of your leap, join a professional association of members in the career field or industry where you want to go. When your change is involuntary and you're suddenly left high and dry, scramble to assemble a skeleton personal network of people who can guide you into your intended field and beef it up as fast as you can. Make friends. Find out who's who and what's happening with professionals who can connect you with employment. Ask what you should read and what workshops you should attend. Ask if you can visit a professional's workplace as an observer.

- ✔ **Educate yourself.** Seek out short-term certificate programs and workshops offered during industry conferences, as well as those available locally. If you study online, get the scoop on pluses and pitfalls about distance learning. One starting spot: www.geteducated.com.

- ✔ **Bone up on the industry.** Even if you're a nonacademic type who always sneaked light rubbish reads or sports sections into your study halls, at this time in your life you really can't afford to skip hard-core research on your proposed destination. (Check back to Chapter 6 for research leads.) Those greener pastures sometimes bleach out when something about the work isn't what a changer realistically expects or can do well. This probably happens as a result of skimpy research.

- ✔ **Talk the talk.** Learn the lingo of prospective new colleagues. You'll seem like one of them already.

- ✔ **Brace yourself for interview pitfalls.** When you find yourself trapped in a behavior-based interview setting (described in Chapter 5) and you're coming up short trying to answer a question about what you have done that's relevant to the new career, answer quickly. And then reframe your response segueing from behavior-based interviewing (the past) to situational interviewing (the future): *That's a good question. And here's what I would do if we decide I'm the right person for this position. I would —.*

✔ **Make the experience connection.** The bridge you use to join the old with the new must be rational and reasonable. Your qualifications have to come from somewhere — skills you already possess, volunteer work, part-time jobs, training, hobbies, and so forth. Strive to present a believable relationship between your qualifications and the career you're targeting. The more convincing your bridge, the easier you make it for an employer to say "Welcome, we want you."

✔ **Accentuate the positive.** Don't say you hope to change careers because there are no more jobs in your field. An exception might be when a condition is well known, such as real estate agents who got out during the recent downturn in home sales. Even then, add that you'd been thinking about making a change for a couple of years and have decided to redesign your life for a better fit with your priorities and goals. As in any job search, you're moving toward a preferred future, not running away from a bad spot or a toxic boss.

✔ **Tell true stories.** Expect to be asked the same kinds of questions that new graduates often face, such as some version of "Why shouldn't we hire someone more experienced in this line of work?" When you work out your answers, remember to storytell — that is, to back up your claims of superior qualities with true examples of achievement. Otherwise, what you claim will likely be blown off as hot air. You must be believable.

✔ **Inventory your core skills and knowledge.** Sort through to see which will crossover to a different industry or career field. Push them to the front of your memory where you can find and translate them as needed. The use of crossover skills is the topic of the next segment.

Leveraging Crossover Skills for Change

In mid-career, Roger (or so I'm calling our hero in this true story) woke up one morning asking himself, "Is this all there is?" Successful but unhappily employed, Roger wanted to find a new way to work, produce, self-actualize, earn a living, and be happy.

Pulling the plug on his job as a controller of a division of a big Midwestern corporation, Roger worked with an experienced career coach on self-analysis; a big part of the analysis focused on identifying Roger's crossover skills. Using judgment born of maturity, Roger realized that what he really wanted to do was work outdoors with boats. After leaving his land-locked state and moving to Florida, Roger's transferable skills, including boating and financial management, built his crossover bridge into a marina business that he liked so much he ended up buying it two years later.

The leadership conundrum

When you're an entrepreneur who wants to come in out of the cold, tell stories about the skills and self-motivation that you developed being on your own. But be vigilant in countering any inference that after being your own boss, you'd be hard to manage. Practice interviewing with a friendly "devil's advocate" who won't pull punches in evaluating your interviewing performance for dominance traits. Unless a company is interviewing for a chief officer, turn down the volume.

Using crossover skills as a bridge from one career (or job) to another is your most important persuasion tool to gain acceptance in job interviews. So what exactly are crossover skills? In a nutshell, crossover skills are those you've gathered through jobs, classes, volunteer work, hobbies, sports, projects, parenting, or any other life experience that can be valuable in your new career.

Blogging, for example, is a crossover skill. Surprised? Don't be. Blogging is more than going online and telling the world about your day or what you think. For starters, blogging requires more than writing skills. As a blogger, you build a loyal readership and study visitor statistics to see what works and what doesn't. You meet self-announced deadlines for new material. You make intelligent responses to comments including those that insult your own intelligence. As an extension of social networking, blogging can benefit many businesses (such as financial services) or causes (such as politics) that depend on large numbers of customers and supporters. Any entity seeking to establish or maintain a blog needs people who can make it work correctly.

A few better known examples of crossover skills include the following

- ✔ Decision-making
- ✔ Oral and written communication
- ✔ Organization
- ✔ Problem-solving
- ✔ Technology

Crossovers are portable skills that you can use in many work settings. They go straight to the heart of an employer's question of "Can you do the job?" Considering the importance of been-there, done-that experience to the success of your career change, be ready to identify your crossover skills to an interviewer, and to translate how they make you immediately productive.

There's a hitch. Even brilliant people have trouble correctly and comprehensively identifying their portable skills. Searching online for "crossover skills" or "transferable skills" is the cheapest and quickest way to get started on identifying yours. Additionally, look for books that contain multipage listings, of portable skills, including my own *Cover Letters For Dummies,* 2nd Edition. When big fat holes remain in your inventory of crossover skills, it's time to return to your college's career center for help or engage a career coach well versed in identifying skills and competencies.

Say What? Say This When You're in Change Mode

You aren't going to ring up a sale trying to explain why your previous experience as a restaurant manager qualifies you to manage a nuclear waste disposal company. But you are going to make headway with hiring decisions when you give convincing reasons why your lack of explicit prior experience doesn't matter. Study these sample answers and then add your own circumstances, interpretations, and phrases to the scripts that follow.

- ✔ To respond to hesitations about your career change:

    This job is a good fit for what I've been interested in throughout my career — working with others to achieve an above-average outcome, the satisfaction of being technically competent, and having a serious interest in sports. For example, my work at Leader Public Relations taught me that a team needs bench strength. When the senior publicist left Leader unexpectedly, I was able to successfully step in and increase placements within six months by 20 percent. The persuasion skills I bring along with seven years of surfing ideally qualify me for this position as assistant manager of surf board production. Do you agree?

- ✔ To respond to concerns that your previous experience is irrelevant to the job you want:

    I am a well-qualified candidate for this educational research position because cost control expertise required by the grant is more than met with my 15 years' experience as a manager with budget and supervisory responsibility.

- ✔ To respond to concerns that your previous position is irrelevant to the job you want:

    Yes, I was a receptionist for twelve years and it was great training to deal with all levels of individuals. Here's why I am so well-matched to your brokerage department. Not only have I interacted with venture and equity capital managers and with retirement fund managers in a high-pressure environment, I have taken a course in financial markets and stock, bonds, and other investments. With the world rushing forward, I think we need new thinking for new times, don't you? My people skills will help me to bring in the kinds of customers you've been losing to online traders. Do you see any reasons why I wouldn't be a great addition to your team?

✔ To demonstrate that you are changing directions with forethought and action:

As I matured and got to know myself better, I realized how I fit into Career X better than what I'd been doing, although my previous work has been fine preparation for what I plan to do with the rest of my life. I've been steadily drawn to Career X for several years and getting ready for this transition, I did the following (attended school, researched and volunteered in the field, took a part-time job in the new industry). Since you didn't screen me out because of my prior experience, I assume you recognize my crossover skills.

I appreciate your valuable time invested in seeing me and so I have taken the initiative of working up a brief ledger sheet that shows you how I qualify for this position. May I come around the desk and walk you through it?

(A ledger sheet in this usage refers to a brief one-page sheet of paper with two columns. Title the left column, "Job Requirements." Title the right column, "My Qualifications." Show the matches item by item. You can do a ledger sheet for interviews on paper or on a laptop.)

✔ Waitress transitioning to wholesale sales rep:

Although I haven't yet specifically sold eyewear accessory products to retailers, I do have sales experience when you consider that in my previous job I was a de facto sales representative for the restaurant.

My upselling record consistently brought in high revenues each week. I've demonstrated that I pay close attention to detail, that I can multitask with precision and accuracy, and that I know how to build a loyal clientele of customers who rave about my service and attention to their requirements. (Smile.) While I'm certainly not the type of person who would lose her head if it weren't attached to her shoulder, I am the type of person who would lose her reading glasses if they weren't attached to lovely eyewear accessory chains such as the one around my neck.

I won't disappoint you. When can I start?

✔ To respond to reason you are interviewing:

As soon as I was sure I wanted to do work that makes a difference in people's lives, I researched this field and reached out to practitioners for informational interviews. I quickly learned that I had to have an associate degree for this work but before I signed up at New School Community College, I researched the reputation of its program by checking with previous graduates and with the employers who hire them. I also went online to a social network and asked for comments on what people really thought about the program I was considering making sacrifices to attend. Everything I heard was good so I attended and now have my degree. It was a great decision!

✔ To the issue of the cause of satisfaction in your last career and concern that you would experience changer's remorse:

I didn't see the results of all the hard work I put in. The structure was overly rigid and bureaucratic and, frankly, I like to feel as though my contributions accomplish a positive outcome. And although I am pretty good with computers, I like to have a slice of my day working with people. I checked out your company with my network and you get glowing reviews for rewarding outstanding performance, for giving employees breathing space to accomplish their assignments, for being able to observe the fruits of their labor and for hiring great teams. Is that how you see this company? Are we made for each other?

More Funny Things That Shouldn't Happen on Your Way to Anywhere

The message is clear: To successfully sell a career change, remember to logically lay out a bridge explaining why you — with no prior matching experience — will be able to handle the job you seek. And take pains to assure that you, as a career changer, aren't given to snap judgments and quick reversal.

Funny stuff will happen if you say either of the following bloopers:

✔ *I saw the job posting and, what the hey, this company is in an industry that I'm willing to give a whirl.*

✔ *I'm changing careers because I can't stand what I've been doing and just need several more quarters for your Social Security.*

People actually say things like this in interviews. They don't realize such rationales are akin to telling a prospective buyer that you're selling your house because the heating bill is too high.

To see more recommended answers to job search questions, go to my Web site, www.sunfeatures.com. Select Columns. At the bottom of the left side of the screen, you see Good Answers to Hard Questions; click on the column in that group that you want to read.

Career change auditions

In a lot of career-changing situations, the company asks the candidate to audition for the job by doing it for a few weeks, usually at peanut wages. This gives the company the opportunity to make a minimum investment in the oyster that may or may not have a pearl in it. The audition similarly gives the candidate a chance to find out whether his or her career change choice was as great as anticipated.

Chapter 17

Spotlighting Prime-Timers over 50

*I*f you'll never see your 20s and 30s again, you may already have run into an age obstacle that puts the brakes on your job hunt in a culture that values youth over experience.

But isn't age discrimination illegal? Of course it is. Does it still happen? Sometimes, depending on your perspective.

From a base in Weston, Conn., Matt Bud works as chairman of The Financial Executives Networking Group, a 27,000-member national organization with local chapters. Most men and women who join The FENG do so when they must find new jobs but once employed tend to stay aboard, bonding with other financial professionals as a kind of safety net against future joblessness.

Running The FENG has given Bud a vault full of experience advising transition-ing executives on the best methods of finding new employment connections. Based on his experience, Bud observes that many employers have a profile of a winning candidate in mind. A rejection decision may not be discrimination but simply that, in the employer's eyes, the candidate has the wrong profile for the job being filled.

So rather than refer to age bias, this chapter covers solutions to what I call age trouble, whether the trouble is due to discrimination or to a wrong pro-file. The following segment focuses on recognizing and overcoming issues of age trouble when it stops you in your tracks.

Showing You Improve with Age

Age trouble shows up in many guises. In this overview, I present examples of questions that may mask common unspoken age-related concerns, followed by sample responses that show there are no expired shelf-life dates stamped on your forehead.

Age and job performance

A big chunk of age trouble is centered on doubts that you can do the work. Here are three masked put-offs and push-backs.

- ✔ This is stressful and demanding work. How well do you work under pressure? (Translation: You may lack the stamina to do the job.)

  I work well in all situations and especially well when I'm under pressure. I like having deadlines. Early on, I learned to set internal deadlines for myself in all my projects, breaking the projects into segments so I always knew how I was doing. I consistently brought my projects in on time and on budget. Internal deadlines are my specialty.

- ✔ What do you do to maintain good health? (Translation: You don't look too healthy to me and you may not be around long enough to justify training costs.)

  Maintaining good health is a passion with me. My body mass index is similar to or better than that of most 30-year-olds. I exercise several times a week. Once a week I play volleyball on the beach. And I watch what I eat.

- ✔ What office software do you use? Do you have a cell phone? (Translation: You look like you do things the old-school way and we're into new-school thinking.)

  I'm proficient with (current business software). I took a class for it on my own time last year at St. Louis community College. My BlackBerry is with me 24/7. I make it a point to stay current with such major trends in our industry as (give one or two examples). I'm a member of the World Future Society.

Age and money

In a world impacted by business budgets, companies may see prime-timers as too pricey for value received, as the following two examples illustrate:

✔ What can you bring to this company? (Translation: You expect to earn more money to start than we want to pay; I can hire someone at half of what you want.)

I bring a background that includes a related degree and successful years of experience in a similar position with another company. The contacts I have already made in my previous positions will help me be productive immediately, saving costs and earning revenues. My background is an open book, showing that by any measure I am a bargain!

✔ What are your monetary expectations of this job? (Translation: You're a seasoned worker accustomed to regular raises; our firm won't be able to make that kind of commitment, so why am I wasting time interviewing you?)

Yes, I've been rewarded for my contributions to the bottom line for previous employers. Sometimes the compensation was in the form of a raise and sometimes it was a performance bonus for meeting goals. If you decide that I'm the right person for this position, I believe the monetary details won't present a problem, and I'll work with you on making that the case.

Age and attitude

Prime-timers may be perceived as living in another dimension of values and viewpoints or as set in their ways, as the following two questions and responses indicate:

The health insurance put-off

Health insurance cost for employees is a monster age-related cost bite for employers who consider hiring prime-timers. It's a tough issue to beat, says ace job connector Tony Beshara: "Boomers' inclusion in a group insurance plan drives up the cost for an average American company. Additionally, older workers are perceived to miss more work because of their own illness or that of their spouse."

So what's the answer? Other than carrying your own health insurance plan and letting the interviewer know you won't be another policy to feed, Beshara says the best you can do is look healthy: "Get in shape, dress sharply, and interview with energy."

Health insurance in America is under scrutiny for change. As I write this book, Massachusetts is the first state to provide nearly universal healthcare coverage. California's talking about it. Other states may follow. Politicians are proposing national plans. Getting insurance costs off the back of employers would help level the global playing field for American enterprise and open more employment doors for prime-timers.

✔ How would you go about doing this job? (Translation: You're accustomed to doing things your way, which may not be our way.)

Although I've been quite successful in previous positions, I don't buy the idea of resting on one's laurels. I'm always happy to learn new and better ways to do things. Before suggesting any innovations, I would first make certain that I understand company policies and ways of working. I am very excited about this work opportunity and look forward to starting to work with you as soon as possible.

✔ You look as though you've led too accomplished a life to be returning to a career now (Translation: You don't fit in with our young culture.)

I believe that my extensive experience in many productive settings will be of great benefit to your company because (give one or two examples). I can work effectively with people of all ages. In fact, I really like working with young people because I respect their energy and vitality and fresh look at challenges.

Outing the Elephant: Addressing Age Concerns

Have you heard the expression "If there's an elephant in the room, introduce it?" That's the topic of Matt Bud's advice to members of his networking group.

Matt Bud is chairman of The Financial Executives Networking Group. He warns prime-timers that it's a huge mistake to avoid an age-related issue that the interviewer may be wary of bringing up directly. That's because an age zinger becomes an elephant in a small room — impossible to overlook, an obvious truth that is being ignored. Instead, get the sensitive question out in the open where you can take control of it.

In a communication to The FENG, Bud wrote of "Ensuring a Productive Interview." What follows is a part of what Bud counseled:

Among difficult questions an interviewer would like to ask you, a big one is age related: How much longer are you planning to work?

Close to being an illegal question even if the job is potentially long term or might involve a move, the interviewer may not ask but the question is hanging out there, and until you get it out of the way, not much will happen during an interview.

If you choose not to address it, the interviewer may be trying to think up a way to politely ask you instead of listening to your very fine offerings about your many talents and how they could be applied to the job in question.

Don't wait to be put on the defensive that may cause you to flush red-faced or stammer. My experience has been that most folks are uncomfortable with the answers to these kinds of questions and hope they won't come up. Wrong! Get your story out in exactly the way you want it to be heard. When an elephant is in the room blocking the doorway to your progress, it is in the best interests of both parties to get this and other difficult questions out of the way early in the interview so that more important matters can be addressed.

The interview won't move forward until you expose and conquer hidden hiring objections.

Overcoming the Overqualified Label

Overqualified may be code for one of five perceptions. Interviewers may use it to indicate that you

- ✔ Have too many years' experience
- ✔ Have too much education
- ✔ Will want to be too highly paid
- ✔ Are too rigid with demands
- ✔ Are too rusted with obsolete skills

In my view, when you're told you're overqualified for a position, you can usually chalk it up to the first perception — age trouble.

But Dallas-based Tony Beshara is a job-finding whiz who disagrees that being rated as overqualified for a position is because of age trouble, and he has strong credentials to back up his opinion. Beshara runs Babich and Associates, one of the nation's most successful job placement firms, and he personally has connected thousands of people with employment. Beshara says:

When a candidate of any age applies for a job one step or more below the level of his or her previous position, a hiring authority is going to be concerned that the candidate will be underemployed, depart as soon as something better turns up, and leave the authority holding the blame for a bad choice. The same overqualified tag could be applied to a 35- or 40-year-old candidate, but since the predominant numbers of people going down the career ladder are in their 50s, the overqualified experience appears to be an age thing, but it's not.

In either case, whether you're dealing with age trouble or not, why go down with the one-word punch of being rated as "overqualified"? Come back with a strong response — or a pre-emptive strike to clear the air.

To combat concerns of overqualification, use the following tactics:

✔ Clarify the interviewer's concerns. Find out whether the interviewer really thinks you're overqualified — or just overaged — and whether you'll want to earn too much money or be bored by the position.

✔ Enthusiastically address the interviewer's concerns, emphasizing the positive. Explain how you can grow in this position.

✔ Show how you can use your experience to benefit the company in solving long-term problems, building profit, or assisting in other departments.

✔ Make sure that the interviewer understands your qualifications.

✔ If you'll be working in an office full of younger people, explain how you're an anchor. You're experienced, calm, stable, reliable, and you can provide day-to-day continuity.

Here are six model responses to the overqualified put-off:

Overqualified? Some would say that I'm not overqualified but fully qualified. With due respect, could you explain the problem with someone doing the job better than expected?

Fortunately, I've lived enough years to have developed the judgment that allows me to focus on the future. Before we speak of past years, past titles, and past salaries, can we look at my strengths and abilities and how I've stayed on the cutting edge of my career field, including its technology?

I hope you're not concerned that hiring someone with my solid experience and competencies would look like age bias if once on the job you decided you'd made a mistake and I had to go. Can I present a creative idea? Why don't I work on a trial basis for a month — no strings — to give you a chance to view me up close? This immediately solves your staffing problem at no risk to you. I can hit the floor running and require less supervision than a less experienced worker. When can I start?

This job is so attractive to me that I'm willing to sign a contract committing to stay for a minimum of 12 months. There's no obligation on your part. How else can I convince you that I'm the best person for this position?

My family's grown. And I'm no longer concerned with title and salary — I like to keep busy. A reference check will show I do my work on time and do it well as a team member. I'm sure we can agree on a salary that fits your budget. When can we make my time your time?

Salary is not my top priority. Not that I have a trust fund, but I will work for less money, will take direction from managers of any age, will continue to stay current on technology and will not leave you in the lurch if Hollywood calls to make me a star. And I don't insist that it's my way or the highway.

Radio babies and retirement reversal

Are you way over 50? If so, you may be in the generation born in the years 1930-1945, sometimes called radio babies (guess why). Perhaps you decided to opt out of the workforce for a period of time and now want back in. How do you best answer the following question?

Why are you looking for a job after being retired for three years?

The effective answer is not that you need the money or that you were bored out of your mind with your job.

For a ShowStopper answer, follow this line of persuasion:

✔ Retired? Who retired? Explain that you didn't actually do the R-word. Discuss positive reasons for taking time off. Everyone needs to refresh and refill from time to time. Now you're opting back in.

✔ Discuss work with enthusiasm and declare that you're itching to get back to it.

✔ Describe how you can contribute to the company in chapter-and-verse detail.

Top Hints for Prime-Timers

As good actors and actresses grow older, they no longer have to prove their talent, but they do have to prove that they still have what it takes to play a demanding role.

Take the following A-game hints to heart, two of which are suggested by contributing experts Liz Ryan, acclaimed speaker and writer on networking and the new-millennium workplace, and Tony Beshara, author of *Acing the Interview: How to Ask and Answer the Questions That Will Get You the Job!* (AMACOM, 2008).

✔ Experiment with statements clarifying that contributing to the employer's goals is your first priority.

✔ Storytell — prepare examples of your high energy, fresh enthusiasm, and willingness to compete.

✔ Carry yourself with a young attitude. Enter the room with pep in your step.

✔ Liz Ryan advises that you think of concrete examples of times when you overcame an obstacle, made a save, and had a breakthrough solution. Talk about how you deal with change. Work these things into the conversation before they're asked. Overcome any sense that people your age can't hustle.

✔ Tony Beshara suggests that you build rapport with an interviewer by mirroring his or her body language in the first few minutes. If the interviewer crosses arms or leans back in the chair, you cross arms and lean back in the chair. But as the interview develops, present yourself in an open, direct, and assertive manner. Keep your feet planted on the floor, your arms open at your sides or on the arms of a chair, and lean forward just enough to make good eye contact. If your body language isn't appropriate, your words may never be heard.

✔ Don't enter an interviewing room with the attitude that your experience should speak for itself. Merely listing your tasks doesn't impress employers. Instead answer the so-what question: Explain what difference you made and how your experience translates to their needs right now.

✔ Downplay ancient history. Unless you have a compelling reason to look way back in your career, focus your comments on the past 10 or 15 years. Talk only about your past experience that relates to the job at hand.

✔ To get around being seen as a tiresome know-it-all, don't constantly say "I know." Instead, acknowledge an interviewer's statement with "That's interesting." "You make a good point." "I see what you mean."

✔ Don't fall into the trap of thinking "uppity child" when you're being interviewed by a younger hiring manager. Your interview mindset should realign your ideas of authority: Mutual respect is the right tone — even when the interviewer is young enough to be your kid.

✔ Use the question technique to avoid seeming to take charge of the interview: "Did I fully explain how I can make a difference in solving the problem we've just discussed?" or "Have I left unanswered any questions that you may have about my being the best person for this position?" When the answer indicates no reservations remain, smile and ask "When do I start?"

When the boss is your kid's age

Tony G., a reader of my newspaper column, wrote to me to say that at age 60 he had just landed an excellent position with a start-up company after being interviewed by the 33-year-old company president, who coincidentally is the same age as his son. The other three employees are in their late 20s, as are Tony's daughters. Tony credits his success to his lack of *neophobia* (fear of new things).

"I think I was offered the job because of my attitude during the interview. I made it clear to the young boss that I would rather work with people in 'your age bracket' because there is so much energy and new, fresh ideas. That's the environment where I want to work," Tony said with conviction.

Advising other prime-timers, Tony added: "Think young, think responsibly, and always be prepared to put something solid and attractive on the interview table."

Greener pastures

Do you know that the Federal government is the nation's largest employer, is age diverse and that 85 percent of federal jobs are located outside of the Washington, D.C., area (including Virginia and Maryland)? Being accepted into the federal workplace is complex. Before you hit the 143 federal job boards (`federal jobs.net/federal.htm`), get the whole picture. Two books excel in shepherding you through the thicket of merit hiring practices. They are

- *The Book of U.S. Government Jobs: Where They Are, What's Available & How to Get One, Tenth Edition*, by Dennis V. Damp (Bookhaven Press, 2008). This excellent guide contains an instructive chapter on federal interviewing.

- *The Federal Resume Guidebook: Strategies for Writing a Winning Federal Electronic Resume, KSAs, and Essays*, by Kathryn Kraemer Troutman, Fourth Edition (JIST Works, 2007). This is a must-have book for the serious federal job hunter who hopes to get as far as the interviewing stage.

Keep Your Career Fit and Stay Out of Corners

Everyone 50 and over knows that scooping up choice jobs isn't the cinch it often was when you were younger. As a prime-timer, you can greatly improve your odds of being chosen by learning new and improved job search skills, particularly the A-game interviewing techniques that determine what comes next in your life.

Part IV
Lights, Camera, Talk! Answering Questions

The 5th Wave   By Rich Tennant

"I see on page 124 of your resume it says you're a concise writer."

In this part . . .

*Q*uestions are the beginning, middle, and end of any interview story. How you respond to them and the questions you ask in return are the primary way interviewers get a feel for who you are and what you can do.

This part runs down the do's and don'ts of answering questions about yourself, your education, and your experience. It fills you in on answering questions about the job you hope is ahead and the jobs you've had in the past. It also covers questions about hard-to-market situations and tells you how to handle sticky questions you might not want to answer.

Chapter 18

What Can You Tell Me about Yourself?

Questions and answers are dialogue on the stage of job interviews. This chapter is devoted to questions and answers that spotlight you and your dreams, talent, and motivation in reaching your audience.

Many of this chapter's questions attempt to examine the kind of person you are. For example:

✔ **Interviewers want to know what's right with you:** *Are you team-oriented about rolling up your sleeves to get a project done even when it's not in your job description? Can you give me an illustration of when that was the case?*

✔ **Interviewers want to know what's wrong with you:** *If I brought up your name with former coworkers, what would they say about you?*

To unearth that information, interviewers often start with one agony-inducing question. In this chapter, I show you how to address that question with a "personal commercial" that makes you a must-hire.

Answering a Very Broad Question Specifically

In trying to figure out whether you're the right person to hire, interviewers usually open fire with the big bazooka of self-revealing questions, often phrased as a statement:

Tell me a little about yourself.

No matter how the question is worded, take care to get your act together for it because it comes early in an interview — at the very time when an interviewer is forming an initial impression of you.

A good beginning sets the stage for the halo effect to kick in (see Chapter 9). The *halo effect* happens when an interviewer is impressed with you right off the bat and may assume that if you excel in one area, you excel in others.

When you start to tell about yourself, focus on aspects of your life that *illustrate your value as a candidate for the position you seek.* In addition to knowing you have competencies, skills, and experience related to the potential work, employers want to feel confident that you're the sort of person who

- ✔ Can do the job
- ✔ Will do the job
- ✔ Gets along with others while doing the job

Employers want to know how well you accept management direction. They want to know whether you have a history of slacking off as you get too comfortable on a job. They want to know whether — despite their lack of long-term commitment to you — you will jump ship at an inconvenient time if another employer dangles more money before your eyes.

When answering the Tell Me About Yourself question, bear the following thought in mind:

Focus on the Best You.

In sticking to the Best You theme, you may ask, "But isn't that kind of like lying?" No. Lying is a time bomb that doesn't travel well.

I know a woman who did not inflate her previous salary — instead, she did the opposite, lowering it because she didn't want to be considered overqualified for a job she wanted. After 11 months she was fired for lying when her reference checks finally caught up with her. The week before that she had been offered a promotion!

Always be honest about the wonderful parts of you. But don't blurt out anything that could make you look like a poor hiring choice. Neither should you wildly exaggerate your best traits to the extent that your performance bears no relationship to your promise — remember that the piper who lives down the road will demand to be paid.

A contrarian expert speaks

In the Different-Strokes-for-Different-Folks Department: Ace placement professional Neil P. McNulty (www.mcnultymanagement.com) of Virginia Beach, Virginia, has made hundreds of individual placements over 25 years. McNulty is a cut-to-the-chase kind of guy who advises his candidates to stick to business. Here's McNulty's take on the Tell Me About Yourself question:

"Job hunting book experts say the question is asked because the interviewer wants to hear how you organize your thoughts, learn how you articulate your career ambitions, and see how you present yourself when under pressure. That's not always the case.

"The real reason it's asked is often because the interviewer is unprepared, doesn't know where to begin, and while you are speaking, he or she is trying to figure out what to ask you next.

"I teach candidates to give a two-minute (max) chronological rundown of their professional history — no personal information — just a list of positions held, ending the rundown with this statement: *This brings us to today. Tell me, what exactly do you want someone to do for you in this position?* The tactic gives the interviewer a direction to go and also gives the candidate a 'needs target' to shoot at as the interview develops."

Shading your answers packs a punch

A careful questioner hears not only your lyrics, or content, in response to the self-defining question. The questioner also listens to your music, or where you choose to play fortissimo:

- Do you focus on your competencies and skills, your education and training as they relate to the job? The interviewer is likely to conclude — *hooray!* — that you're work-oriented.

- Do you focus on your hobbies? The interviewer may decide that you're more interested in your leisure hours, working only because you don't want to starve to death.

- Do you focus on your present job? The employer may think that you're still attached to your current haunts and not ready to move on. Or that you'll cynically use a job offer merely to leverage a counteroffer from your boss.

Narrow the question

You can jump right in and answer the Tell Me About Yourself, or you can ask for prompts:

I can tell you about experience and accomplishments in this industry, or the education and training that qualify me for this position, or about my personal history. Where shall I start?

Employers typically answer that they want to hear about both your work and relevant background — or a little bit of everything.

Write Your Marketing Pitch

The sensible way to make star tracks in responding to a request to tell about yourself is to memorize — literally memorize — a personal commercial about yourself. Your "show and sell" bit should run between one and two minutes.

Think for a few seconds about what a commercial does. It focuses on selling a product in a blink of time. It grabs your attention fast with information of interest to you. Then it tells why you should buy the product.

Your personal commercial works exactly the same way by enabling you to

- ✔ Grab employers' interest with a confident statement about yourself and your value related to the job you want.
- ✔ Support that statement with specific facts.
- ✔ Sell employers on why they should hire you instead of someone else.

I wasn't kidding about memorizing your personal commercial. Practice until it sounds natural. Just like an actor, you need to learn your script and deliver it in character. No stumbling. No ad-libbing.

Perhaps you're not so sure about that advice. Won't all this memorization make you sound as canned as a tin of tuna? Maybe. But which would you prefer — to sound a bit stiff or to flounder about as though you have no idea why you're there or why you're right for the job or why you have marbles in your mouth? Duh.

Depending on your experience level and the job you're trying to land, your personal commercial can include any or all of the following information:

- ✔ Competencies, skills, and experience for the job
- ✔ Academic degree
- ✔ Positions of leadership
- ✔ Specific job training
- ✔ Date of expected graduation (if applicable)

✔ Honors or achievements

✔ General goals

✔ A branding brief (See the sidebar, "New tool: A branding brief," at the end of this chapter.)

Sample Personal Commercials

A prospective new graduate applying for a Web news site start-up might use a personal commercial something like this:

> *Your need for a Web editor who can handle breaking news deadlines is just what I want and am qualified to handle. Working and attending school full time taught me to organize and prioritize for superior time management skills — I wouldn't have succeeded without mastering these skills. Considering the demand of deadlines, I see multitasking skills as especially important in a journalism career.*
>
> *I will graduate in May from the University of Kansas with a Bachelor of Arts in Journalism. I was a feature writer on the school's Web site and the student newspaper. I would have been named editor, but I worked throughout my education to pay for 80 percent of my school expenses. At the same time, I managed to maintain a high GPA, so I expect to graduate cum laude.*

A seasoned manager's personal commercial highlights accomplishments and experience. For example:

> *I am an experienced line manager with extensive knowledge in team-building that ranges from organizing project teams to informally encouraging people to work together. I've developed solid skills in hiring and retaining employees.*
>
> *I also have incorporated technological advances into a company where such advances require a significant amount of employee retraining.*
>
> *Additionally, my track record is substantial in major presentations to clients, which has led to as much as an 87 percent increase in product adoption from the year I took over.*
>
> *In summary, I believe I have the required skills and experience you seek for this position, as well as the technological savvy and a positive attitude toward implementing change. Is my background on the mark?*

You can create one all-purpose personal commercial (think core commercial) and edit it on your feet to make it fit the requirements of the position you seek.

Or if — like me — you're not too hot at instant editing, prepare several different personal commercials aimed at related but different types of jobs. Tweak the appropriate version and rehearse yourself before each interview.

Admittedly, this tip is a no-brainer, but recruiters tell me that surprisingly few candidates include personal commercial prep in their interview planning.

Try writing your own personal commercial. Describe your experience, competencies, and skills that are relevant to the type of position you want. Make the information interesting and remember to sell rather than tell employers what you've got and why they should want it.

The Questions

Readers of previous editions of this book tell me that they need more help with two other questions: What is your greatest weakness? Why should I hire you? This edition elaborates on those puzzlers.

For the following questions in this chapter, *ShowStoppers* are answers that work for you; *Clunkers and Bloopers* are answers that work against you.

What is your most memorable accomplishment?

ShowStoppers

- ✔ Relate an accomplishment directly to the job for which you're interviewing.
- ✔ Give details about the accomplishment, as if you're telling a story.
- ✔ Describe results.

Clunkers and Bloopers

- ✔ Give a vague or unfocused answer.
- ✔ Discuss an accomplishment with no connection to the job you want.
- ✔ Discuss responsibilities instead of results.

Where do you see yourself five years from now? How does this position fit with your long-term career objectives?

ShowStoppers

- ✔ Say you hope your hard work has moved you appropriately forward on your career track.

✔ Answer realistically: In a changed business world where a long-term job may mean three years, speak of lifelong education to keep abreast of changes in your field and self-reliance for your own career.

✔ Describe short-term, achievable goals and discuss how they will help you reach your long-term goals.

✔ Explain how the position you want will help you to reach your goals.

✔ Strive to look ambitious, but not too much so that you threaten the hiring manager.

Clunkers and Bloopers

✔ Say that you want the interviewer's job.

✔ Describe unrealistic goals.

✔ State goals that aren't consistent with the company's needs or ability to satisfy.

What is your greatest strength?

ShowStoppers

✔ Anticipate and prepare to discuss up to five strengths, such as

- Skill in managing your work schedule
- Willingness to do extra
- Ability to learn quickly
- Proactivity in solving problems
- Team-building
- Leadership
- Cool-headed temperament under pressure

✔ Discuss only strengths related to the position you want.

✔ Use specific examples to illustrate. Include statistics and testimonials.

Clunkers and Bloopers

✔ Discuss strengths unrelated to the job you want.

✔ Fumble around, saying that you don't feel comfortable bragging on yourself.

✔ For women only: Bring up the fact that you're president of your child's PTA, (unless you're interviewing for a job selling school supplies). Discriminatory? Yes, but studies show that moms may be seen as less committed to jobs than childless women or men with or without kids.

Expert contrarian discusses strengths

Virginia Beach, Virginia placement pro Neil P. McNulty notes that placement experts advise you to have at least two or three significant achievements to describe, preferably in mini-story format.

"That is good information," McNulty says. "What they leave out is the fact that most of the entire job-hunting populace consists simply of average, hardworking, everyday people — most of whom have not done anything of tremendous importance. I teach such candidates that I place to answer this way:

I have done many things that I consider significant, but nothing that really rocked the business world. The bottom line is that I am a hardworking, results-oriented, high-energy individual who gets the job done — and done right. My work is always on time, of correct quantity and quality, and if you hire me, you can expect nothing less, whatever the task.

My two cents: Rarely is there a job search question so universal in outcome that any given rule must always be followed. Thanks, Neil McNulty, for another slant.

What is your greatest weakness?

ShowStoppers

✔ Because of the corrective action you took, you were able to transform a starting point of failure into a success story of strength. Three examples follow:

- *I didn't always know what I was doing — right or wrong — when I took my first managerial position. So I took online classes in managerial techniques, read management books, and paid attention to how managers whom I admired operated. As a result, I give careful thought to the quality of guidance that I give my direct reports before launching a project. I'm not yet perfect and may never be — I'm my own toughest critic — but, as the record shows, my leadership has improved dramatically in motivating the productivity achievements of my teams.*

- *Not being a natural techie, I was underperforming when I first worked with X word processing software. So I took a class in that software program at a community college on my own time and now I'm the best administrative assistant in my office.*

- *I've had trouble in the past with remembering the timing of every appointment when I had to move like lightning across town from one sales call to another sales call. But I've corrected that scheduling problem with this terrific digital device — let me show it to you. I haven't missed a call since I got it.*

✔ Balance a weakness with a compensating strength. Three examples follow:

✔ *I'm not a global thinker. But, being detail-minded, I'm a topnotch staffer to an executive who is a big-picture guy.*

✔ *I don't pretend to be a gifted trial lawyer. But I'll stack my legal research and business structure skills up against any other lawyer in town.*

✔ *As a newcomer to this city, I can't bring a clientele to this job but I can use my talent for public presentations to build one faster than you can say "Give me a quote." I have a plan to attract clients by quickly becoming known as a speaker at local club meetings and civic events.*

Clunkers and Bloopers

✔ Mention a brutally honest negative, such as you're hard to work with, you're easily bored, you don't get along well with minority coworkers, you have a poor memory, or that stress exhausts you.

✔ Fall back on clichés. Examples: You're a workaholic. (*My boss has to shove me out the door every night to make me go home.*) You're a perfectionist. (*The devil is in the time-eating details and I sweat every one.*) But even clichés sometimes work for very young candidates.

✔ Say you have no weaknesses.

✔ Volunteer key weaknesses that are likely to go unnoticed in the hiring decision.

What are your outside interests, including sports? Do you IM (instant message)? What books/magazine/blogs have you read recently? What movies/TV have you seen?

ShowStoppers

✔ Be enthusiastic.

✔ Tell why you enjoy the activities you mention.

✔ Focus on team-oriented, active hobbies — usually sports over reading.

✔ If possible, show how your hobbies or reading materials help you in your work.

✔ Focus on traditional or new media that relate to personal growth.

Clunkers and Bloopers

✔ Say that you don't have any outside interests. Just work.

✔ Discuss extreme solo sports, unless applicable to the job you want.

✔ Mention vampire-like fiction, horror, or violent media. (Stick to business and news.)

More strong weakness answers

Find additional answers to the weakness question on my Web site, www.sunfeatures.com; click on Columns, and then, at the bottom of the columns page on the left hand side of the screen, on Good Answers to Hard Questions, where you find the question, *What is your biggest weakness?*

You also find my answers to other questions:

✔ *Why do you want to change jobs?*

✔ *Why were you fired?*

✔ *Why do you want this job?*

✔ *Are you overqualified for this job?*

Would you rather work with others or alone? How about teams?

ShowStoppers

  ✔ Discuss your adaptability and flexibility in working with others or alone, as a leader or a follower.

  ✔ Give concrete examples.

  ✔ Mention the importance of every team member's contribution.

Clunkers and Bloopers

  ✔ Let the interviewer think that you're a pushover, willing to carry the load of team members who don't contribute.

  ✔ Say you don't like to work on teams.

What is your definition of success? Of failure?

ShowStoppers

  ✔ Show that your success is balanced between your professional and personal lives.

  ✔ Relate success to the position you want.

  ✔ If you have to talk about failure, do so positively. Show how you turned a failure into a success or discuss how and what you learned from the failure.

  ✔ Demonstrate that you're a happy person who thinks the world is more good than bad.

Clunkers and Bloopers

✔ Spend a great deal of time talking about failure.

✔ Say that you've never failed, made no mistakes.

✔ Discuss success as a ruthless, take-no-prisoners shot to the top.

How do you handle stressful situations?

ShowStoppers

✔ Give examples of how you've dealt with job stress.

✔ Discuss what you do to relax, refresh, and refill.

✔ Give positive illustrations of how job stress makes you work harder or more efficiently.

Clunkers and Bloopers

✔ Say that you avoid stress. (What, me worry?)

✔ Imply that stress is usually the result of lack of preparation or knowledge.

Is there anything else I should know about you?

ShowStoppers

✔ Discuss any selling points the interview failed to uncover and relate those selling points to the job you want.

✔ Repeat the selling points you've already discussed and remind the interviewer why you're the best candidate for the job.

Clunkers and Bloopers

✔ Say "No." And not another word.

✔ Remark that you will require the first two weeks off every June for vacation because that's when your timeshare is available.

Why should I hire you?

This is the worst of questions, and the best of questions.

The worst because it's one that many (perhaps most) candidates are unprepared for and often botch. It causes clueless candidates to say the darnedest things (*Because I live nearby*) or mumble threadbare clichés (*Because I'm honest and show up*).

The best because it's an invitation to repeat your strengths and other factors that distinguish you as the perfect person for the job.

Moreover, because it's usually the last question, your answer may stick in the interviewer's memory.

Your basic answer relates the work (in the workplace or in school) that you've done to the work you're going to do. It covers your unique combination of specific skills, knowledge (including education and training), and experience. Get ready to own this question with the help of these four steps:

1. **Review your research on the company (see Chapter 6). Review the job description.**

   When you lack a job description or research, ask questions: Can you tell me a bit about what problems you need solved? What would you expect the person hired for this position to accomplish in the first six months?

2. **Show how the work you've done relates to the work you're going to do. Or, if you're a rookie or a career-changer, show how your skills cross over.**

   Explain how your education qualifies you. Make the connection memorable with behavioral storytelling (see Chapter 5). Refer to your personal commercial or branding brief (the latter is described at the end of this chapter).

3. **Mention shared values, which you glean from the company's mission statement and reputation:** *I totally agree with and applaud the company's strong stand against setting up debt traps for the nation's working poor.*

4. **Declare your interest in wanting the job.**

Here are three examples of how you might style your answer:

✔ *Your job posting says you're looking for an administrative assistant who can help keep the IT department functioning smoothly. That's what I've done almost all of my career, which means I have 12 years' experience in exactly this function. I am very familiar with software, contract administration, and sleuthing out trouble spots. My former and present employers say I helped them grow their business each year. I feel confident that I can do the same for you.*

✔ *You told me earlier in this meeting that your main concern in filling this position is that the customer service trainee manager focuses on improving communications with our customer base. I can do that! During my internships at X and Y Corporations, I observed a number of techniques that you may want to think about implementing here. For example, (name two techniques). The techniques are credited with boosting customer satisfaction and retention by 14 percent.*

Do performance reviews belong at a job interview?

Displaying actual copies of your review data on an interview is risky for two reasons, advises James M. Lemke, director of organizational development for Opportunity International, and this book's technical reviewer.

First, the review data is usually considered a company's proprietary information. Second, a perfect review is rare and Murphy's Law (If anything can go wrong, it will.) periodically surfaces in job interviews.

"Most review documents include spaces to suggest areas that need improvement, such as organizational skills or written communication abilities," Lemke says. "If Murphy is at work the day you show off your review, you may lose out on a job opportunity by giving too much information."

Here's a better way to get your points across. Compile a quotation sheet (Q sheet) with excerpts of complimentary statements from your reviews. Hold your Q sheet until the interview is drawing to a close. You need not go into detail about the source. Just suggest: "Perhaps you'd like to see what some of my previous managers have said about me." A well-done Q sheet adds extra punch to your exit.

> *In addition to my management studies (name them) that provided the useful knowledge to do this job better than the typical applicant, I showed leadership in restructuring the mechanics of my college's student government office while serving as secretary. Additionally, I was one of five senior students voted most likely to succeed in business. I want this job, and I hope I have given you the reasons why you want me in this job.*

> ✔ *As I understand your needs in this law firm, you're looking for an attorney who can provide specialist topnotch legal research to meet a challenge to one of a client's best-selling drugs. In addition to my five years of general research experience at respected law firms, my work on the Excalibur vs. Marston case last year was described in law journals as central to the client's win.*

> *I share your enthusiasm for chasing down every last lead to maintain quality advocacy, counsel and integrity in client service. I've got my eye on this position. How do I rank in the candidate pool at this point?*

As you work out your own unique response, you may have to think on your feet if the interviewer surprises you with new facts or a call for skills you hadn't anticipated. In the meantime, review the basics to answer Why Should I Hire You?

ShowStoppers

✔ Prepare at least three key reasons to roll off your tongue that show how you're better than the other candidates.

✔ Use specific examples to illustrate your reasons.

New tool: The branding brief

Kathryn Kraemer Troutman, executive career consultant and CEO of The Resume Place, Inc. (www.resume-place.com) in Baltimore, recommends that job seekers devise an abbreviated personal marketing message, one that she terms a *branding brief*. The length of a branding brief is 20-30 seconds, or about 100 words.

A similar synoposis may also be called an *elevator speech, personal branding message*, or *profile summary*; all these terms refer to a capsule of your "story" as it relates to an employer. All are shorter than your personal commercial, which I describe earlier in this chapter.

Consider incorporating a branding brief within your one-to-two minute personal commercial for interviews, or use it as a stand-alone statement in networking.

A branding brief headlines what you are known for. It identifies your special characteristics and achievements of interest to an employer. You can use a branding brief to help people remember who you are, why you're memorable, and when they should seek you, Troutman explains.

"In constructing a branding brief, describe your top characteristics and how they can contribute to the mission of an organization that you hope to join. And clearly state how you can help achieve the organization's mission." Here are a half-dozen of Troutman's examples:

✔ As a kid, I listened to old radio programs that said things like "The Shadow Knows..." Right then I developed a life-long passion for radio. In a complex media marketplace, you can count on me as a proven programming manager to target and deliver larger audiences.

I offer expert marketing and distribution skills that I'll stack up against anyone's in the business. As a programming chief, I've got the whole package of skills, from affiliate contract negotiation and content, to audience and technology. In short, I hope you'll agree that I know more about leading a programming effort than the Shadow ever knew ... although the Shadow knew a lot!

✔ My name is Keri Bright and I formerly taught English at Martingale High School, where I was known for establishing community literacy programs to teach immigrants how to read and write English. My bilingual skills would be useful as an aide in the Congressman's office.

✔ I'm JoAnn Thomas Reed, and I'm a people-friendly IT specialist. I offer expert consulting services to your staff and managers for data management services you can be proud of. Think of me when you want a real pro who speaks plain English. I've always believed that geek is chic and nerd is nice. Give me a chance to prove it and you'll be glad you did.

✔ I'm a cosmos professional. After managing Space Shuttle Orbit Operations for 16 years, I'm well qualified to contribute to Space Station operations. My number-one goal will be the efficient, cost-effective management of resources to achieve our mission objective of building a new shuttle by 2010.

My 16 years of NASA science includes direction of space engineering technology, leadership of engineers and technicians, and performance measurements. I am passionate about contributing to the operational success of the Space Shuttle missions now and in the future.

✔ *I successfully worked as a library technician in the James River Free Library, with diverse accomplishments ranging from multimedia productions and program development, to speaker recruitment and publication selection for special markets.*

After getting real library experience for six years, I invested in a library science degree program to upgrade my professional competencies and skills. Now I am ready to begin work on blending technology, archives and library services in efficient and affordable programs to excite library patrons.

✔ *My career as a logistics specialist — some people call that supply-chain specialist — is very rewarding as I work to see that important materials and resources get to the right place at the right time for the right price. I'm a perfect fit for your position, where I would continue working my magic for your customers — managing inventory, distributing goods, and monitoring the quality of materials provided.*

✔ Tell something unusual or unique about you that will make the interviewer remember you. You can use a branding brief, described in the sidebar "New tool: The branding brief," for this purpose.

Clunkers and Bloopers

✔ Dance around this question (*Because I want the job.*), leaving without really addressing it.

✔ You would be an asset to the company bowling team; you have a winning smile; you are tired of living with your parents; you can lie with a straight face; your house payment is overdue; your brother needs help paying off his gambling debts.

✔ Say, "Because you're trying to fill a position."

Chapter 19

What Do You Know about This Job and Our Company?

. . . .

In This Chapter

▶ Proving that you understand the job

▶ Showing savvy about the company

▶ Confirming that you know the industry

▶ Answering sample questions for practice

. . . .

*W*hen you're aiming for a professional or managerial job, expect a number of questions to be fired across the footlights that test your knowledge of the position, company, and industry.

Even when your aspirations are less lofty and your goal is to be hired as a supporting player, knowing something about some of the topics in this chapter can put you in the take-a-bow category of candidates.

Understand Job, Company, Industry — and How They All Fit Together

Employers expect you to grasp what the job entails and how the job fits into the overall company picture. For responsible professional jobs, they're even more impressed if you have looked into what the company does and where it stands in its industry.

An interviewer may test your knowledge with questions like this:

Where would you rank this company in the marketplace and why?

Such a question requires you to go into some detail about the company's place in the scheme of things — its products, profitability, industry position, goals, and vulnerability to buyout.

An interviewer may not look at your answers for definitive details, but he is interested in how you arrived at your conclusions. You could say:

> *You ranked second in the industry in total earnings last year, so that's a positive. Your level of debt is a little high, but that was the result of tooling up for your next line of products due out in June. If the new line is as successful as forecast, then most of the rest of the company debt will be wiped out by new sales, leaving the company with a shot at being the most financially secure in the industry. Plus, you still enjoy an enormous potential for growth in the near future.*

If you mention problems in the company's performance, offer general solutions (additional training, financial fixes, workforce restructuring, and the like). Otherwise you appear clueless, or as some interviewers may say: *Nice cage, no bird.* Or, *all foam, no beer.* Or, *all hat, no cattle.* You get the idea.

To model credibility, you can beef up your general solutions with specifics that suggest you're doing more than merely guessing. That is, cite statistics and figures to back up the problems you note along with your bright ideas to remedy them.

A caution: Reflect before following interviewing advice you may have read elsewhere that urges you to Superman-leap tall problems in a single bound. Certain difficulties may have eluded resolution by company managers for good reasons. On the outside looking in, chances are you don't have all the facts on the ground.

The Questions

Look at the following questions and the strategies you can use to answer them as you gear up to show perfect casting between yourself, the job, and the company.

Choose strategies marked as ShowStoppers; avoid those indicated to be Clunkers and Bloopers.

What do you know about this position?

ShowStoppers

✔ From your research, discuss how the position fits into the company structure and how you would fit like a glove into that position.

✔ Mention how you can help the company achieve its goals.

✔ Confirm your understanding of the broad responsibilities of the position. Ask whether you missed any key points (thereby setting up topics to discuss your qualifications).

Clunkers and Bloopers

✔ Ask what the company makes.

✔ Use out-of-date data.

What do you know about our competition?

ShowStoppers

✔ Discuss the current climate of the industry and how competitors are affected.

✔ Add details that show you truly understand the industry and the competition.

✔ Analyze the impact global competition is having on industry.

Clunkers and Bloopers

✔ Say you know very little about the competition.

✔ Admit you recently interviewed with the competition.

✔ Reveal trade secrets from your current employer.

What are your opinions about some of the challenges facing our company?

ShowStoppers

✔ Show the depth of your research by discussing some of the company's upcoming projects.

✔ Mention several possible solutions to potential problems the company may be facing, acknowledging that you lack certainty without proprietary facts.

Clunkers and Bloopers

✔ Say you don't know of any challenges, but you're all ears.

✔ Mention problems but add no possible solutions.

What do you see as the direction of this company?

ShowStoppers

- ✔ Give a brief but somewhat detailed answer, displaying a solid grasp of the company's movement in the industry. Add how you can help.
- ✔ Support your answer with facts and figures, citing their source.

Clunkers and Bloopers

- ✔ Make guesses because you haven't a clue.
- ✔ Offer no data to back up your comments.

Why did you apply to this company?

ShowStoppers

- ✔ The position is a compelling opportunity and the company a place where your qualifications can make a difference. Explain why.
- ✔ You heard about a new service the company is launching, which is somewhat related to a project you helped create in a (college) senior year project; you find the potential exciting. Ask if the interviewer would like to hear about your project.

Clunkers and Bloopers

- ✔ The company is in an industry you've always wanted to try.
- ✔ Say you've always wanted to live in the Southwest.

Our company has a mission statement; do you have a personal mission statement — or personal vision?

ShowStoppers

- ✔ In one or two sentences, give examples of your values (customer service, ethics, honor, keeping one's word, and so on) that are compatible with the company's.
- ✔ Review the company's mission statement on its Web site and describe a compatible aim.

Clunkers and Bloopers

- ✔ Ask what a mission statement is.
- ✔ Ask for clarification on the meaning of values.

How will you help our company?

ShowStoppers

- ✔ Summarize how your key skills can help the company toward its goals.
- ✔ Describe the wide circle of contacts and other intangible benefits you can bring to the company.

Clunkers and Bloopers

- ✔ Give a short answer with no specifics.
- ✔ Say you'll have to get back on that one.

Chapter 20

What Are Your Skills and Competencies?

*W*ith job security in today's market going the way of the ozone layer, the operative words are *skills* (what you can do) and, increasingly, a newer and broader employment concept termed *competencies* (how well you do what you do using natural talents).

The competencies concept includes skills and such related characteristics and natural abilities as motivation, industriousness, and attitudes.

In other words, the *competency-based interviewing approach* attempts to look at the whole package where you're concerned. Suppose, for example, that you're a certified expert in Java and there's no question about your skill level. Competency questions attempt to uncover whether you also have the soft skills you need to pursue successful work projects where organization, cooperation, and communication ease are essential. (Or whether your quirky personality drives colleagues to the aspirin bottle.)

Competency-based models fall into two categories:

✔ *Work-based competencies* describe job-specific characteristics, skills, and abilities, such as fluency in the English language or the ability to read topographical maps.

✔ *Behavior-based competencies* describe all the other personal stuff you need, in addition to technical skills, to do the job well. Competencies include abilities like:

- Prioritizing and planning work

- Using time efficiently

- Planning for additional resources

- Adapting to new technologies

- Keeping technical skills up to date

A *competency-based interview* is highly-structured and based on the premise that past success is the best predictor of future success. Many questions designed to reveal behavioral competencies begin with "Tell me about a time when . . ." (See Chapter 5 to find out about the behavior-based interview.)

How much must you know about competency-based interviewing? That depends upon where you're interviewing. The competency-based interviewing approach is on the rise but isn't yet a mainstream interviewing method for the majority of jobs in the United States. You can expect competency-based interviewing at larger companies and the federal government.

By contrast, small and medium-sized employers (where most of the jobs are) tend to stick to skills discovery in their interview questions. Their interviewers make informal judgments about how well candidates will use their skills on the job.

Be aware that some overlap in everyday usage of terminology occurs: That is, one interviewer's *skills* is another interviewer's *competencies.* To keep it simple, in this chapter I use the s-word — *skills.*

When you expect to be heading into a competencies-based quizzing, consider reading an entire book on the approach: *Competency-Based Interviews: Master the Tough New Interview Style and Give Them the Answers That Will Win You the Job,* by Robin Kessler (Career Press, 2006).

Recognizing Questions about Your Skills

Accomplishments, like some wines, don't always travel well. You catch an employer's eye with accomplishments, but when you change jobs, you leave your accomplishments behind.

What you do pack along with you are the skills that enabled you to achieve those accomplishments: subject mastery, meeting deadlines, and researching on the Internet, for instance.

Experienced interviewers move past the citations of *what* you did to discover *how* you did it — the essence of your skills.

Interviewers may be straightforward in trying to determine your skills through questions about specific work experiences:

> *Tell me about a time that a supervisor gave you a new project when you were racing the clock to complete an earlier-assigned project.*

Or you may be tossed a pretend workplace scenario and asked how you'd handle the situation:

> *You're monitoring and integrating control feedback in a petrochemical processing facility to maintain production flow when the system suddenly goes down; what do you do?*

Other questions are less direct, going in a conversational side door to see how you react using such skills as conflict-management and interpersonal relationships:

> *How would you deal with a difficult boss?*

To pull off a ShowStopper interview, learn to recognize questions that spotlight the skills you bring to a job stage.

Answering Questions about Your Skills

Use storytelling (Check out Chapter 5.) to comprehensively answer skills questions. Remember, too, that social, or soft, skills (people skills) play a significant role in determining the winning candidate. Take pains to convince the interviewer that you're a pleasant individual who gets along with people.

Take that question in the previous section about how you'd deal with a difficult boss. Here's an answer, underscored with storytelling that makes you look like a reasonable and conscientious person:

> *I would first try to make sure that the difficulty isn't walking around in my shoes. Then I'd read a few books on how to interact with difficult people. I've never had a boss I didn't like, but I have had to use tact on occasion.*
>
> *On my last job, my boss and I didn't see eye to eye on the best software for an office application. I researched the issue in detail and wrote a short, fact-filled report for my boss. Based on this new information, my boss then bought the software I recommended.*

This answer centers on research skills but also highlights patience and acceptance of supervision.

The Questions

The sample skills questions in this chapter are generalized for wider application, although in an interview you should expect skills questions that relate to your career field: *What computer skills do you have? Why do you think your technical skills are a match for this job? When is the best time to close a sale? What was your most difficult auditing problem and how did you solve it? Tell me about your typical workday as a probation officer.*

Note that questions in this chapter may seem to be close relatives of the questions in Chapter 19. The difference is that those in Chapter 19 are intended to draw out your qualities as a human being; those in this chapter go after your skills. Is it a big goof if you mix them up? Not at all. Both are reminders to keep your self-marketing pitch up and running.

What is the toughest job problem you've ever faced?

ShowStoppers

- ✔ Recall a problem, the *skills used in your action* to deal with it, and the successful results; this is a skills-detailed version of PAR (problem, action, result).

- ✔ Explain how you could apply those same skills to the prospective job.

Clunkers and Bloopers

- ✔ Recall a problem but not an accomplishment or skill related to it.

- ✔ Say you've searched your memory and can't recall a problem you couldn't handle.

What do you like least about gathering information to deal with a problem (research)?

ShowStoppers

- ✔ Comment that wanting to do a first-rate job, you're uncomfortable when you're uncertain that you've compiled enough research to quit and make a decision that affects the well-being of others.

- ✔ Reveal that you enjoy solving problems but become impatient with repetitive sameo-sameo answers leading to dead ends.

- ✔ Explain that you use multiple resources — Web, books, journals, and expert people — and you become frustrated when key resources aren't adequate.

Clunkers and Bloopers

⟟ ✔ Dismiss researching as work for the scholars among us, and say you prefer to be an action hero. (Even bank robbers have to case the job.)

⟟ ✔ Admit you prefer outdoor work and aren't sure why you're here.

How good are you at making oral presentations?

ShowStoppers

⟟ ✔ Discuss how you prepare. Name presentation skills. Mention specific instances where you've given a good show.

⟟ ✔ Offer to give a one-minute oral presentation on a topic you've practiced.

Clunkers and Bloopers

⟟ ✔ Say that you never do them because you're terrified of speaking in front of large crowds.

⟟ ✔ Admit you were roundly booed at your last political protest speech.

How would you rate your writing skills in comparison to your verbal skills?

ShowStoppers

⟟ ✔ Discuss how both skills — as well as listening — are important to being a good communicator, and that while one or the other may be your strong suit, you're working to become strongly proficient at both speaking and writing. Explain how you're doing so — class work, independent study, membership in Toastmasters International or a writing group; show brief writing samples.

⟟ ✔ Concretely explain a real communication situation in your past; describe how you communicated the information and the result.

⟟ ✔ If you're a weak communicator, give a compensatory response that substitutes another skill for writing or verbal skills; for example, in a technical call center, problem-solving outweighs the need for golden tonsils and laudable business writing.

Clunkers and Bloopers

⟟ ✔ Rate your skill in one area as better than the other and clam up.

⟟ ✔ Say public speaking gives you sweaty palms and you don't like it.

How do you deal with unexpected events on the job?

ShowStoppers

- ✔ Discuss how you immediately reprioritize your assignments in emergencies.
- ✔ Mention specific instances where you were able to complete a project (or projects) on time despite unforeseen complications.

Clunkers and Bloopers

- ✔ Tell how you just keep doing what you were doing until you're finished.
- ✔ Discuss an instance when an unexpected event resulted in disaster.

How do you organize your time?

ShowStoppers

- ✔ Affirm that you put first things first. Each day you identify A-level tasks and get those done before moving on to B-level tasks. You return voice-mail messages once or twice daily and urgent messages immediately.
- ✔ Comment that you use up-to-date planning products. These include planning software such as PlanPlusOnline, and PDA (personal digital assistant) hand-held devices, such as a BlackBerry. These kinds of mentions show that you are techno-current. If you organize yourself on paper, mention a formal business product such as a Franklin Planner. (Pulling out a pocket calendar is like pulling out a slide rule.) Conclude with true examples showing that you completed multiple tasks on time.
- ✔ Discuss how you went through a typical day on one of your previous jobs.

Clunkers and Bloopers

- ✔ Say that you don't usually handle more than one task at a time.
- ✔ Reply that you don't wear a watch.

How do you delegate responsibility?

ShowStoppers

- ✔ Discuss how you involve everyone in the overall picture.
- ✔ Discuss specific projects that were successful because of your team effort.

Clunkers and Bloopers

- ✔ Reveal that you like process detail; admit your micromanaging tendencies to tell direct reports how to connect every dot.
- ✔ Mention your belief that a task will be done right only if you do it yourself.

What's your experience with group projects (teamwork)?

ShowStoppers

- ✔ Mention a specific project, including the group goals and your particular responsibilities.
- ✔ Discuss your positive relationship with the project supervisor; compliment coworkers.

Clunkers and Bloopers

- ✔ Don't identify your responsibilities; just say you all worked together.
- ✔ Rip your coworkers as laggards and say you're sick of doing most of the heavy lifting without credit.

Why should I hire you?

ShowStoppers

- ✔ Summarize point-by-point why your qualifications match the employer's needs to a tee, adding any additional competitive edge you can honestly claim. (Rehearse in advance to avoid stumbles.)
- ✔ Include accomplishments and the skills that facilitated those accomplishments, plus relevant experience and training.

Clunkers and Bloopers

- ✔ Fail to make the "perfect match" connection.
- ✔ Offer only clichés, such as "I'm honest, hardworking, and a fast learner" without factual backup illustrations.

Chapter 21

How Does Your Experience Help Us?

*I*n the classic adventure film *Raiders of the Lost Ark,* Karen Allen (playing Marion Ravenwood) hasn't seen Harrison Ford (playing Indiana Jones) for awhile when she comments that he's not the same man she knew ten years ago. Ford's Indiana Jones has a great comeback:

> *It's not the years, honey, it's the mileage.*

And so it goes with experience. You can have ten years of skill-building experience — or you can have one year's experience with nine years of reruns. Solid experience is yet one more confirmation of your ability to do a job.

Make Your Experience Relevant

Psychologists insist that past behavior predicts future behavior. True or not, interviewers look at your yesterdays for clues on how well you'll perform tomorrow.

Simply reciting your experience isn't going to wow an employer. You have to make the connection between then and now. You have to show exactly how your experience-based accomplishments make you the perfect candidate for the job opening. Here's a straightforward example:

As you'll note on my resume, I've had five years of praised experience as an instructor and training coordinator. I'd like to tell you a few details about my work as an office-work trainer for military spouses, which has a direct application to your project to retrain a portion of the company's plant workers. Would you like to hear a bit about that?

Whether you have a lot or a little experience, employers want to hire people who will continue to learn and grow to the benefit of their company. So as you answer the experience questions, focus not only on your experience, but also on how your efforts served the changing needs of your previous employer.

I started training the military wives on word processing programs from 9 am until 12 noon, three days a week. After several months I was asked to add evening hours two nights a week to train a class on spreadsheet programs, which I myself had to quickly get up to steam on — and was glad to do so.

When you can show how you've successfully adapted in the past, convincing employers that you have what it takes to adapt your experience to their workplaces is easier.

After the interviewing Q & A begins, what should you do if you don't understand one of the questions? Don't be afraid to ask for clarification — *I'm not sure I understand your question, and I don't want to give you an irrelevant or incorrect answer.*

The Questions

Questions that you may be asked about your work experience, along with suggested answering techniques (ShowStoppers) and definite mistakes (Clunkers and Bloopers) include the following:

What kind of experience do you have for this job?

ShowStoppers

- ✔ Gather information before answering. Ask what projects you would be working on in the first six months. Relate your experience to those projects, detailing exactly how you would go about working on them.

- ✔ Give specific examples of your success in dealing with similar projects in the past, focusing on results.

- ✔ Show how transferable skills drawn from even seemingly unrelated experience (waiting tables or planning club functions) apply to this project. You learned the value of being reliable, of coordinating efforts, of organization, and so forth.

When you're technically great but quiet and shy

Some people, including those who have technical talents, are sometimes very shy at interviews, appearing introverted and timid. Is that you?

Here's a trick around that problem from Martin Yate, author of *Knock 'em Dead: The Ultimate Job Seeker's Guide* (Adams Media Corporation, 2005) and other best-selling job search books.

Yate says that if you reach across the desk to hand the interviewer papers, graphs, and reports from your portfolio of work samples, the interviewer will ask you questions about the samples. Your answers will keep the flow of conversation going — and you'll answer the questions and won't come across as, well, bashful.

Clunkers and Bloopers

✔ Say you have no experience. Next question!

✔ Show that your experience overreaches this particular job — unless you know your overqualification is a plus or your real agenda is to angle for a higher-level position.

In what ways has your job status changed since you got into this field?

ShowStoppers

✔ Mention that you've worked in X number of positions — from small to larger employers — with increasing responsibility; this position is a logical next level in your upward track record.

✔ Describe how you've continued your education and training to be sure you're moving forward with the technology and the times.

✔ With brief, broad verbal brush strokes, sketch advances in your line of work over the years. The point is to show that you recognize epic change.

✔ Ask whether you failed to cover any key responsibilities. If there's a gap, show how you've handled missing responsibilities, perhaps in earlier positions.

Clunkers and Bloopers

✔ Leave out important functions in your move upward. You'll look like you may need to catch up.

✔ Confirm that you've held the same job for 10 years with little change.

How long would it take you to make a contribution to our company?

ShowStoppers

- ✔ Ask the interviewer to explain which areas need the greatest contribution, perhaps focusing on a specific project.

- ✔ Estimate how long it would realistically take you to get settled and get working. Then detail how you would go about working on the particular project, showing how much time you estimate that each step would take. Be realistic, yet optimistic, in your time estimation.

Clunkers and Bloopers

- ✔ Say you'll make a contribution the very first day, unless you can support that claim with facts.

- ✔ Estimate that you won't become productive for at least four months (unless you're headed for an incredibly complex job in which a settling-in period lasting beyond three months is normal).

What are your qualifications?

ShowStoppers

- ✔ Connect your close fit between the job's requirements and your qualifications.

- ✔ Ask whether you should first focus on academic and training or job-related qualifications.

- ✔ Ask what specific projects or problems you may be expected to deal with and which have the highest priority.

- ✔ Identify the projects you've accomplished in the past that qualify you to work successfully on the projects the interviewer mentioned.

Clunkers and Bloopers

- ✔ Assume you know what the interviewer wants to hear about, plunge in, and fail to check the interviewer's interest after a minute or so.

- ✔ Speak only of your education when you have the wrong or limited work experience without working in nuggets of experience in your school lab work, volunteer work, or student jobs.

How did you resolve a tense situation with a coworker? Have you ever had to fire someone?

ShowStoppers

- ✔ Discuss your analytical process for solving any problem involving coworkers (as advocated in conflict-resolution guides).

- ✔ Give a specific example of a difficulty that you've dealt with (conflict resolution or discipline), focusing on how you used your analytical skills to effectively solve the problem.

- ✔ Illustrate how you go about collecting information, stating the steps you took to help the fired person improve and save his or her job before making a termination decision.

- ✔ Emphasize that you follow company policy and that you're fair and tactful in dealing with employee problems.

Clunkers and Bloopers

- ✔ Explain that colleagues unfairly ganged up on you.

- ✔ Discuss an example where you fired someone because you just didn't like the person.

- ✔ Focus on how horrible the problem or employee was, naming names.

Give a specific example of a time that you had to put your needs aside to help a coworker (teamwork).

ShowStoppers

- ✔ Mention teamwork and the importance of coworkers being able to rely on each other.

- ✔ Give a specific example, showing that the reliance wasn't one-sided.

- ✔ Show either how your efforts contributed to getting the work done or how the help you gave didn't cause problems with your own work.

Clunkers and Bloopers

- ✔ Comment that it happens all the time and leave it at that.

- ✔ Say you can't recall any examples.

What did you like best at your last job?

ShowStoppers

- ✔ Mention specific work experiences you were good at and enjoyed that are likely to be present in the prospective position (leading the interviewer to see a match from past to future).

✔ Speak about opportunities to plan your own day or think out of the box. (If you've made a hit, the interviewer may encouragingly say you'll find similar opportunities in this position.)

✔ Confirm that you enjoyed the accomplishment opportunities, that you liked being visible in a high-stakes effort, knowing that your contributions directly affected the company's bottom line.

Clunkers and Bloopers

✔ Blast your ex-job as a loser and say that's why you're here. (Unless your previous employment was at Enron or your former boss is doing hard time.)

✔ Explain that nothing stood out as being especially rewarding.

Based on your experience, what problems do team-focused companies face?

ShowStoppers

✔ Document, with storytelling, that your experience includes being a successful leader or member of teams.

✔ Discuss teams as an overall positive factor in the work world of the 21st century.

✔ Discuss a minor negative aspect of teams and show how that negative aspect can be overcome. (Magazine articles and books about teamwork are helpful for developing teamwork language skills.)

Clunkers and Bloopers

✔ Say that you've always preferred to work alone or to let the people who report to you handle the grunts down the line.

✔ Explain why teamwork is overrated in business today.

Describe a time that you had to work without direct supervision. Have you ever had to make department decisions when your supervisor was not available?

ShowStoppers

✔ Discuss your decision-making process. You don't rattle easily.

✔ Show that you're self-directed and self-motivated, but still willing to follow others' directions or to ask for assistance when needed.

✔ Storytell: Discuss a specific example of a time you had to make a decision without supervision. Preferably, discuss a time that you anticipated company needs and finished a project ahead of time or made a beneficial decision.

Clunkers and Bloopers

🖙 Whine about being forced into a decision that turned sour.

🖙 Admit that you've never worked without someone looking over your shoulder or telling you what to do.

Have you ever misjudged something? How could you have prevented the mistake?

ShowStoppers

🖙 Briefly discuss a specific — but minor — example.

🖙 Briefly discuss what the mistake taught you and how it led you to improve your system for making decisions or solving problems.

🖙 After talking about your example and what you learned from it, refocus the discussion on your accomplishments.

Clunkers and Bloopers

🖙 Discuss a mistake that cost your employer plenty of time and money.

🖙 Pass the blame to someone else.

🖙 Say you've never misjudged anything.

Has a supervisor ever challenged one of your decisions? How did you respond?

ShowStoppers

🖙 Discuss an example of being challenged where you listened politely but supported your decision with research or analytical data and you prevailed.

🖙 Add that even though you supported your decision, you were open to suggestions or comments. You're confident in your abilities but not closed-minded or foolishly stubborn.

Clunkers and Bloopers

🖙 Castigate your supervisor for micromanaging.

🖙 Insist that you were right even though management reversed your decision.

In your current position, what are your three most important accomplishments?

ShowStoppers

- ✔ Name your best work accomplishment stories. Ask which ones the interviewer would like to hear more about.

- ✔ Explain why the three accomplishments are your top picks, adding that you can expand the list. Reach across the desk to hand over an index card with your name and as many as 10 accomplishments.

Clunkers and Bloopers

- ✔ Laughingly remark that you have so many accomplishments that it's hard to choose just three.

- ✔ Admit that you're not sure what counts as an accomplishment.

Your experience doesn't exactly match our needs right now, does it?

ShowStoppers

- ✔ Don't agree. Instead, say that you see your fit with the job through a rosier lens. Your skills are cross-functional. Speak the language of transferable skills and focus on how you can easily transfer your experience in other areas to learning this new job.

- ✔ Stress that you're dedicated to learning the new job quickly. Give two true examples of how you learned a job skill much faster than usual.

- ✔ Say you don't have any bad habits to unlearn and discuss your good work habits that will help you get the job done efficiently and well.

Clunkers and Bloopers

- ✔ Agree, smile, and say nothing to compensate for the mismatch — unless, of course, you don't want the job.

- ✔ Let the door hit you on the way out.

Chapter 22

What Education Do You Have?

*I*nterviewers glean more from your answers about education and training than just the facts. What you say reveals your decision-making processes, your values, your ability to keep up with the times, and your willingness to adapt to a technology-driven global economy.

In addition to dealing with touchy issues that job seekers of any age or experience level may encounter — like not having a degree or other educational credential — this chapter homes in on inquiries often directed at two specific groups:

- ✔ *Boomers,* a young-at-heart generation toting around a few extra years of experience. (See Chapter 17 for interviewing tips for people over 50.)

- ✔ *Millennials* (those born after 1980), fresh faces on the work scene and typically recent college gradates. (See Chapter 15 for interviewing tips for new college graduates.)

When You Are Degree-less

What can you do when all the jobs you want seem to require a college degree and you don't have one? Or you have an undergraduate degree and the job requires a graduate degree? Or you have the "wrong" degree?

Your moves depend upon whether you want to make a play for the degree-requiring job without additional education or make a commitment to higher learning.

Talking around an education obstacle

If you must address your lack of required education, discuss your experience and skills as education. Speak of *experience-based knowledge and skills*, for instance, and redirect the conversation to your self-teaching efforts. Assure the interviewer that your degree-less state does not affect your ability to do the job well. Use specific examples from your experience to prove this point.

Using experience as education won't change anyone's mind when the education requirement is rigid — as it is in health fields, for example. But it may keep your candidacy afloat when an educational requirement is simply a convenient screening device.

You have at your disposal three more strategies that don't require returning to school:

- ✔ **Persevere:** Continue interviewing at companies too small to operate a human resource department. HR staffers are paid to exclude applicants who miss job criteria, including education.

- ✔ **Work short-term:** Seek staffing firms that will send you on temporary or contract assignments so that employers can see how good you are and offer you a regular-status job.

- ✔ **Network:** Try an online career network, such as LinkedIn.com to find a contact within your target company who will see that you're interviewed by a hiring manager. The hiring manager is advised that you are so talented that your experience is more than equivalent to a degree.

For talented liars, warnings against telling big, fat lies fall on deaf ears. But rarely a month passes without headlines revealing that yet another liar has been busted. As I write this, stories are in every newspaper about an often-quoted dean of admissions for a top East Coast university who was canned for claiming imaginary degrees from three institutions of higher education.

Although her lies didn't catch up with her for 28 years, the time period of discovery may shrink dramatically as Google and other search engines make headway on providing Internet surfers easy access to reams of public records — including education.

Heading back to school

If you enroll in a formal degree program, be sure to mention this fact when explaining that you don't have a sheepskin now but are hot on the trail of a degree.

My experience in the point-of-sale industry more than compensates for my present lack of a marketing degree. (Cite several examples showing you know what you're talking about.) However, I can see that a degree is important to you, and I want to mention that I'm enrolled in a degree program now, with expected graduation in 20XX. So you have the best of both worlds with me — heavy-duty experience, plus current academic knowledge.

But if smoothing out the scratches on your blackboard with a heavy schedule of classes at a four-year campus while pounding away at your day job is more than you can tackle right now, consider these options:

- ✔ Kick off your educational comeback in slow motion. Begin with one class in a modestly-priced community college course.

- ✔ Enroll in distance education degree programs. Costs vary considerably, from such private institutions as the University of Phoenix on the high end, to such public institutions as New Jersey's Thomas Edison State College on the low end. Look online at www.geteducated.com and www.petersons.com/distancelearning.

- ✔ Take advantage of a new kind of free online "auditing" opportunity offered by some of the nation's finest colleges and universities.

  The trend started with Massachusetts Institute of Technology's *Open-CourseWare* in 2003; by the end of 2007, MIT hopes to publish materials from virtually all of its 1,800 courses.

  Joining the list of name colleges and universities offering free course materials online are Yale, Notre Dame, Bryn Mawr, University of California, Berkeley, and Stanford. Specifics vary by school but institutions are posting everything from lecture notes and sample tests to actual audio and video.

- ✔ Sign up for lectures. These are not degree-granting programs, but if you enroll in one for the joy of learning, you can mention in a job interview that you are "enrolled at MIT, 2007, Physics II."

You're probably besieged with Internet spam advertising "overnight" delivery of impressive college degrees: *Get a Harvard law degree tomorrow, only $29.95.* Don't fall for such nonsense. Degree-mill documents are suitable for shredding. In a new age of instant Internet sleuthing, truth will out.

Boomers: High on Adaptability

Interviewers concentrate on your work experience, but you should still expect them to ask about your education or training. They want to know whether you're rusted out or ready to keep up with your industry by making the effort to learn new skills.

Education and training come in many forms. In addition to colleges and universities, vocational-technical institutions, private career schools, and military schools, discuss other learning resources such as the following:

- Company training programs you've participated in and what you learned in those training programs.

- Trade or professional journals that you read regularly, in print or online.

- Professional conferences, seminars, and workshops that you've attended recently (or plan to attend soon), especially those offering CEUs (continuing education credits).

- Teleseminars and Webinars through which you find new information.

- Computer training that you've had, are taking, or expect to take; when appropriate, use computer jargon during your interviews.

However you address employers' questions about education and training, communicate that although you're focused, you're flexible about the way you get the work done. You don't expect to do a job the same way tomorrow that you did yesterday. You've continued to learn new trends and developments in your field throughout your career — and certainly you're always willing to learn more.

The Questions

What do you do to keep up to date in your job? How do you improve yourself professionally?

ShowStoppers

- Describe your participation in professional associations, seminars, meetings and activities, and Internet professional discussion groups.

- Say you study professional magazines and online professional sites, look for technical breakthroughs, and seek certifications that document your continued skill-building (describe certifications).

- Discuss classes and programs in which you're enrolled.

Clunkers and Bloopers

- Be nonspecific in saying you keep your radar up.

- Look uncomfortable and mumble that you plan to return to school soon.

Of what value do you consider academic degrees?

ShowStoppers

- ✔ Comment that when matched with solid experience, the degrees are excellent.

- ✔ Remark that degrees are essential but you must continue to learn throughout your life.

- ✔ If you have no degree, assert that human traits and skills are as important as education and that your record shows you have the background to succeed in this position.

- ✔ Reply that you'll let your work achievements and interpersonal skills speak for you.

Clunkers and Bloopers

- ✔ Knock the value of formal education. Say it's overrated.

- ✔ Observe that you've been too busy at home raising a family to stay current with all the things changing in the world today.

I see you've been attending a training program online. Do you believe distance education is as beneficial as sitting in a classroom?

ShowStoppers

- ✔ Say *yes*. Defend your education. Be positive, responding that what you know is the important issue — not where you learned it.

- ✔ Identify the institution's accreditation. Say that your study was designed by the best minds in the field. Mention any honors accorded your online program.

- ✔ Be confident, noting that some educators think online students are more committed than campus students — that their motivation is stronger. Say that from personal perseverance, you agree.

- ✔ Add that the experience immensely improved your computer skills.

Clunkers and Bloopers

- ✔ Apologize, lamenting that distance education was the only way you could manage to work and learn.

- ✔ Explain that your only online class was really for life enrichment, not for work.

Boomers: Updated education is marketable

"Once we thought that you went to college or career training, graduated, and went on with your life,"observes **Mark S. James** CPC, President and CEO of Hire Consulting Services (www.hireconsultant.com). "Now we know that lifelong employability and enjoyability come with the price tag of constant vigilance in keeping your skills up to date."

Millennials: High on Education, Low on Experience

Education is magnificent, but you can't count on education.

You have to look focused. You have to look passionate about what you want to do. You have to show how your education has prepared you for the job you target.

Whenever possible, present your education as work experience. If that seems like a reach, think of it this way:

- ✔ You have experience working with deadlines and with applying skills that you've learned throughout the years as you completed various projects.

- ✔ You've probably given at least one presentation, so you've had experience preparing it, and you have experience communicating to a group of people.

- ✔ To get through school without killing yourself, you probably had to develop some type of time schedule, so you have valuable experience in time management — organizing your time for greatest efficiency.

Don't neglect any of these important experiences.

The Questions

Questions you may be asked that are related to education and training include the following:

Why did you attend (name of school)? What factors influenced your choice of school?

ShowStoppers

- ✔ Describe the process that you went through to determine which school you wanted to attend, such as matching the schools to your career plans, visiting the schools, and talking to faculty.

- ✔ Discuss at least four specific reasons why you chose your school, focusing on career-related programs and academic considerations such as distinguished faculty, research opportunities, student government programs, leadership opportunities in campus organizations, or school reputation.

Clunkers and Bloopers

- ✔ Say you chose your school because of its great social life or because your best friend went there.

- ✔ Say you made a mistake in choosing your school.

How or why did you choose your major? What factors led to your decision to choose your major?

ShowStoppers

- ✔ Show that you took a deliberate, systematic approach in choosing your major, focusing on future career goals.

- ✔ If you studied liberal arts, respond that you sought to learn how to reason, research, and communicate as well as do. Explain that you put meat on academic bones with practical, career-oriented courses, seminars, internships, co-op education programs, and extracurricular activities.

- ✔ Discuss the courses you've taken that are most job-related and show how they can help you meet the challenges of the job.

- ✔ Show that your choice was logical considering your interests and skills.

Clunkers and Bloopers

- ✔ Ramble or give vague answers.

- ✔ Say you chose the same major as the Homecoming Queen, based on her advice.

How has your education prepared you for working as a (job title)? How has your education benefited you? What specific work-related courses have you taken? How has your education helped with your current job?

ShowStoppers

- ✔ Give specific examples of how the skills and abilities you learned in school can be transferred to the job.
- ✔ Emphasize that your education has not only provided you with job skills but has prepared you to learn new skills throughout your career.
- ✔ Discuss the online research skills you learned at school.
- ✔ Cover your leadership activities and how that leadership experience transfers to the job.
- ✔ Mention experience you have with teamwork and how that will help you on the job.
- ✔ Explain how your education has expanded your mind, opening you up to new ideas or perspectives.
- ✔ Give specific examples of career-related problems you solved or results you have achieved.
- ✔ Observe that your college internships (or co-op education) gave you good work experience you can apply on this job, such as the necessity to meet deadlines, work within a budget, follow your boss's lead, and more.

Clunkers and Bloopers

- ✔ Give vague grasping-for-straws answers.
- ✔ Recite a list of the courses you took (unless asked to do so).

What was your grade point average?

ShowStoppers

If your grade point average was low

- ✔ Give positive reasons for a poor or marginal grade point average (GPA). You had to work virtually full time to pay for your school and living expenses. For jobs working with people, you devoted much time to "real life" experiences, such as leadership positions in campus organizations.
- ✔ Emphasize that your grades within your major are excellent or that they improved dramatically the last two years. Cite reasons why your grades improved.

✔ Emphasize that success in academics and in the job requires more than a high GPA. Discuss the skills you learned outside of your course work that can contribute to your success.

✔ Remark how your GPA gradually rose as you learned better study habits and say that you wish you had learned them sooner.

✔ Answer the question and quickly redirect the discussion to your skills and how you can apply those skills to the job.

✔ Give specific examples of your success in job-related pursuits, outside of your GPA.

If you have an impressive GPA

✔ Emphasize that your education extends beyond the classroom. Discuss extracurricular activities and what you learned from them that you can apply to the job.

✔ Explain the factors that are common between a high GPA and success on the job, such as organizing, prioritizing, and commitment to goals.

Clunkers and Bloopers

✔ Say you don't know why you got a low GPA.

✔ Confess any weaknesses, unless you can show how you have overcome them.

✔ Offer transparent alibis for poor grades.

✔ Assert that grades aren't important or be defensively arrogant.

What extracurricular activities did you participate in? What leadership positions did you hold?

ShowStoppers

✔ Emphasize goal-oriented activities or groups over "fun" ones. About sororities and fraternities — carefully mention only leadership and doing good works, not the social aspect; otherwise, nonmembers may think "party animal" and write you off.

✔ Discuss all leadership roles, teamwork, and self-motivation; explain how those experiences will help you in the job.

✔ Discuss skills you learned from the activities or groups and how those skills apply to the job.

✔ Explain that you had to work so many hours that being active in campus groups would have left you with too little time for your course work.

- ✔ If you didn't join campus organizations until later in your education, say you wish you had joined them sooner, emphasizing what those organizations taught you.

- ✔ Mention all elected offices you held.

Clunkers and Bloopers

- ✔ Mention only good-time social activities without articulating leadership or teamwork experiences drawn from them.

- ✔ Dwell on membership in political or religious groups (unless you know you are talking to a kindred soul who shares your beliefs).

If you could do it over again, would you change your university/major? What didn't you like about school?

ShowStoppers

- ✔ Say you made the right choice and discuss why.

- ✔ Discuss education as more than just courses and college life; it's a broad base for learning and a training ground for meeting challenges.

- ✔ You liked everything about your school — except maybe the high cost of tuition. You have student loan money to pay back and look forward to working hard at a job to do so.

Clunkers and Bloopers

- ✔ Be negative about the school or faculty.

- ✔ Admit that you made a poor decision.

In what areas could your education have better prepared you for your career?

ShowStoppers

- ✔ Your academic studies did not include the quality of hands-on experience you hope to have here, but all-around, your education superbly prepared you for this job.

- ✔ Explain how you made up for lack of experience with student jobs, co-op education, internships, or unpaid work with campus organizations or nonprofit organizations.

Clunkers and Bloopers

✔ Insist that you're totally prepared for your career — you could be vice president of Google tomorrow.

✔ Say that you're not sure how your degree in fine arts will translate to selling medical supplies.

Academically, what were your best and worst courses? What courses did you like best and least?

ShowStoppers

✔ For best courses, choose those that you got the best grades in that were most related to the job.

✔ For worst courses, choose those least related to the job and avoid mentioning courses you did poorly in.

✔ Discuss course content or presentation as reasons for liking or not liking a course.

Clunkers and Bloopers

✔ Name and criticize courses you did poorly in.

✔ Cite poor academic performance as a reason for not liking a course.

Chapter 23

What about Your Special Situation?

The job of the interviewer is two-fold:

- ✔ To find the best match at the best price between the position's requirements and your qualifications

- ✔ To ferret out disqualifications about you — which can range from a mild to serious stumbling block in the interviewer's perception — even though you're not anxious to talk about a particular topic

Perhaps you've been in the same job too long, making you appear to be unmotivated. Maybe you have employment gaps or too many jobs hanging around your neck.

Conceivably you're battling bias against a disability or sexual orientation. Could be that you're a woman who knows an underlying concern may be parental absenteeism — or whether you can supervise men. Or suppose you're in alcohol or drug recovery and crashing into brick walls.

Sometimes you're pretty sure that you're running into rejection because you were fired for cause or demoted. You're very sure that you don't know what to say because you've been convicted of a crime.

Think carefully before discussing special issues. Even a question that seems innocent may cause you to reveal things you didn't mean to tell. For non-sensitive questions, asking for more time to think about your answer is okay. But for special issue answers, you seem more straightforward and sure of yourself when you anticipate the question and are ready with a good answer.

This chapter provides comments and response strategies to help shape your special issue.

When You've Long Been in the Same Job

What could be considered stability by some is increasingly seen as fossilization by others. Your chief strategy is to look industrious, ready to take on any challenge that comes your way, and adaptable to new ideas.

Because you've been with your last employer for so long, do you think you may have a hard time adjusting to a new company's way of working?

ShowStoppers

✔ Not at all. Give examples of how you've already learned to be adaptable — how your previous job was dynamic, provided a constantly changing environment, and shared common links with the new company. Note parallels of budget, business philosophy, and work ethics. You plan to take up mountain climbing and sky diving when you're 80 — figuratively speaking.

✔ Emphasize your commitment to your previous company as one of many assets you bring with you to the new position — and then name more of your assets.

Clunkers and Bloopers

✔ Discuss your relief at escaping that old awful job — at last!

✔ Say you're ready to try something new.

You've been in your previous position an unusually long period of time — why haven't you been promoted?

ShowStoppers

✔ Present the old job in modules (by clusters of skills you developed instead of by your periods of employment). Concentrate on all increases in responsibility (to show upward mobility within the position) and on relevant accomplishments. Note raises.

✔ Say that you're interested in this new job precisely because of the inertia of your previous position. Mention any lifestyle changes (grown kids, second family income) freeing you to make a vigorous move at this time.

✔ Agree that your career hasn't progressed much, but note that many talented people are forced to root or to accept lateral moves because few upwardly mobile job slots are available. Say your career plateau gave you time to reflect, lighting a fire under your motivation.

✔ Explain that you had reached the highest position the company offered individuals in your specialty.

Clunkers and Bloopers

✔ Complain about office politics keeping you down.

✔ Say you were happy where you were and ask, "Why fix what isn't broken?"

When You've Served Prison Time

The key to dealing with prison time is to make the experience as positive as possible. Work double-time to outshine the other candidates with your positive outlook and qualifications for the job.

Here are several tips you may find useful:

✔ Find the best collection of resources that address the criminal record employment dilemma on the following Web site: www.exoffender reentry.com. The resources include books, DVDs, free articles and more. An especially helpful book is *Ex-Offender's Job Hunting Guide: 10 Steps to a New Life in the Work World,* by Ron and Caryl Krannich, PhDs (Impact Publications, 2005). Inmates without access to the Internet will have to rely on family and friends to obtain these resources.

✔ Don't count on *expungement* — the court sealing of criminal records — to keep employers from knowing that you've served time in prison. Expungement is no longer a reliable strategy for ex-offender job seekers because in this digital era, commercial databases are slow to update what courts have forgiven; expunged records now often turn up in criminal background checks ordered by employers.

✔ Job seekers with prison records should be aware of the *Federal Bonding Program* (www.bonds4jobs.com). It basically provides insurance guaranteeing worker honesty — an incentive to employers to hire an at-risk applicant.

✔ The *Work Opportunity Tax Credit* is a tax break for employers who hire certain workers, including ex-offenders. Learn more at this Web site: www.doleta.gov/business/incentives/opptax.

> ✔ The U.S. Military accepts enrollments from those who have served time for misdemeanors and felonies. The pathway to enlist begins with applying for a *moral waiver.* The moral waiver process varies with each military service. Ask military recruiters for more information.

Tell me about your incarceration.

ShowStoppers

> ✔ Describe how it was one of the best learning experiences you've ever had. Explain the crossover (transferable) skills and education you acquired in prison.

> ✔ Say that it helped you make changes in your life so that the behavior that got you in trouble is history. Part of your old problem was hanging out with the wrong people. In your new life you hang out with a different group of people who do not get into trouble.

Clunkers and Bloopers

> ✔ Lie about your conviction, figuring no one will learn about it until after you've been hired. (Why risk a firing on top of your criminal record?)

> ✔ Say you're a victim of bad police work and never should have been in prison (unless technology has cleared you of all charges).

When You're Shoved out the Door

The number-one rule in explaining why you were fired is to keep it brief, keep it honest, and keep it moving. Say what you need to say and redirect the conversation to your qualifications. As for what you should say, you have two core options.

Were you fired from your last job?

ShowStoppers

> ✔ **If it wasn't your fault:**
>
> Explain the firing as a result of downsizing, mergers, company closure, or some other act beyond your control. Sometimes firing happens several times in a row to good people who figuratively happen to be standing on the wrong street corner when the wrong bus comes along. So many people have been on that bus these days that being terminated is no longer a big deal. Being let go wasn't your fault, so you have no reason to feel guilty. Go on with the interview.

✔ **If it was your fault:**

Say you learned an enormous lesson during the experience. You messed up, but you know better now, and you won't make the same mistakes again. Explain briefly how you benefited from this learning experience. Then quickly turn the interview back to the better you and go on to explain how you're the best candidate for the job.

Clunkers and Bloopers

✔ Give interviewers the impression that you're hiding something, that you're not being absolutely honest and open with them.

✔ Bad-mouth your former boss. Say your former coworkers were a freak show.

✔ Tell the interviewer that you've had personality conflicts on more than one job. That admission sets off blaring smoke detectors warning that you're a fiery troublemaker.

Have you ever been asked to resign? Why?

ShowStoppers

✔ Being allowed to resign (a gentler process than being fired for cause) suggests that you may be able to work out a mutually agreeable rationale with your former employer. Do so and stick to that rationale.

✔ When you have no rationale, admit your mistake and say it was a painful lesson that caused a change in your work habits.

Sidelining a series of firings

If you've been fired from a significant number of jobs, few employers will be willing to give you a second chance; understandably, they don't want to deal with the same problems your previous employers did.

The best course for you to take in this situation is to call on a third party's help. Appeal to your family and friends to step in and recommend you to people they know personally who can hire you. Make sure that the people with hiring power are aware of your past mistakes and assure them (honestly) that you've learned from the experiences and have reformed your wicked ways.

Your other most likely options are to obtain additional education or training for a fresh start or consider self-employment.

More answers to why you were fired

To see an additional 12 positive answers to the question, "Why were you fired?" visit my Web site, www.sunfeatures.com; click on Columns; then at the bottom of the left screen, click on Good Answers to Hard Questions.

Clunkers and Bloopers

- ✔ Lie or give excuses to justify why you shouldn't have been treated so unfairly.
- ✔ Rip on your ex-bosses or coworkers for forcing you out.
- ✔ Give multiple examples of your interpersonal conflicts.

When Sexual Orientation Is up for Discussion

"A record number of U.S. companies are competing to expand benefits and protections for their gay, lesbian, bisexual and transgender (GLBT) employees . . ." says a 2006 Human Rights Campaign Foundation (www.hrc.org) report.

In a statement the following year, HRC measured the progress of workplace fairness finding that nine out of ten Fortune 500 (the largest U.S.-based corporations) included gender identity in their non-discrimination policies in 2007. That's ten times as many as were doing so in 2001.

Observers of GLBT employment trends believe that many mid-sized companies also have established formal non-discrimination policies concerning sexual minorities. Arguably, as Monster.com writer Dan Woog put it: "The workplace has come a long way from the days when homosexuality was the elephant in the cubicle."

My research suggests that a generational component is an influential factor in the spread of fairness in workplace sexual orientation issues. As a generality, most younger interviewers seem to be flat-out neutral — not affected one way or the other by a candidate's sexuality. Some older interviewers, who've lived through changing times, may be affected but lean over backwards making sure that all questions are job-related.

But another group of interviewers — of any age— continues to form the "third rail" of interviewing for you. Because of their belief systems or the culture that produced them, these interviewers operate with hard-wired predispositions against sexual minorities, rain or shine.

Even in companies or locales where sexual orientation discrimination is forbidden, homophobic interviewers get away with it because that won't be the reason they give when you're turned down (if you ever even hear back). They find other reasons for your rejection when they have any reason to suspect your sexual orientation is one they disapprove of.

Don't be lulled into complacent mistakes because of the rapid acceleration during the past decade of sexual orientation as a protected class by both company declarations and government (state and local) laws. Discrimination is alive and well.

When you suspect that for a screening interview you've been paired with a closet homophobic whom you'll never see again, don't worry too much because that individual could be an anomaly; if the interviewer is the hiring manager to whom you'd report, worry.

As you evaluate how to move forward in your job search, note that a growing number of job seekers with same-sex orientation reject out of hand the notion of working for companies where they can't be open about their sexual orientation. They say the effort to hide sexual orientation takes a toll on their productivity, as well as their emotional and physical health.

But sometimes the need for employment takes over. When you can't find a workplace where your sexual orientation won't be used against you, and you have rent to pay, you may choose not to disclose.

Here are a few suggestions to smooth your interviewing experience:

- ✔ If you choose to disclose, wait until the interviewer either shows enormous interest in your qualifications and you know an offer is eminent, or until the offer is actually made. Some savvy advisers recommend that you wait until you have a written offer letter in hand.

- ✔ Thoroughly research the company's culture and civil rights policies before the interview. Look for companies that proclaim a nondiscriminatory policy on sexual orientation. Look for a company that offers a domestic partner benefits plan to life partners.

✔ How can you tell whether fairness happy talk is real or window dressing? Ask members of GLBT support networks what they know about a company where you plan to interview. And look at GLBT Web sites and job boards for lists of friendly employers and detailed job hunting advice. Key resources include the following:

- Human Rights Campaign (www.hrc.org)

- Gay Financial Network (www.gfn.com)

- Progayjobs.com (www.progayjobs.com)

- GayJob.biz (www.gayjob.biz)

- Diversity Working (www.diversityworking.com)

- Monster.com (career-advice.monster.com/gay-lesbian-bisexual-transgender/home.aspx) and in Canada (diversity.monster.ca)

Although you won't be asked directly about your sexual orientation, an interviewer may — inadvertently or purposely — nibble around the edges with inappropriate personal questions.

ShowStoppers

Is there a special woman in your life? How's your marriage?

✔ *A nondisclosure answer:* You consider a number of women special in your life (meaning your mother, your sister, and your aunt), or just say you're not married yet.

✔ *A confirming but neutral answer:* Say you're gay and in a stable relationship. Your sexual orientation bears no relationship to your work. It's not a problem for you and you hope it isn't a problem for the company.

Clunkers and Bloopers

✔ Bluntly refuse to discuss your personal life.

✔ Ask whether the interviewer is married.

I see you that when you were a college student, you were president for a year of the Fairness Group — can you tell me about that?

ShowStoppers

✔ Note that the Fairness Group is a campus anti-discrimination organization. It has 75 members. As president for two years, you were the group's representative in student government and participated in official greeting events with visiting dignitaries. All your duties weren't so visible — you also led planning for fundraising activities, balanced the checkbook and helped clean up after events.

✔ Explaining that after leading the Fairness Group as president for two years, you received a Campus Leader Award from the university's chancellor; ask whether the interviewer would like to see it (from your portfolio).

Clunkers and Bloopers

✔ Answer only that it was a political action group for GLBT students.

✔ State that the Fairness Group is an organization purposed to be fair to all students in all ways.

When You've Worked Everywhere

In an era of contract workers and just-in-time temporary hirings and tossing employees overboard to boost already healthy profits for stockholders, I'm always surprised to hear employers object to "job hopping." I shouldn't be.

Employers favor candidates with a track record of staying a "reasonable" amount of time at previous jobs. They assume the past predicts the future and so the candidate will stay as long as they're wanted at their company.

The kicker is the meaning of "reasonable amount of time." The current group-think narrative places a minimum stay in a job at two to three years. This arbitrary time frame does not mean that you shouldn't cut your losses and leave if you're in a bad job — circumstances vary widely. It does mean you need to give plenty of thought to how you handle a job-hopper question and deal with it in a logical, convincing, and upbeat answer.

You've changed jobs more frequently than is usual — why is that?

ShowStoppers

✔ List accomplishments on each job that relate to the position you seek. Note that you built new skills in each job. Say that you're a person who contributes value wherever you go.

✔ Give acceptable, verifiable reasons why you changed jobs so frequently — project-oriented work, downsizing, dead-end positions, company sold out, or the department shut down.

✔ Say that you've become more selective lately, and you hadn't been able to find the right job until this opportunity came along; explain your employment travels as a quest for a fulfilling job.

✔ If this move is a career change for you, show how your experience and skills support this change and how the position fits your revised career goals.

✔ If your positions were for temporary agencies, cluster them by responsibility and recast them as evidence of your use of cross-functional skills in many situations.

✔ Ask whether this is regular-status employment. If so, admit you've lacked some commitment in the past, but now you're ready to settle down with a good company such as this one. If not, say a temporary job is just what you have in mind to keep your skills refreshed with experiences gained at various companies.

Clunkers and Bloopers

✔ Complain about what was wrong with each of your ex-employers that made you quit. Say you didn't want to waste your time working for dysfunctional people and organizations.

✔ Show a lack of focus — you just couldn't get into your jobs.

✔ Say you're looking for something that pays more.

When Gaps Shred Your History

Employers may rush to judgment when gaps are found in your job history.

If your job history has as many gaps as a hockey player's teeth, try to find growth experiences (self-directed study or broadening travel). If you must blame your jobless patches on sick leave, emphasize that you have recovered and are in excellent health. If personal problems take the hit (ill parent or sick child), again follow up with facts that indicate the personal problems are history.

When your record is spotty beyond belief, try to get on with a temporary job and then prove by your work record that you've turned over a new leaf.

Sometimes the gaps in your record are of recent vintage — you've been looking for employment without success for a very long time. In current periods of unemployment, your posture is commitment — you throw yourself heart and soul into your work and you want to be very sure to find a good fit. Explain your waiting period as a quest for a fulfilling job.

How long have you been job hunting? Wow! That's a long time — what's the problem? Why haven't you had any job offers yet?

ShowStoppers

✔ Say you've become more selective lately, and you hadn't been able to find the right job until this opportunity came along.

- ✔ If you were given a sizable severance package, explain how it financially allowed you to take your time searching for the perfect next move.

- ✔ Admit your career hasn't progressed as much as you'd like, but the good news is you've had time to think through your life direction, you've re-assessed your career, and you feel focused now. You're fueled up and ready to go!

- ✔ Explain that while you're good at building consensus (through compromise) with others, you haven't been willing to settle for a job that doesn't maximize your skills and qualifications. And that low-end jobs are all that have turned up in this market until now. Clarify that you've taken your time to find the perfect job fit because the position is very important to you.

Clunkers and Bloopers

- ✔ Say you don't know what the problem is.

- ✔ Gripe abut how many opportunities you've missed out on because recruiters don't recognize your true worth.

- ✔ Look depressed and admit that you're becoming discouraged.

When You're Demoted a Notch

Oddly, demotion carries more negative weight than does firing today. Demotion suggests personal failure; firing doesn't, unless you're fired for cause.

Do I read this resume right — were you demoted?

ShowStoppers

- ✔ Your best move is to deal with demotions before you reach the interview. Ask your demoting boss for a positive reference (see my book, *Resumes For Dummies,* 5th Edition) and come to an agreement about what happened that's favorable to you — assuming your boss knows you're looking around and doesn't mind helping you leave.

- ✔ Explain honestly and as positively as possible the reasons for your send-down.

- ✔ Admit that you weren't ready for the responsibility at that time, but now you are. Describe the actions you have taken to grow professionally — school courses in deficient areas, management seminars, management books, and introspection.

> ✔ Affirm that you're looking for a good place to put your new and improved management skills to use, and you hope that place is where you are interviewing. Quickly remind interviewers that you're qualified for the job you're interviewing for, and back that up with examples of your skills and quantified achievements.

Clunkers and Bloopers

> ✔ Lie or try to shift the blame to ABY (anybody but you).
>
> ✔ Accuse management of unreasonable expectations.

When People in Recovery Interview

Networking is the way many people in substance recovery get job interviews, with the result that the referring party often has revealed your background to the interviewer.

When you're sure that the interviewer is well aware of your substance history, find a way to introduce the topic on your terms: *I am a better-than-average qualified candidate for this job. As you know, I have fought the substance abuse battle and won.*

Emphasize that you are a tested, proven individual who has survived a crucible, taken control of your life, and grown into a stronger person. Try not to become mired in interminable details of your recovery, but stick to your main theme of being a well-qualified applicant who overcame an illness and is now better equipped to meet new challenges.

As soon as you think you have tapped into the interviewer's sense of fairness, redirect the conversation to reasons that you should be hired. But until you calm the interviewer's anxiety about your recovery, the interviewer won't truly hear anything you say about your strengths and qualifications.

 Seek more advice on doing well in job interviews when you have red flags such as drug or alcohol abuse in your background. Read *Job Interview Tips for People With Not-So-Hot Backgrounds,* by Ron and Caryl Krannich, PhDs (Impact Publications, 2004).

Head-on questions in a job interview are unlikely to be asked — *Do you drink more than you should? Do you use drugs?* But you may be indirectly questioned.

We have a drug testing policy for all employees. Do you object to that?

ShowStoppers

- ✔ Answer that no, you don't object. You don't use drugs or alcohol. You are very healthy, clear-thinking, and reliable. You are in a 12-step or another recovery program and have been substance-free for a year. Discuss your qualifications for the position.

- ✔ Tell the interviewer *no* and add that you have no health problems that would prevent you from giving 100-percent effort on every assignment.

Clunkers and Bloopers

- ✔ Say you're doing your best to get your life back together; to prove it you've attended four rehab programs in the past two years. You just need a chance at a good job to keep you clean (sober).

- ✔ Say you had some problems in the past and give no details about how you kicked substance abuse.

When Women Are Put on the Spot

News flash! Young women of child-bearing age battle questions about family matters.

Research companies for family-friendly policies before you apply. For example, women's magazines regularly run stories identifying the best of national companies that promote work-life balance. Use your networks and search local newspaper stories to find similar small and mid-sized companies where you live.

When you have small fry and you choose to stay home with them but you still need the pay, contemplate alternatives: working part-time, pairing up with another person to do the same job (job sharing), taking your work home (telecommuting), and rearranging work schedules without cutting productive hours (flextime).

Get quality career advice and job postings for all types of jobs by visiting Nancy Collamer's JobsandMoms.com (www.jobsandmoms.com). Check out the expanding and unique long-term, part-time placement service for college-educated individuals at 10 til 2 (www.tentiltwo.com).

Is becoming a major business player more your dream than hanging out with growing kids? Lois Frankel, PhD, has long had her finger on the pulse of why women succeed or stumble. She's the author of a shelf of widely acclaimed books of what works for women who work; find her wisdom — which includes good ammo for answers to gender questions — at www.drloisfrankel.com.

In the meantime, standard responses to the subtle (or not so subtle) probes about the patter of little feet: Kids are way, way in the future because (say why); the lifestyle you'd like to grow accustomed to requires a two-income family; you have super-reliable child care (explain).

When cornered, try this tactic to assure you won't become a staffing problem down the line: *Whether or not I plan to have children in the future is not central to my career. Like so many other energetic women today, I intend to work and have a career no matter what happens in my personal life.*

What are your career plans?

ShowStoppers

✔ This job meets your immediate career plan. It allows you to be a solid producer yet build on your already strong skills. You will work hard at this job to prove yourself and accept greater responsibility as it is offered. You're reasonably ambitious. You don't plan to relocate.

✔ Making career plans five years out is not realistic in today's rapidly changing job market. But you're excited about developing new nanotechnology (or whatever) engineering and this job is exactly what you seek. Your background makes you a perfect fit — (details).

Clunkers and Bloopers

✔ You expect a promotion within a year (suggesting that you'll be unhappy if you don't quickly rise through the ranks).

✔ You haven't a particular goal in mind.

What is your management style?

ShowStoppers

✔ Explain how your management style is compatible with the company culture (you researched that culture on the company Web site). Incorporate contemporary management style language (you read a few magazines and recent books on the language of business today). No marbles in your mouth when you state how you handle insubordination, motivation, serious mistakes, and other supervisory issues.

✔ Explain that you don't flinch at making tough decisions and implementing them. But you're not a bully or a screamer. Storytell: Give true examples of how you've handled past supervisory problems.

Clunkers and Bloopers

✔ Give a vague answer on management style revealing your naiveté.

✔ Out-macho a male interviewer or seem to be too lightweight for the job.

When Disabilities Are up for Disclosure

The Americans with Disabilities Act severely limits what interviewers can ask people with disabilities prior to offering a job. If you have a visible disability, you may benefit by giving an explanation of how you're able to do the job.

Essentially, the ADA permits an interviewer to ask you about your abilities to perform a job, but not about your disabilities. As an astute employer once said, "We are not interviewing a disability. We are not hiring a disability. We are looking to hire a person who can do the job we want done."

Suppose an interviewer asks: "How is your health?" Just explain that you're able to perform tasks that the job requires. (But if you have an obvious disability, the ADA makes the question illegal at the pre-offer stage.)

For a quick brush-up on your rights in job interviews, scour the federal Labor Department's Office of Disability Employment Policy (`www.dol.gov/odep`; click on Frequently Asked Questions).

Examples of questions to expect include the following:

You say you can do the job. How would that work? Can you explain more?

ShowStoppers

✔ When practical, ask to give a demonstration — if practical, bring your own equipment.

✔ When a demonstration is impractical, pull an example from your last job (paid or volunteer) or educational experience. Storytell: Recount a true tale of your having been there, done that.

✔ Anticipate essentials to job performance (anything in the job description) the interviewer may be worried about — such as physical mobility, safety, and motor coordination. If you have vision or hearing impairment, expect some concerns that you'll miss visual or aural cues essential to job performance. Explain how you've adapted in these areas or will overcome obstacles.

✔ Suggest a few references (previous teachers, counselors, employers, or coworkers) who can testify to your abilities to do the job.

Clunkers and Bloopers

- ✔ Show you're offended by the question — soapbox about unspoken bias.
- ✔ Explain that your coworkers have always set aside their work to assist you with problematic tasks.
- ✔ Without examples to support your claims, assert you have no problems with job performance.

Because you're our first applicant with a disability, we've never dealt with accommodations before. How much are these accommodations going to cost us?

ShowStoppers

- ✔ Promise that your requirements are minimal and give examples of how your skills will merit the company's small investment. Get cost estimates on the Job Accommodation Network (www.jan.wvu.edu).
- ✔ Offer to provide some of your own equipment (you aren't required to do so, but the offer shows serious interest in contributing to the company).
- ✔ Offer information on accommodations, such as telephone numbers for companies that sell accommodations devices or consultant organizations specializing in accommodations.

Clunkers and Bloopers

- ✔ Name a costly price for all the equipment you could possibly need, assuming the company can afford the expense.
- ✔ Act demanding because you think that the ADA is protecting you — the interviewer on the lookout for litigious types won't hire a bad attitude.
- ✔ Cite the ADA requirements and threaten to sic your attorney on them. If you sue, hope you win enough money to not need a job — ever! (Companies have access to databases of individuals who have sued other employers, and they resist hiring litigious applicants.)

Chapter 24

How Should You Answer an Inappropriate Question?

Is that a Spanish name?

What year did you graduate from high school?

Are you a Christian?

All of the above are foolish questions in a job interview. Every human resource specialist in America knows this. But other interviewers who don't deal with employment issues on a regular basis and who are unsophisticated cross the line and ask personal, intrusive, discriminatory questions all the time.

You find a sample of risky questions in Table 24-1. But, in general, employers shouldn't ask about any of the following topics:

✔ Age

✔ Birthplace

✔ Color

✔ Disability

✔ Marital/family status

✔ National origin

✔ Race

✔ Religion

✔ Sex

Should you set off sirens if an interviewer has the audacity to toss you a possibly discriminatory question that shouldn't be asked? Should you flame the transgressor with passive-aggressive answers like the following:

How is my marital status a factor in the selection process for this job?

As you know, under Title VII, basing employment decisions on sex is illegal, and I feel that this question is discriminatory in nature.

Think twice about verbally punching out an interviewer — especially if job talk is going well otherwise and you're thinking that this could be the right place for you.

The landscape has changed during the past decade, and maybe you should revise your attitude about the need to stand up for your rights in response to every single questionable question — for your own advantage. Consider these factors:

✔ People incautiously are posting their inner moments and life events on social networking and blog Web sites. That's where recruiters are discovering revelations about family plans, church activities, health issues, personal disasters, and more. When so much voluntarily announced personal information is posted online for all eyes, there's no need for employers to resort to asking risky questions.

✔ More ways your past and current situation can be revealed include the employment background check, of which a credit report may be a part.

From a relatively few employers who did so a dozen years ago, today most companies conduct employment background checks on potential employees. The check-ups range from criminal records searches and civil litigation history to educational background, job history, credit reports, and Social Security verifications.

The use of employment background checks has skyrocketed because of three main reasons:

• Post-9/11 security cautions.

• Workplace violence concerns about hiring potentially violent people.

• Lack of information from references. Background checks serve as the reference of last resort in a time of tight-lipped employers. (Employers are stingy with reference information to avoid legal liability by revealing more about former employees than the "name/rank/serial number" basics.)

✔ People who suspect their rights have been trampled aren't so quick to pull the legal trigger these days in part because of the growing realization that employment discrimination litigation isn't famous for big money awards.

And employment litigation can drag on and on. Even preliminary action by the Equal Employment Opportunity Commission doesn't happen overnight (if ever).

When you sue, your name is likely to end up in a civil litigation database that future potential employers may see, perhaps causing them to decide that you're a troublemaker. Can you spell *pariah?*

Defining Illegal Questions

Let's talk terms. An *illegal question* is one that the interviewer has no legal right to ask. Most states and large cities have laws restraining employers from going hog-wild with intrusive questions covering civil rights — age, sex, religion, race, ethnicity, sexual orientation, and so forth. Asking illegal questions can get the interviewer (in a company that retains lawyers) in big trouble.

To find out what's what in your locale, get the facts. You can inquire at your state or city attorney general's office. A library may have a list of questions that shouldn't be asked, according to state or local laws.

Why Interviewers Ask Inappropriate Questions

In large companies where interviewers should know better but don't, interviewers may go on fishing expeditions, hoping that weird, unexpected questions catch candidates without prepared answers, causing them to make unintended revelations.

In companies where interviewers do know better, some go ahead and ask risky questions because they want the information and are willing to gamble that they won't be challenged.

An *inappropriate* question is one the interviewer can legally ask, but probably shouldn't. Depending on whether the information is used to discriminate, inappropriate questions set up employers for lawsuits, a threat their corporate lawyers constantly warn against. Inappropriate questions range from civil rights and privacy issues to hard-to-classify bizarre inquiries:

- *Is your girlfriend white?*
- *How would you go about making a pizza?*
- *If you were at a departmental meeting and a coworker put his hand on your thigh, what would you do?*

Club fed's forbidden questions

Discrimination law is ever-changing and complex. Contrary to popular understanding, no such thing as a list of questions prohibited by federal law exists, except for these two questions:

1. *Have you ever been arrested?*

2. *How's your health?*

An employer can't ask about your arrest record because an arrest isn't an admission of guilt. The Americans with Disabilities Act forbids pre-employment questions asking about a candidate's health, but asking about an individual's ability to perform job-related tasks — *Can you stand for long periods of time?* — is okay.

Other than questions about arrests and health, interviewers can ask any questions they wish as far as the feds are concerned. (Of course, they may pay a stiff penalty for bias.) Federal law merely notes subjects — based on disability and civil rights, such as visible and invisible impairments, race, sex, age, and so on — that can be the basis for bias complaints and prohibit discriminatory treatment on these grounds.

Illegal questions are always inappropriate, but inappropriate questions are not always illegal.

Redirect Inappropriate Questions

If you're a crusader and fighting injustice is your priority, by all means tell the interviewer the illegal or inappropriate question is off-base and shame on the interviewer.

But perhaps another, frankly foxier, approach will work better for you, especially if you think the interviewer's questions come from ignorance rather than bias. Redirect the offensive question.

Suppose the interviewer asks a question about age:

> *I see you went to the University of Colorado. My son's there now. When did you graduate?*

The smooth candidate directly responds to the question, sort of:

> *I don't think your son and I know each other. I'm sure he's a fine young man. As for me, fortunately, I've been out of school long enough to have developed good judgment. Would you like to know a little about how my good judgment saved a previous employer $25,000?*

Another way to redirect is to answer the question you want to answer, not necessarily the question that's asked. (Politicians do so all the time.) Using the same situation, here's an example of how a smooth candidate cherry-picks the conversation:

> _You mention the University of Colorado, such a fine school. In addition to taking my undergraduate degree there, I returned last summer for an intensive executive management course that prepared me for exactly the kind of position we're discussing now. Would you like to hear more about how I am a good match for the financial oversight functions of this position?_

Religion is another slippery-slope question not to answer directly. Suppose, for example, you're asked if you'll need time off to celebrate Passover — or any religious holiday. Try this approach:

> _I understand your concern about the time I will need to observe my religious beliefs, but let me assure you that if this time has any bearing on my job performance at all, it will only be positive, because the inspiration of my beliefs will help me stay renewed, fresh, and mentally focused._

Notice the answer makes no mention of specific religious holidays, it doesn't refuse to answer, and it doesn't confront the interviewer with the discriminatory nature of the question.

If a question is repugnant or blatantly discriminatory, don't answer it at all or answer it your way — unless the question is off the wall, and then you may need to stand firm. For example, an in-your-face answer to an earlier question — _Is your girlfriend white?_ — might be

> _I do not feel that specific, intimate details of my personal life would be appropriate to discuss here. They do not affect my ability to effectively perform the duties of this position._ (Translation: Back off.)

Sometimes you have to establish your boundaries firmly. But in general, if you want the job, avoid becoming confrontational and answer all the questions to your benefit. If the questioner would be your boss and is such a jerk that you don't want the job, find a polite way of uttering your exit line and just get out.

Inappropriate and Illegal Questions

Table 24-1 illustrates inappropriate or illegal questions you hope you never hear. Decide in advance how you'll respond to clunkers like these — just in case. When the question is expressed in an appropriate version, give a straightforward answer.

Table 24-1:	Questions That Shouldn't Be Asked	
Topic	**Inappropriate or Illegal Questions**	**Appropriate Versions**
Age	• What is your date of birth? • How old are you?	• If hired, can you furnish proof that you are over age 18? • None.
Arrest and Conviction	• Have you ever been arrested?	• Have you ever been convicted of a crime? If so, when, where, and what was the disposition of the case?
Citizenship/ National Origin	• What is your national origin? • Where are your parents from?	• Are you legally eligible for employment in the United States?
Credit Record	• Have your wages ever been garnished? • Have you ever declared bankruptcy?	• Credit references may be used if in compliance with the Fair Credit Reporting Act of 1970 and the Consumer Credit Reporting Reform Act of 1996.
Disabilities	• Do you have any disabilities?	• Can you perform the duties of the job you are applying for?
Education	• When did you graduate from high school or college?	• Do you have a high school diploma or equivalent? • Do you have a university or college degree?
Family	• Number of children? • Who is going to baby-sit? • Do you have pre-school age children at home? • What is your marital status?	• What hours and days can you work? • Do you have responsibilities other than work that will interfere with specific job requirements such as traveling?
Home	• Do you own your own home?	• None.

Topic	Inappropriate or Illegal Questions	Appropriate Versions
Language	• What is your native language?	• Inquiry into use of how candidate acquired ability to read, write or speak a foreign language. • Inquiry into languages candidate speaks and writes fluently. (If the job requires additional languages.)
Military Record	• What type of discharge did you receive?	• What type of education, training, work experience, did you receive while in the military?
Organizations	• List all clubs, societies and lodges to which you belong. • Are you a union member?	• Inquiry into candidate's membership in organizations which the candidate considers relevant to his or her ability to perform job.
Personal	• What color are your eyes, hair? • What is your weight?	• Only permissible if there is a bona fide occupational qualification.
Religion	• Inquiry into candidate's religious denomination, religious affiliations, church, parish, pastor or religious holidays observed.	• Are there specific times that you cannot work?
Worker's Compensation	• Have you ever filed for worker's compensation? • Have you had any prior work injuries?	• None. • None.

Part V
The Part of Tens

The 5th Wave   By Rich Tennant

"It was an interview at a law firm. I thought they'd appreciate my creative use of the 5th Amendment."

In this part . . .

Here you find the short films of job interview information. I give you three quick chapters — one that leads you through ten ways to show off your star quality in an interview and another full of fun takes on job interviews from superstars. The final chapter runs down personalities you might encounter in the interview theater.

Chapter 25

Ten Tips to Avoid Wretched Reviews

*T*hink klieg lights sweeping the Hollywood sky, stretch limos pulling up to a theater entrance, and celebrities being interviewed by television entertainment show hosts as they make their way up a red carpet into a much ballyhooed movie premiere.

Crazy exciting, right? Until the next morning when the reviews appear. Uh oh. Critics think the movie was a dog. The film's actors and their colleagues are spun off center with verbal depth charges instead of hoped-for praise.

Wretched reviews affect job interviewees too, even though shortcomings in their performances won't become public. When interviewees just don't hear back, they feel the same way as panned actors: awful.

Don't let that unhappy ending happen to you. Do everything you can to make your interview performance earn rich reviews. And to help, a master of job search, Joe Turner (www.jobchangesecrets.com), CEO of Swenson Turner, Inc., a career coaching firm in Phoenix, shares 10 ways you can do just that.

Bring Storytelling into Prime Time

An interview is a conversation. Don't fall into an answers-only rut. That's why you've spent time learning to storytell with true prepared stories that highlight your accomplishments (see Chapter 5). Remember, a conversation is really a series of questions and answers. As soon as you answer a question, try following up with a question of your own.

Go In Knowing Your Lines

About 90 percent of candidates "didn't get the wiki" that their purpose in an interview is to do infinitely more than ask for a job. Not you. You got the wiki.

Your goal is two-fold: First, to demonstrate that you are a good "fit" for the organization — like salt and pepper, bread and butter, Arnold Schwarzenegger and Hummers.

Second, you're looking for breaking news on whether the position is really something you want to invest your life in.

Leave the Begging to Others

Neediness is one of the all-time deal killers in the job market. Whisper in your own ear before walking in the door: "I don't need this job. I do need air, food, and water." Keep things in perspective. Sell your strengths and your ability to do the job. Employers don't hire because they feel sorry for you; they hire because they want you to solve their problems.

Share the Stage with Dignity

Generally speaking, participate in an interview as an equal, not as a subordinate of the person conducting the interview. This doesn't mean you shouldn't show courteous respect to the interviewer, especially if the interviewer is a general and you're a buck private. Participating as an equal is a subtle matter of self-perception, so remind yourself of your status before the interview begins.

Remember How a Star Is Born

From the moment you walk into an interview room, demonstrate confidence. Your first impression makes a difference. Stand up straight, make eye contact, and offer an enthusiastic handshake with your interviewer. If you don't remember names well, jot down the interviewer's name on your notepad as soon as you're seated. Ditto for any other person you're meeting with.

Avoid Ad Libbing Ad Infinitum

Although you should always do your share to keep the conversational flow going, droning on loses your audience. Telling your interviewer more than he or she needs to know could be fatal.

Your stories should be no longer than 60 to 90 seconds and they must — repeat, *must* — have a relevant point related to your topic. Stick with your rehearsed stories, your research, your adequate answers, and the questions you need to ask.

You're looking for an easy give-and-take in your interview without coming across as a motor-mouth.

Keep in Mind That "Friends" Is a Television Show

Don't make the mistake of being overly familiar. A good interviewer is skilled enough to put you at ease within the first 10 minutes of the interview. That doesn't mean that the interviewer has become your best friend. Never let your guard down. Remember that you're there to give and receive information about a position that you may want. From start to finish, treat this encounter as the professional business meeting that it is.

Know That Faulty Assumptions Equal Faulty Interviewing

Think about this scene on a stage: The leading lady is supposed to rush to the leading man as he enters stage right; for some reason, she assumes he'll enter stage left and rushes to an empty space. She looks as though she doesn't know what she's doing.

The same is true when you make a wrong guess at what your interviewer has in mind with a particular question. When in doubt, ask! You don't lose points at an interview for asking questions when you don't have a clear understanding of a point.

Keep Emotions out of the Interview

Sure, this might be a time of stress in your life. The rent's due, the car's on the fritz, or you recently had an argument with your significant other.

Put it all behind you while you're on stage in the spotlight. Here's why: The interviewer may at times consciously attempt to provoke you into a temperamental outburst. Don't fall for it or take it personally. This may be only a part of the interviewing process. Remember, your role is to be cool, calm, and collected — so play the part. When emotions enter an interview, failure follows.

Ask Questions That Show You Care Where You Go

You want to be sure you're getting the true picture of what this job is really about and whether you want it. Arrive with a list of several prepared questions about the company, the position, and the people who work there. Ask questions that begin with "what," "how," and "why." Avoid simple "yes" or "no" questions. Take notes. Most interviewers are unimpressed by a candidate who has no questions — are you disinterested, or do you think you already know everything?

Chapter 26

Tens of Lines on the Cutting Room Floor

In This Chapter

▶ Made-up wacky quotes from famous folks

▶ Have a laugh on me

*Y*ou dutifully finished a whole book of savvy strategies and astute responses. Your big reward arrives when you get the job offer you want. But your immediate reward starts now.

From the Time Machine: News You Can't Use

Job interviews have been around since God interviewed Noah for ship's captain. Here's a totally made-up collection of lines that famous figures in history, literature, and pop culture might say to a job interviewer today. The quips are the creative contribution of Jeffery R. Cox, an attorney in Indianapolis who has a wickedly wild sense of humor. What do you think — would these comments get the job?

Hester Pryne — I bring a talent for marketing, with specific experience in branding.

William the Conqueror — I know I have a reputation for hostile takeovers, but I like to think of them as friendly mergers.

Don Vito Corleone — I was a good boss. I treated my employees like a family, and as you know, nothing is more important than the family.

The Joker — My past employers were all happy with me . . . HA HA . . . my work left them all smiling . . . still does . . . HA HA HA HA . . . I can make you smile, too . . . HA HA HA HA HA HA HA HA.

Zeus — I have to go through a job interview? I used to be the King of the Gods, for cryin' out loud!

Captain Kirk — I boldly took my department where no one had gone before.

Joan of Arc — I may look a little wet behind the ears, but I defeated the world's greatest army, liberated my country, changed the course of history, and my last boss called me a saint.

Sauron — I am proud of my management skills. I like to think I keep a good eye on my employees.

Isaac Newton — My last boss thought I took direction well. I didn't need to be hit on the head to do something.

David — I'm not into size. When it comes to the competition, my thinking is "The bigger they are, the harder they fall."

Harriet Tubman — My specialty is discreet outplacement.

Julius Caesar — My previous job involved a lot of office politics and back-stabbing. I'd like to get away from all that.

Cleopatra — The office politics at my last job were a nightmare. I worked with a bunch of snakes.

Tony Soprano — Would I go after my boss's job? Do I look like the kind of guy who would knock off his boss for a promotion?

Lady Godiva — So, this isn't what you meant by "business casual"?

Genghis Khan — My primary talent is downsizing. On my last job I downsized my staff, my organization, and the populations of a number of countries.

Albert Einstein — I brought my major research project with me. Do you have time for a demonstration?

Pandora — I think I can bring a lot to your company. I like discovering new things.

James Brown — I feel good about your company. OW!

Dracula — I sucked everything I could out of my employees, but I got them to produce. No mean feat since I could only work the night shift.

Hannibal Lecter — I was the victim of communications problems with my old boss. I had him over for dinner and he practically disappeared after that.

Odysseus — We didn't reach our goals overnight, but we got there . . . eventually.

Michelangelo — Can we negotiate on the Sistine ceiling? I'll do the job for 50 percent less if I can use a roller.

Pharaoh (Ramses II) — My main accomplishment? My entire labor force walked out on me, but I still produced.

Robin Hood — My financial management experience? Some may consider it stealing from the rich and giving to the poor, but I saw it as creative reinvestment.

Archimedes — I can do whatever floats your boat.

Faust — I had to make a deal with the devil, but I kept my department under budget.

Cassandra — My greatest weakness? Perhaps it is my skill at seeing the future.

Helen of Troy — I'm not just another pretty face. Although I've been known to launch a thousand ships, I'd like to be known for the skills I bring to the job.

George Washington — If I can lead a successful rebellion and a fledgling country, I'm sure I can lead your insignificant department.

Moses — I can part the red tape to get the job done.

Christopher Columbus — You bet I can open new markets for your company. Put me on the road, and I'll discover a world of opportunity, the likes of which you've never seen.

Napoleon Bonaparte — Okay, I'll start today in the mailroom, but tomorrow . . . the world.

John F. Kennedy — In preparation for this interview, I asked myself not what this company can do for me, but what I can do for this company.

Joseph Guillotine — I think I can give your company a head start on the competition.

William Tell — My last boss told me I always gave everything I did my best shot.

Othello — I demand performance. Even those closest to me were axed when I was told they had let me down.

Lewis & Clark — Big land development plans? Yes, we have experience in scouting out new real estate.

Chiang Kai-shek — While my division was reduced in size, our performance was so excellent that we became a target for takeover.

Richard III — A job! A job! My kingdom for a job!

Chapter 27

Ten Interviewer Personality Types

In This Chapter
▶ Interviewer styles you may encounter
▶ Amusing but useful information

*L*iking people who are like you is human nature. Moreover, job interviewers for companies tend to be representative of the kinds of people at their respective companies.

Using general perspectives (see Chapter 1) as a starting point, look over the following personality types, presented according to my "Latin" designations. Without resorting to a personality transplant, try to strike a pose harmonious with that of your interviewer. For example, if your interviewer is full of courtly charm, let honey drip from your lips; if your interviewer is brisk to the point of brusqueness, stick to the verbal point with virtually no detours.

Heed this mirroring strategy, and you have a better chance of establishing a good rapport.

Achieveus Youngius (Young Achiever)

Achieveus youngius: *A twentysomething, fresh-faced, conservatively dressed, preppie type most commonly seen on college campuses during job fairs; easily tamed; demeanor is cheerful and positive — friendly.*

Approach these specimens with down-home charm, and you have them eating out of your hand. Encourage conversations about extracurricular activities, common interests, leadership positions, admiration for the company, and a lot of enthusiasm. But not for too long.

Specimens of this type have little or no interviewing experience, so help out by asking questions. Doing so puts them at ease. To get the job, focus on demonstrating traits, skills, goals, and experiences that the *achieveus youngius* can relate to.

Businessius Serious (Serious Businessperson)

Businessius serious: Gray-haired, successful, most often seen wearing a slightly rumpled, expensive suit; females are less common than males; demeanor is serious and businesslike.

Approach these specimens with confidence and humility and let them know that you're willing to work your way to the top. Discuss your academic or work achievements, strict work ethic, steadfast dedication to a goal, and leadership skills. Let the *businessius serious* see that you have broad knowledge of the company.

Let this specimen control the interview. To get the job, focus on showing the *businessius serious* exactly what skills you bring to the company and how you can apply those skills toward the position you seek.

Caution: Most specimens of this type are friendly. However, a few have a mutant gene that makes them very dangerous. Watch out for the ones who try to bite you with stress-inducing situations and off-the-wall questions.

Bossus Potentialus (Potential Boss)

Bossus potentialus: Of variegated descriptions; similar to businessius serious; usually found at top of department, looking for help; demeanor is serious and practical.

To identify these specimens, ask whether the *businessius serious* interviewing you would be your direct boss. If so, ask questions about management philosophy. Then present your skills as compatible with that philosophy. For example, if the *bossus potentialus* mentions teamwork, show yourself as a team player.

The *bossus potentialus* values common sense, work experience, and a positive attitude and despises arrogance and immaturity. Use level-headed practicality when approaching these specimens and let them control the interview.

Contemplativius Coldius (Cold Contemplator)

> ***Contemplativius coldius:*** *Usually found in comfortable, uninteresting clothing in a practical environment; doesn't collect personal items; likes to be alone; methodical, precise, and work-oriented; demeanor is quiet and self-sufficient.*

If you have any discrepancies on your resume, beware — *contemplativius coldius* wants a logical explanation. These specimens are thinkers — analytical and critical. Approach them with reserve and self-confidence. Don't talk too much and don't try to be their new best friend. Focus your answers so that you do not stray into irrelevant information — doing so drives *contemplativius coldius* crazy.

Do give plenty of information for them to mull over; they love details, so tell them the *who, what, why, when,* and *how.* These specimens love analyzing, but they need something to analyze. Offer your skills, achievements, and experience as a rich analytic possibility, more interesting than any other yet offered, and they'll be happy.

Fuzzius Warmus (Warm Fuzzies Person)

> ***Fuzzius warmus:*** *Nonthreatening, friendly, likes people; several personal items in office; usually involved in several things at once; smiles often and genuinely; demeanor is concerned, comfortable, and thoughtful.*

These specimens make sure that you're happy and comfortable before they start the interview. In fact, you may find that they spend so much time caring for you that you never get interviewed.

Start by establishing a connection and then steer the interview toward more serious matters. *Fuzzius warmus* is delighted to follow your lead; after all, they just want you to be happy. Don't expect them to be very skilled at interviewing — they hate making decisions. So be ready to present all of your qualifications for the job.

Interviewus Incompetus (Incompetent Interviewer)

Interviewus incompetus: Of all shapes, colors, and sizes; found in various environments; identified by a poor interviewing technique; demeanor varies.

Unlike its distant relative, the *interviewus competus*, the *interviewus incompetus* either has little training or experience in interviewing or has personality problems. If your interview seems unfocused, or you find yourself asked unethical or irrelevant questions, or you're faced with an arrogant brute who never lets you speak, you can be fairly sure that you've entered the lair of *interviewus incompetus*.

To escape this specimen unscathed and leave the best impression possible, gracefully take control of the situation by repeating the questions for focus, asking questions that demonstrate your skills or knowledge in a particular area, staying calm, and initiating discussion of your skills and their application to the position you seek. Don't overestimate this specimen's ability to uncover your potential.

Intimidatus Serious (Serious Intimidator)

Intimidatus serious: Impeccably dressed, conservative; very neat and organized; prefers expensive, classic furnishings; work-oriented; always on time; demeanor is reserved, dedicated, and critical.

Approach these specimens quietly and seriously. Don't scare them away with chatter, false friendliness, or insincerity. *Intimidatus serious* doesn't go to work to make friends, but to work — only work. So don't waste time with pleasantries; get right to the point as succinctly as possible.

Whatever you do, don't let these specimens see your fear or intimidation. They'll kick you right out and race to the next interview.

Recruiterus Professionalus (Professional Recruiter)

Recruiterus professionalus: Suave, professional, well dressed; demeanor is quiet and confident, measuring.

These specimens spend their days interviewing people for specific companies. Their goal is more to screen you out than in, as they narrow their list of applicants. They won't let you ask many questions, so concentrate on answering their questions with as many specifics as possible about your skills, experience, and accomplishments.

To get this specimen on your side, focus on presenting the best possible you. Make sure that your appearance is impeccable and that your enthusiasm and interest in the job shine forth. Answer confidently and communicate clearly.

Talkus Alotus (Person Talks a Lot)

Talkus alotus: Fashionable, often individualistic in dress; hoards sentimental items like pictures or mementos; prefers clutter to order; often runs late; demeanor is talkative and upbeat.

The *talkus alotus* enjoys company. These specimens gravitate toward busy offices where they're surrounded by many others. They like to talk and they talk fast, so keep up.

Start by establishing a personal connection with these specimens. They probably won't pay much attention to you if they don't like you, so work on creating a friendly foundation by pasting a wide, sincere smile on your face and exuding enthusiasm. Focus on keeping these specimens interested throughout the interview — beware of boring them.

Technicus Strictus (Strictly Technical Person)

Technicus strictus: No definite description; look for pencils, notepads, and gadgets, like a pocket calculator or laptop computer; often found behind a technical title, like accountant, marketing assistant, or chemical engineer; demeanor is friendly but distant.

The *technicus strictus* doesn't mix well with other species, so camouflage yourself in the tools of your trade. Focus on your technical knowledge and achievements. Get this specimen excited by discussing common interests in your field.

These specimens usually have little interviewing experience, so make sure that you discuss your skills in detail. Don't assume that they will be able to uncover all of your strengths — *technicus strictus* are undoubtedly skilled in their fields, but not in interviewing, so be ready to ask good questions.

Too Muchus of a Good Thing?

If you're not flatlined after reading this good but goofyius list of interview types, reinforce your understanding by trying to think of a person you know who fits each category. Or meet with friends and pretend you're trying out for the cast of a sitcom. Each friend assumes a personality type and role-plays an interview with you. Good luck with *contemplativus coldius* and *technicus strictus*.

Index

• U •

• V •

BUSINESS, CAREERS & PERSONAL FINANCE

0-7645-9847-3

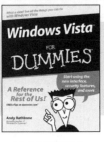

0-7645-2431-3

Also available:
- Business Plans Kit For Dummies
  0-7645-9794-9
- Economics For Dummies
  0-7645-5726-2
- Grant Writing For Dummies
  0-7645-8416-2
- Home Buying For Dummies
  0-7645-5331-3
- Managing For Dummies
  0-7645-1771-6
- Marketing For Dummies
  0-7645-5600-2

- Personal Finance For Dummies
  0-7645-2590-5*
- Resumes For Dummies
  0-7645-5471-9
- Selling For Dummies
  0-7645-5363-1
- Six Sigma For Dummies
  0-7645-6798-5
- Small Business Kit For Dummies
  0-7645-5984-2
- Starting an eBay Business For Dummies
  0-7645-6924-4
- Your Dream Career For Dummies
  0-7645-9795-7

HOME & BUSINESS COMPUTER BASICS

0-470-05432-8

0-471-75421-8

Also available:
- Cleaning Windows Vista For Dummies
  0-471-78293-9
- Excel 2007 For Dummies
  0-470-03737-7
- Mac OS X Tiger For Dummies
  0-7645-7675-5
- MacBook For Dummies
  0-470-04859-X
- Macs For Dummies
  0-470-04849-2
- Office 2007 For Dummies
  0-470-00923-3

- Outlook 2007 For Dummies
  0-470-03830-6
- PCs For Dummies
  0-7645-8958-X
- Salesforce.com For Dummies
  0-470-04893-X
- Upgrading & Fixing Laptops For Dummies
  0-7645-8959-8
- Word 2007 For Dummies
  0-470-03658-3
- Quicken 2007 For Dummies
  0-470-04600-7

FOOD, HOME, GARDEN, HOBBIES, MUSIC & PETS

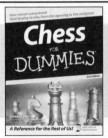

0-7645-8404-9

0-7645-9904-6

Also available:
- Candy Making For Dummies
  0-7645-9734-5
- Card Games For Dummies
  0-7645-9910-0
- Crocheting For Dummies
  0-7645-4151-X
- Dog Training For Dummies
  0-7645-8418-9
- Healthy Carb Cookbook For Dummies
  0-7645-8476-6
- Home Maintenance For Dummies
  0-7645-5215-5

- Horses For Dummies
  0-7645-9797-3
- Jewelry Making & Beading For Dummies
  0-7645-2571-9
- Orchids For Dummies
  0-7645-6759-4
- Puppies For Dummies
  0-7645-5255-4
- Rock Guitar For Dummies
  0-7645-5356-9
- Sewing For Dummies
  0-7645-6847-7
- Singing For Dummies
  0-7645-2475-5

INTERNET & DIGITAL MEDIA

0-470-04529-9

0-470-04894-8

Also available:
- Blogging For Dummies
  0-471-77084-1
- Digital Photography For Dummies
  0-7645-9802-3
- Digital Photography All-in-One Desk Reference For Dummies
  0-470-03743-1
- Digital SLR Cameras and Photography For Dummies
  0-7645-9803-1
- eBay Business All-in-One Desk Reference For Dummies
  0-7645-8438-3
- HDTV For Dummies
  0-470-09673-X

- Home Entertainment PCs For Dummies
  0-470-05523-5
- MySpace For Dummies
  0-470-09529-6
- Search Engine Optimization For Dummies
  0-471-97998-8
- Skype For Dummies
  0-470-04891-3
- The Internet For Dummies
  0-7645-8996-2
- Wiring Your Digital Home For Dummies
  0-471-91830-X

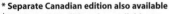

* Separate Canadian edition also available
† Separate U.K. edition also available

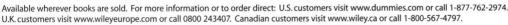

SPORTS, FITNESS, PARENTING, RELIGION & SPIRITUALITY

0-471-76871-5

0-7645-7841-3

Also available:

- Catholicism For Dummies
  0-7645-5391-7
- Exercise Balls For Dummies
  0-7645-5623-1
- Fitness For Dummies
  0-7645-7851-0
- Football For Dummies
  0-7645-3936-1
- Judaism For Dummies
  0-7645-5299-6
- Potty Training For Dummies
  0-7645-5417-4
- Buddhism For Dummies
  0-7645-5359-3

- Pregnancy For Dummies
  0-7645-4483-7 †
- Ten Minute Tone-Ups For Dummies
  0-7645-7207-5
- NASCAR For Dummies
  0-7645-7681-X
- Religion For Dummies
  0-7645-5264-3
- Soccer For Dummies
  0-7645-5229-5
- Women in the Bible For Dummies
  0-7645-8475-8

TRAVEL

0-7645-7749-2

0-7645-6945-7

Also available:

- Alaska For Dummies
  0-7645-7746-8
- Cruise Vacations For Dummies
  0-7645-6941-4
- England For Dummies
  0-7645-4276-1
- Europe For Dummies
  0-7645-7529-5
- Germany For Dummies
  0-7645-7823-5
- Hawaii For Dummies
  0-7645-7402-7

- Italy For Dummies
  0-7645-7386-1
- Las Vegas For Dummies
  0-7645-7382-9
- London For Dummies
  0-7645-4277-X
- Paris For Dummies
  0-7645-7630-5
- RV Vacations For Dummies
  0-7645-4442-X
- Walt Disney World & Orlando
  For Dummies
  0-7645-9660-8

GRAPHICS, DESIGN & WEB DEVELOPMENT

0-7645-8815-X

0-7645-9571-7

Also available:

- 3D Game Animation For Dummies
  0-7645-8789-7
- AutoCAD 2006 For Dummies
  0-7645-8925-3
- Building a Web Site For Dummies
  0-7645-7144-3
- Creating Web Pages For Dummies
  0-470-08030-2
- Creating Web Pages All-in-One Desk
  Reference For Dummies
  0-7645-4345-8
- Dreamweaver 8 For Dummies
  0-7645-9649-7

- InDesign CS2 For Dummies
  0-7645-9572-5
- Macromedia Flash 8 For Dummies
  0-7645-9691-8
- Photoshop CS2 and Digital
  Photography For Dummies
  0-7645-9580-6
- Photoshop Elements 4 For Dummies
  0-471-77483-9
- Syndicating Web Sites with RSS Feeds
  For Dummies
  0-7645-8848-6
- Yahoo! SiteBuilder For Dummies
  0-7645-9800-7

NETWORKING, SECURITY, PROGRAMMING & DATABASES

0-7645-7728-X

0-471-74940-0

Also available:

- Access 2007 For Dummies
  0-470-04612-0
- ASP.NET 2 For Dummies
  0-7645-7907-X
- C# 2005 For Dummies
  0-7645-9704-3
- Hacking For Dummies
  0-470-05235-X
- Hacking Wireless Networks
  For Dummies
  0-7645-9730-2
- Java For Dummies
  0-470-08716-1

- Microsoft SQL Server 2005 For Dummies
  0-7645-7755-7
- Networking All-in-One Desk Reference
  For Dummies
  0-7645-9939-9
- Preventing Identity Theft For Dummies
  0-7645-7336-5
- Telecom For Dummies
  0-471-77085-X
- Visual Studio 2005 All-in-One Desk
  Reference For Dummies
  0-7645-9775-2
- XML For Dummies
  0-7645-8845-1